Celebrating
Children's Literature in Education

Celebrating Children's Literature in Education

A selection by Geoff Fox

Hodder & Stoughton

A MEMBER OF THE HODDER HEADLINE GROUP

British Library Cataloguing in Publication Data

Celebrating "Children's Literature in Education"
I. Fox, Geoff
820.99282

ISBN 0–340–61863–9

First published 1995
Impression number 10 9 8 7 6 5 4 3 2 1
Year 1999 1998 1997 1996 1995

Typeset by Wearset, Boldon, Tyne and Wear.
Printed in Great Britain for Hodder & Stoughton Educational, a division of Hodder Headline Plc, 338 Euston Road, London NW1 3BH by Redwood Books, Trowbridge.

Contents

FOREWORD

The articles in this book originally appeared in the quarterly *Children's Literature in Education (CLE)*; this selection of essays celebrates twenty-five years of the journal's publication. *CLE* was established by a British editorial committee in Devon, but as circulation became international North American editors were appointed, an arrangement which persists to the present time. Submissions to the journal come from virtually every continent, though the majority of the subscribers are to be found in the United Kingdom, North America and Australia.

In the early 1970s, the children's book world was enjoying what some called a modern Golden Age. Many new, young writers emerged in the sixties and enthusiasm for their work developed vigorously among teachers, librarians, reviewers and a small number of scholars. It is less certain, however, that there was a comparable enthusiasm among children and young adult readers. A survey of Children's Reading Interests which took its sample in 1971[1] showed readers apparently ignoring the new wave of writers who so excited adults. *Jane Eyre* headed the list of most-read books among fourteen-year-old girls, whilst the salacious *Skinhead* was the boys' current favourite. (*CLE* published a critical appraisal of the latter alongside an account of a teacher talking with his pupils about the book at their request, albeit out of school hours.) With hindsight, it seems possible that much of the enthusiasm at this time was generated by adults who read recent children's books for their own satisfaction, rather than with children in view.

Twenty-five years have witnessed considerable changes in the field of children's books. There have been undoubted advances, among them some fine poetry for young readers and writing originating in different ethnic groups. An increasing awareness of the part played by a reader in creating a text influenced the classroom practice of many teachers. The creators of information books at last began to take account of how their young readers might engage with the words and pictures effectively. Most exciting of all, perhaps, have been radical innovations in the creation of picture books.

Articles in the journal reflected many of these changes. In this book, for example, Peter Neumeyer explores Maurice Sendak's *We Are All in the Dumps with Jack and Guy* with an attention which would have surprised readers in 1970. Margaret Mackey's discussion of the process of rereading carries implications for teaching fiction which most of us would not have understood twenty-five years ago. Margaret Meek opens up the issues of children's engagement with information books in a pioneering article which appeared as recently as the 25th Anniversary issue of *CLE* in Spring, 1995.[2]

Modern literary theory had made little impact on the discussion of children's books in 1970; much of that theory was yet to be developed. Some of the most perceptive contributions to the journal have grown from recent critical theory, although the editors occasionally reject submissions because they are embedded in language which would be impenetrable to a diverse international readership. *CLE* has chosen to be eclectic, not aligning itself with one critical perspective. The editors have always believed, however, that discussion of children's books should never lose sight of young readers themselves.

In other ways, the children's book world seems little changed. The popularity of *Skinhead* in 1971 is matched by the series of horror novels in 1995. In 1970, as Aidan Chambers reminds us in the final essay in this collection, some children's librarians banned *Where the Wild Things Are* because it was too frightening. Twenty-five years later, a Canadian author discovers that an illustration of a fox with a chicken in its mouth has been withdrawn from one of his books in response to pressure that such terrors are unfit for children's consumption. If Chaucer were alive today, we might never have heard of Chanticleer. The most lunatic pronouncements on literature in England, however, have not come from the fringes, but from the government. Prescribed, or even exemplary, lists of authors in the National Curriculum (mostly dead, mostly male, mostly beyond the reach of most young readers and almost all white) take no account of how readers read, and how children grow up to be readers.

Twenty-five years have yielded some six hundred articles in the journal, and as I made this selection, I searched above all for distinctive 'voices'. What those voices have to say will prove, I believe, as informative, interesting and even as provocative now as when they were first heard. Back numbers of a journal are hard to obtain and the pieces reprinted here deserve a wider audience. Glimpses of some of the many articles reluctantly excluded are contained in a section of extracts entitled *In Essence.*

Nothing, in many teachers' experience, welds a group of children or students into a good-humoured, learning community so effectively as the sharing of literature in all its forms. I hope **Celebrating Children's Literature in Education** reaffirms a belief in the centrality of novels, poems, picture books and information books in classrooms and the experience of young readers. In the first issue of *CLE* and the first article in this book, Ted Hughes writes, 'A simple tale, told at the right moment, transforms a person's life with the order its pattern brings to incoherent energies'. This book celebrates that kind of transformation.

Notes

1 In *Children and their Books*, Frank Whitehead *et al.*, Macmillan Education, 1977

2 There have been changes also in social awareness. The articles appear as they were originally published. Earlier pieces may thus employ 'he' where later contributors use 'he or she' or the plural form. I hope that no offence or distraction results.

Geoff Fox
May 1995

Acknowledgements

I am grateful to Human Sciences Press, New York, the publishers of *Children's Literature in Education,* who readily gave permission for the reprinting of the articles which make up this collection; I am also grateful that most of those articles passed at some time through the meticulous hands of Henry Bashwiner, desk-editor of the journal for many years.

Different editors had a share in preparing these pieces for their original publication in the journal. From the United Kingdom editorial committee, I must thank Pam Barnard, Graham Hammond, David Lewis and Anne Merrick; and my particular thanks to Terry Jones and Frederic Smith, my colleagues on this committee since its first meeting in 1969. Some of the articles initially reached *CLE's* pages by way of the American editorial board, whose members I also thank.

My suggestion that an anniversary selection of articles would be appropriate was enthusiastically supported by Dr Roger Beard of the University of Leeds, who reread all the back numbers and gave invaluable advice to the publisher and to myself. At Hodder & Stoughton, Elizabeth Wright and Lesley Staff could not have been more helpful.

Lastly, my thanks to the contributors of articles and extracts in the book itself; in a sense, they represent all those who have written for the journal over the years. I hope they find pleasure in this celebration of their work.

CHILDREN'S LITERATURE IN EDUCATION: INFORMATION

CLE is a quarterly journal published by Human Sciences Press, New York. Editorial Boards from the United Kingdom and North America each provide 50 per cent of the copy, though contributions come from all over the world. Subscription information is available from: (UK and Europe) Eurospan Ltd., 3 Henrietta Street, London, WC2E 8LU, United Kingdom (fax 0171-379 0609); (Rest of the World) Subscription Department, Human Sciences Press Inc., 233 Spring Street, New York, NY 10013–1578, USA (fax (212) 807–1047). Editorial correspondence, including submissions, to: (Outside North America) Geoff Fox, School of Education, Exeter University, St Luke's, Heavitree Road, Exeter EX1 2LU, United Kingdom; (North America) Anita Moss, English Department, University of North Carolina at Charlotte, UNCC Station, Charlotte, North Carolina 28223, USA.

Blueprints for Imagination

Ted Hughes

Ted Hughes has been Poet Laureate since 1984. His work for children includes *The Iron Man* (1968) and several collections of poetry, among them *What is the Truth?* (1984) which won the *Guardian* Fiction Award. *Poetry in the Making* (1967) based on a series of radio broadcasts, remains an indispensible text for all concerned to help children write their own poems.

In its earliest form, this article was delivered as an address to one of a series of conferences on children's literature at St Luke's College, Exeter, from which *Children's Literature in Education* derived. It was included in Issue No. 1 (1970), and since that time has often been quoted as a seminal discussion of the nature and power of story. Ted Hughes revised the article for an earlier collection of *CLE* pieces, *Writers, Critics, and Children* (1976), and it is this revision which is printed here. The article also appeared in *Winter Pollen* (1994), a collection of Ted Hughes's essays, published by Faber & Faber.

MYTH AND EDUCATION

Somewhere in *The Republic*, where he describes the constitution of his ideal State, Plato talks a little about the education of the people who will live in it. He makes the famous point that quite advanced mathematical truths can be drawn from children when they are asked the right questions in the right order, and his own philosophical method in his dialogues is very like this. He treats his interlocutors as children and by small, simple, logical, stealthy questions gradually draws out of them some part of the Platonic system of ideas – a system which has in one way or another dominated the mental life of the Western world ever since. Nevertheless he goes on to say that a formal education – by which he means a mathematical, philosophical and ethical education – is not for children. The proper education for his future ideal citizens, he suggests, is something quite different: it is to be found in the traditional myths and tales of which Greece possessed such a huge abundance.

Plato was nothing if not an educationalist. His writings can be seen as a prolonged and many-sided debate on just how the ideal citizen is to be shaped. It seemed to him quite possible to create an élite of philosophers who would also be wise and responsible rulers, with a perfect apprehension of the Good. Yet he proposed to start their training with the incredible fantasies of these myths. Everyone knows that the first lessons, with human beings just as with dogs, are the most important of all. So what would be the effect of laying at the foundations of their mental life this mass of supernatural figures and their impossible antics? Later philosophers, throughout history, who have come near often enough to worshipping Plato, have dismissed these tales as absurdities. So how did he come to recommend them?

They were the material of the Greek poets. Many of them had been recreated by poets into works that have been the model and despair of later writers. Yet we know what Plato thought about poets. He wanted them suppressed – much as it is said he suppressed his own poems when he first encountered Socrates. If he wanted nothing of the poets, why was he so respectful of the myths and tales which formed the imaginative world of the poets?

He had no religious motives. For Plato, those Gods and Goddesses were hardly more serious, as religious symbols, than they are for us. Yet they evidently did contain something important. What exactly was it, then, that made them in his opinion the best possible grounding for his future enlightened, realistic, perfectly adjusted citizen?

Let us suppose he thought about it as carefully as he thought about everything else. What did he have in mind? Trying to answer that question leads us in interesting directions.

Plato was preceded in Greece by more shadowy figures. They are a unique collection. Even what fragments remain of their writings reveal a cauldron of titanic ideas, from which Plato drew only a spoonful. Wherever we look around us now, in the modern world, it is not easy to find anything that was not somehow prefigured in the conceptions of those early Greeks. And nothing is more striking about their ideas than the strange, visionary atmosphere from which they emerge. Plato is human and familiar; he invented that careful, logical step-by-step style of investigation, in which all his great dialogues are conducted, and which almost all later philosophers developed, until it evolved finally into the scientific method itself. But his predecessors stand in a different world. By comparison they seem like mythical figures, living in myth, dreaming mythical dreams.

And so they were. We find them embedded in myth. Their vast

powerful notions are emerging, like figures in half-relief, from the massif of myth, which in turn is lifting from the human/animal darkness of early Greece.

Why did they rise in Greece and not somewhere else? What was so special about early Greece? The various peoples of Greece had created their own religions and mythologies, more or less related but with differences. Further abroad, other nations had created theirs, again often borrowing from common sources, but evolving separate systems, sometimes gigantic systems. Those supernatural seeming dreams, full of conflict and authority and unearthly states of feeling, were projections of man's inner and outer world. They developed their ritual, their dogma, their hierarchy of spiritual values in a particular way in each separated group. Then at the beginning of the first millennium they began to converge, by one means or another, on Greece. They came from Africa via Egypt, from Asia via Persia and the Middle East, from Europe and from all the shores of the Mediterranean. Meeting in Greece, they mingled with those rising from the soil of Greece itself. Wherever two cultures with their religious ideas are brought sharply together, there is an inner explosion. Greece had become the battleground of the religious and mythological inspirations of much of the archaic world. The conflict was severe, and the effort to find solutions and make peace among all those contradictory elements was correspondingly great. And the heroes of the struggle were those early philosophers. The struggle created them, it opened the depths of spirit and imagination to them, and they made sense of it. What was religious passion in the religions became in them a special sense of the holiness and seriousness of existence. What was obscure symbolic mystery in the mythologies became in them a bright, manifold perception of universal and human truths. In their works we see the transformation from one to the other taking place. And the great age which immediately followed them, in the fifth century B.C., was the culmination of the activity.

It seems proper, then, that the fantastic dimension of those tales should have appeared to Plato as something very much other than frivolous or absurd. We can begin to guess, maybe, at what he wanted, in familiarising children with as much as possible of that teeming repertoire.

To begin with, we can say that an education of the sort Plato proposes would work on a child in the following way.

A child takes possession of a story as what might be called a unit of imagination. A story which engages, say, earth and the underworld is a unit correspondingly flexible. It contains not merely the space and in some form or other the contents of those two places; it reconciles their contradictions in a workable fashion and holds open the way between them. The child can re-enter the story at will, look around him, find all those things and consider them at his leisure. In attending to the world of such a story there is the beginning of imaginative and mental control. There is the beginning of a form of contemplation. And to begin with, each story is separate from every other story. Each unit of imagination is like a whole separate imagination, no matter how many the head holds.

If the story is learned well, so that all its parts can be seen at a glance, as if we looked through a window into it, then that story has become like the complicated hinterland of a single word. It has become a word. Any fragment of the story serves as the 'word' by which the whole story's electrical circuit is switched into consciousness, and all its light and power brought to bear. As a rather extreme example, take the story of Christ. No matter what point of that story we touch, the whole story hits us. If we mention the Nativity, or the miracle of the loaves and fishes, or Lazarus, or the Crucifixion, the voltage and inner brightness of the whole story is instantly there. A single word of reference is enough – just as you need to touch a power-line with only the tip of your finger.

The story itself is an acquisition, a kind of wealth. We only have to imagine for a moment an individual who knows nothing of it at all. His ignorance would shock us, and, in a real way, he would be outside our society. How would he even begin to understand most of the ideas which are at the roots of our culture and appear everywhere among the branches? To follow the meanings behind the one word Crucifixion would take us through most of European history, and much of Roman and Middle Eastern too. It would take us into every corner of our private life. And before long, it would compel us to acknowledge much more important meanings than merely informative ones. Openings of spiritual experience, a dedication to final realities which might well stop us dead in our tracks and demand of us personally a sacrifice which we could never otherwise have conceived. A word of that sort has magnetised our life into a special pattern. And behind it stands not just the crowded breadth of the world, but all the depths and intensities of it too. Those things have been raised out of chaos and brought into our ken by the story in a word. The word holds them all there, like a constellation, floating and shining, and though we may draw back from tangling with them too closely, nevertheless they are present. And they remain, part of the head that lives our life, and they grow as we grow. A story can wield so much! And a word wields the story.

Imagine hearing, somewhere in the middle of a poem being recited, the phrase 'The Crucifixion of Hitler'. The word 'Hitler' is as much of a hieroglyph as the word 'Crucifixion'. Individually, those two words bear the consciousness of much of our civilisation. But they are meaningless hieroglyphs, unless the stories behind the words are known. We could almost say it is only by possessing these stories that we possess that consciousness. And in those who possess both stories, the collision of those two words, in that phrase, cannot fail to detonate a psychic depth-charge. Whether we like it or not, a huge inner working starts up. How can Hitler and Crucifixion exist together in that way? Can they or can't they? The struggle to sort it out throws up ethical and philosophical implications which could absorb our attention for a very long time. All our static and maybe dormant understanding of good and evil and what opens beyond good and evil is shocked into activity. Many unconscious assumptions and intuitions come up into the light to declare themselves and explain themselves and reassess each other. For some temperaments, those two words twinned in that way might well point to wholly fresh appraisals of good and evil and the underground psychological or even actual connections between them. Yet the visible combatants here are two stories.

Without those stories, how could we have grasped those meanings? Without those stories, how could we have reduced those meanings to two words? The stories have gathered up huge charges of reality, and illuminated us with them, and given us their energy, just as those colliding worlds in early Greece roused the philosophers and the poets. If we argue that a grasp of good and evil has nothing to do with a knowledge of historical anecdotes, we have only to compare what we felt of Hitler's particular evil when our knowledge of his story was only general with what we felt when we learned more details. It is just those details of Hitler's story that have changed the consciousness of modern man. The story hasn't stuck onto us something that was never there before. It has revealed to us something that was always there. And no other story, no other anything, ever did it so powerfully. Just as it needed the story of Christ to change the consciousness of our ancestors. The better we know these stories as stories, the more of ourselves and the world is revealed to us through them.

The story of Christ came to us first of all as two or three sentences.

That tiny seed held all the rest in potential form. Like the blueprint of a city. Once we laid it down firmly in imagination, it became the foundation for everything that could subsequently build and live there. Just the same with the story of Hitler.

Are those two stories extreme examples? They would not have appeared so for the early Greeks, who had several Christs and several Bibles and quite a few Hitlers to deal with. Are Aesop's fables more to our scale? They operate in exactly the same way. Grimms' tales are similar oracles.

But what these two stories show very clearly is how stories think for themselves, once we know them. They not only attract and light up everything relevant in our own experience, they are also in continual private meditation, as it were, on their own implications. They are little factories of understanding. New revelations of meaning open out of their images and patterns continually, stirred into reach by our own growth and changing circumstances.

Then at a certain point in our lives, they begin to combine. What happened forcibly between Hitler and the Crucifixion in that phrase, begins to happen naturally. The head that holds many stories becomes a small early Greece.

It does not matter, either, how old the stories are. Stories are old the way human biology is old. No matter how much they have produced in the past in the way of fruitful inspirations, they are never exhausted. The story of Christ, to stick to our example, can never be diminished by the seemingly infinite mass of theological agonising and insipid homilies which have attempted to translate it into something more manageable. It remains, like any other genuine story, irreducible, a lump of the world, like the body of a new-born child. There is little doubt that, if the world lasts, pretty soon someone will come along and understand the story as if for the first time. He will look back and see two thousand years of somnolent fumbling with the theme. Out of that, and the collision of other things, he will produce, very likely, something totally new and overwhelming, some whole new direction for human life. The same possibility holds for the ancient stories of many another deity. Why not? History is really no older than that new-born baby. And every story is still the original cauldron of wisdom, full of new visions and new life.

What do we mean by 'imagination'? There are obviously many degrees of it. Are there different kinds?

The word 'imagination' usually denotes not much more than the faculty of creating a picture of something in our heads and holding it there while we think about it. Since this is the basis of nearly everything we do, clearly it's very important that our imagination should be strong rather than weak. Education neglects this faculty completely. How is the imagination to be strengthened and trained? A student has imagination, we seem to suppose, much as he has a face, and nothing can be done about it. We use what we've got.

We do realise that it can vary enormously from one person to the next, and from almost non-existent upwards. Of a person who simply cannot think what will happen if he does such and such a thing, we say he has no imagination. He has to work on principles, or orders, or by precedent, and he will always be marked by extreme rigidity, because he is after all moving in the dark. We all know such people, and we all recognise that they are dangerous, since if they have strong temperaments in other respects they end up by destroying their environment and everybody near them. The terrible thing is that they are the planners, and ruthless slaves to the plan – which substitutes for the faculty they do not possess. And they have the will of desperation: where others see alternative courses, they see only a gulf.

Of the person who imagines vividly what will happen if he acts in a certain way, and then turns out to be wrong, we say he is dealing with an unpredictable situation or else, just as likely, he has an inaccurate imagination. Lively, maybe, but inaccurate. There is no innate law that makes a very real-seeming picture of things an accurate picture. That person will be a great nuisance, and as destructive as the other, because he will be full of confident schemes and solutions, which will seem to him foolproof, but which will simply be false, because somehow his sense of reality is defective. In other words, his ordinary perception of reality, by which the imagination regulates all its images, overlooks too much, or misinterprets too much. Many disturbances can account for some of this, but simple sloppiness of attention accounts for most of it.

Those two classes of people contain the majority of us for much of the time. The third class of people is quite rare. Or our own moments of belonging to that class are rare. Imagination which is both accurate and strong is so rare, that when somebody appears in possession of it they are regarded as something more than human. We see that with the few great generals. Normally, it occurs patchily. It is usually no more than patchy because accurate perceptions are rarely more than patchy. We have only to make the simplest test on ourselves to reconfirm this. And where our perceptions are blind, our speculations are pure invention.

This basic type of imagination, with its delicate wiring of perceptions, is our most valuable piece of practical equipment. It is the control panel for everything we think and do, so it ought to be education's first concern. Yet whoever spent half an hour in any classroom trying to strengthen it in any way? Even in the sciences, where accurate perception is recognisably crucial, is this faculty ever deliberately trained?

Sharpness, clarity and scope of the mental eye are all-important in our dealings with the outer world, and that is plenty. And if we were machines it would be enough. But the outer world is only one of the worlds we live in. For better or worse we have another, and that is the inner world of our bodies and everything pertaining. It is closer than the outer world, more decisive, and utterly different. So here are two worlds, which we have to live in simultaneously. And because they are intricately interdependent at every moment, we can't ignore one and concentrate on the other without accidents. Probably fatal accidents.

But why can't this inner world of the body be regarded as an extension of the outer world – in other words why isn't the sharp, clear, objective eye of the mind as adequate for this world as it is for the other more obviously outer world? And if it isn't, why isn't it?

The inner world is not so easily talked about because nobody has ever come near to understanding it. Though it is the closest thing to us – though it is, indeed, us – we live in it as on an unexplored planet in space. It is not so much a place, either, as a region of events. And the first thing we have to confess is that it cannot be seen objectively. How does the biological craving for water turn into the precise notion that it is water that we want? How do we 'see' the make-up of an emotion that we do not even feel – though electrodes on our skin will register its presence? The word 'subjective' was invented for a good reason – but under that vaguest of general terms lies the most important half of our experience.

After all, what exactly is going on in there? It is quite frightening, how little we know about it. We can't say there's nothing – that 'nothing' is merely the shutness of the shut door. And if we say there's something – how much more specific can we get?

We quickly realise that the inner world is indescribable, impenetrable, and invisible. We try to grapple with it, and all we meet is one provisional dream after another. It dawns on us that in order to look at the inner world 'objectively' we have had to separate ourselves from what is an exclusively 'subjective' world, and it has vanished. In the end, we acknowledge that the objective imagination, and the objective perceptions, those sharp clear instruments which cope so well with the outer world, are of very little use here.

By speculating backwards from effects, we can possibly make out a rough plan of what ought to be in there. The incessant bombardment of raw perceptions must land somewhere. And we have been able to notice that any one perception can stir up a host of small feelings, which excite further feelings not necessarily so small, in a turmoil of memory and association. And we do get some evidence, we think, that our emotional and instinctive life, which seems to be on a somewhat bigger scale and not so tied to momentary perceptions, is mustering and regrouping in response to outer circumstances. But these bigger and more dramatic energies are also occasionally yoked to the pettiest of those perceptions, and driven off on some journey. And now and again we are made aware of what seems to be an even larger drama of moods and energies which it is hard to name – psychic, spiritual, cosmic. Any name we give them seems metaphorical, since in that world everything is relative, and we are never sure of the scale of magnification or miniaturisation of the signals. We can guess, with a fair sense of confidence, that all these intervolved processes, which seem like the electrical fields of our body's electrical installations – our glands, organs, chemical transmutations and so on – are striving to tell about themselves. They are all trying to make their needs known, much as thirst imparts its sharp request for water. They are talking incessantly, in a dumb radiating way, about themselves, about their relationships with each other, about the situation of the moment in the main overall drama of the living and growing and dying body in which they are assembled, and also about the outer world, because all these *dramatis personae* are really striving to live, in some way or other, in the outer world. That is the world for which they have been created. That is the world which created them. And so they are highly concerned about the doings of the individual behind whose face they hide. Because they are him. And they want him to live in the way that will give them the greatest satisfaction.

This description is bald enough, but it is as much as the objective eye can be reasonably sure of. And then only in a detached way, the way we think we are sure of the workings of an electrical circuit. But for more intimate negotiations with that world, for genuine contact with its powers and genuine exploration of its regions, it turns out that the eye of the objective imagination is blind.

We solve the problem by never looking inward. We identify ourselves and all that is wakeful and intelligent with our objective eye, saying, 'Let's be objective'. That is really no more than saying 'Let's be happy'. But we sit, closely cramped in the cockpit behind the eyes, steering through the brilliantly crowded landscape beyond the lenses, focused on details and distinctions. In the end, since all our attention from birth has been narrowed into the outward beam, we come to regard our body as no more than a somewhat stupid-vehicle. All the urgent information coming towards us from that inner world sounds to us like a blank, or at best the occasional grunt, or a twinge. Because we have no equipment to receive it and decode it. The body, with its spirits, is the antennae of all perceptions, the receiving aerial for all wavelengths. But we are disconnected. The exclusiveness of our objective eye, the very strength and brilliance of our objective intelligence, suddenly turns into stupidity – of the most rigid and suicidal kind.

That condition certainly sounds extreme, yet most of the people we know, particularly older people, are likely to regard it as ideal. It is a modern ideal. The educational tendencies of the last three hundred years, and especially of the last fifty, corresponding to the rising prestige of scientific objectivity and the lowering prestige of religious awareness, have combined to make it so. It is a scientific ideal. And it is a powerful ideal, it has created the modern world. And without it, the modern world would fall to pieces: infinite misery would result. The disaster is, that it is heading straight towards infinite misery, because it has persuaded human beings to identify themselves with what is no more than a narrow mode of perception. And the more rigorously the ideal is achieved, the more likely it is to be disastrous. A bright, intelligent eye, full of exact images, set in a head of the most frightful stupidity.

The drive towards this ideal is so strong that it has materialised in the outer world. A perfect mechanism of objective perception has been precipitated: the camera. Scientific objectivity, as we all know, has its own morality, which has nothing to do with human morality. It is the morality of the camera. And this is the prevailing morality of our time. It is a morality utterly devoid of any awareness of the requirements of the inner world. It is contemptuous of the 'human element'. That is its purity and its strength. The prevailing philosophies and political ideologies of our time subscribe to this contempt, with a nearly religious fanaticism, just as science itself does.

Some years ago in an American picture magazine I saw a collection of photographs which showed the process of a tiger killing a woman. The story behind this was as follows. The tiger, a tame tiger, belonged to the woman. A professional photographer had wanted to take photographs of her strolling with her tiger. Something – maybe his incessant camera – had upset the tiger, the woman had tried to pacify it, whereupon it attacked her and started to kill her. So what did that hero of the objective attitude do then? Among Jim Corbett's wonderful stories about man-eating tigers and leopards there are occasions when some man-eater, with a terrifying reputation, was driven off its victim by some other person. On one occasion by a girl who beat the animal over the head with a digging stick. But this photographer – we can easily understand him because we all belong to this modern world – had become his camera. What were his thoughts? 'Now that the tiger has started in on her it would be cruelty to save her and prolong her sufferings', or 'If I just stand here making the minimum noise it might leave her, whereas if I interfere it will certainly give her the death bite, just as a cat does when you try to rescue its mouse', or 'If I get involved, who knows what will happen, then I might miss my plane', or 'I can't affect the outcome of this in any way. And who am I to interfere with the cycles of nature? This has happened countless millions of times and always will happen while there are tigers and women', or did he just think 'Oh my God, Oh my God, what a chance!'? Whatever his thoughts were he went on taking photographs of the whole procedure while the tiger killed the woman, because the pictures were there in the magazine. And the story was told as if the photographer had indeed been absent. As if the camera had simply gone on doing what any camera would be expected to do, being a mere mechanical device for registering outer appearances. I may be doing the photographer an injustice. It may be I have forgotten some mention that eventully when he had enough pictures he ran in and hit the tiger with his camera or something else. Or maybe he was just wisely cowardly as many another of us might be. Whatever it was, he got his pictures.

The same paralysis comes to many of us when we watch television. After the interesting bit is over, what keeps us mesmerised by that bright little eye? It can't be the horrors and inanities and killings that jog along there between the curtains and the mantelpiece after supper. Why can't we move? Reality has been removed beyond our participation, behind that very tough screen, and into another dimension. Our inner world, of natural impulsive response, is safely in neutral. Like broiler killers, we are reduced to a state of pure observation. Everything that passes in front of our eyes is equally important, equally unimportant. As far as what we see is concerned, and in a truly practical way, we are paralysed. Even people who profess to dislike television fall under the same spell of passivity. They can only free themselves by a convulsive effort of will. The precious tool of objective imagination has taken control of us there. Materialised in the camera, it has imprisoned us in the lens.

In England, not very long ago, the inner world and Christianity were closely identified. Even the conflicts within Christianity only revealed and consolidated more inner world. When religious knowledge lost the last rags of its credibility, earlier this century, psychoanalysis appeared as if to fill the gap. Both attempt to give form to the inner world. But with a difference.

When it came the turn of the Christian Church to embody the laws of the inner world, it made the mistake of claiming that they were objective laws. That might have passed, if Science had not come along, whose laws were so demonstrably objective that it was able to impose them on the whole world. As the mistaken claims of Christianity became scientifically meaningless, the inner world which it had clothed became incomprehensible, absurd and finally invisible. Objective imagination, in the light of science, rejected religion as charlatanism, and the inner world as a bundle of fairy tales, a relic of primeval superstition. People rushed towards the idea of living without any religion or any inner life whatsoever as if towards some great new freedom. A great final awakening. The most energetic intellectual and political movements of this century wrote the manifestos of the new liberation. The great artistic statements have recorded the true emptiness of the new prison.

The inner world, of course, could not evaporate, just because it no longer had a religion to give it a visible body. A person's own inner world cannot fold up its spirit wings, and shut down all its tuned circuits, and become a mechanical business of nuts and bolts, just because a political or intellectual ideology requires it to. As the religion was stripped away, the defrocked inner world became a waif, an outcast, a tramp. And denied its one great health – acceptance into life – it fell into a huge sickness. A huge collection of deprivation sicknesses. And this is how psychoanalysis found it.

The small piloting consciousness of the bright-eyed objective intelligence had steered its body and soul into a hell. Religious negotiations had formerly embraced and humanised the archaic energies of instinct and feeling. They had conversed in simple but profound terms with the forces struggling inside people, and had civilised them, or attempted to. Without religion, those powers have become dehumanised. The whole inner world has become elemental, chaotic, continually more primitive and beyond our control. It has become a place of demons. But of course, insofar as we are disconnected anyway from that world, and lack the equipment to pick up its signals, we are not aware of it. All we register is the vast absence, the emptiness, the sterility, the meaninglessness, the loneliness. If we do manage to catch a glimpse of our inner selves, by some contraption of mirrors, we recognise it with horror – it is an animal crawling and decomposing in a hell. We refuse to own it.

In the last decade or two, the imprisonment of the camera lens has begun to crack. The demonised state of our inner world has made itself felt in a million ways. How is it that children are so attracted towards it? Every new child is nature's chance to correct culture's error. Children are most sensitive to it, because they are the least conditioned by scientific objectivity to life in the camera lens. They have a double motive, in attempting to break from the lens. They want to escape the ugliness of the despiritualised world in which they see their parents imprisoned. And they are aware that this inner world we have rejected is not merely an inferno of depraved impulses and crazy explosions of embittered energy. Our real selves lie down there. Down there, mixed up among all the madness, is everything that once made life worth living. All the lost awareness and powers and allegiances of our biological and spiritual being. The attempt to re-enter that lost inheritance takes many forms, but it is the chief business of the swarming cults.

Drugs cannot take us there. If we cite the lofty religions in which drugs did take the initiates to where they needed to go, we ought to remember that here again the mythology was crucial. The journey was undertaken as part of an elaborately mythologised ritual. It was the mythology which consolidated the inner world, gave human form to its experiences, and connected them to daily life. Without that preparation a drug carries its user to a prison in the inner world as passive and isolated and meaningless as the camera's eye from which he escaped.

Objective imagination, then, important as it is, is not enough. What about a 'subjective' imagination? It is only logical to suppose that a faculty developed specially for peering into the inner world might end up as specialised and destructive as the faculty for peering into the outer one. Besides, the real problem comes from the fact that outer world and inner world are interdependent at every moment. We are simply the locus of their collision. Two worlds, with mutually contradictory laws, or laws that seem to us to be so, colliding afresh every second, struggling for peaceful coexistence. And whether we like it or not our life is what we are able to make of that collision and struggle.

So what we need, evidently, is a faculty that embraces both worlds simultaneously. A large, flexible grasp, an inner vision which holds wide open, like a great theatre, the arena of contention, and which pays equal respects to both sides. Which keeps faith, as Goethe says, with the world of things and the world of spirits equally.

This really is imagination. This is the faculty we mean when we talk about the imagination of the great artists. The character of great works is exactly this: that in them the full presence of the inner world combines with and is reconciled to the full presence of the outer world. And in them we see that the laws of these two worlds are not contradictory at all; they are one all-inclusive system; they are laws that somehow we find it all but impossible to keep, laws that only the greatest artists are able to restate. They are the laws, simply, of human nature. And men have recognised all through history that the restating of these laws, in one medium or another, in great works of art, are the greatest human acts. They are the greatest acts and they are the most human. We recognise these works because we are all struggling to find those laws, as a man on a tightrope struggles for balance, because they are the formula that reconciles everything, and balances every imbalance.

So it comes about that once we recognise their terms, these works seem to heal us. More important, it is in these works that humanity is truly formed. And it has to be done again and again, as circumstances change, and the balance of power between outer and inner world shifts, showing everybody the gulf. The inner world, separated from the outer world, is a place of demons. The outer world, separated from the inner world, is a place of meaningless objects and machines. The faculty that makes the human being out of these two worlds is called divine. That is only a way of saying that it is the faculty without which humanity cannot really exist. It can be called religious or visionary. More essentially, it is imagination which embraces both outer and inner worlds in a creative spirit.

Laying down blueprints for imagination of that sort is a matter of education, as Plato divined.

The myths and legends, which Plato proposed as the ideal educational material for his young citizens, can be seen as large-scale accounts of negotiations between the powers of the inner world and the stubborn conditions of the outer world, under which ordinary men and women have to live. They are immense and at the same time highly detailed sketches for the possibilities of understanding and reconciling the two. They are, in other words, an archive of draft plans for the kind of imagination we have been discussing.

Their accuracy and usefulness, in this sense, depend on the fact that they were originally the genuine projections of genuine understanding. They were tribal dreams of the highest order of inspiration and truth, at their best. They gave a true account of what really happens in that inner region where the two worlds collide. This has been attested over and over again by the way in which the imaginative men of every subsequent age have had recourse to their basic patterns and images.

But the Greek myths were not the only true myths. The unspoken definition of myth is that it carries truth of this sort. These big dreams only become the treasured property of a people when they express the real state of affairs. Priests continually elaborate the myths, but what is not true is forgotten again. So every real people has its true myths. One of the first surprises of mythographers was to find how uncannily similar these myths are all over the world. They are as alike as the lines on the palm of the human hand.

But Plato implied that all traditional stories, big and small, were part of his syllabus. And indeed the smaller stories come from the same place. If a tale can last, in oral tradition, for two or three generations, then it has either come from the real place, or it has found its way there. And these small tales are just as vigorous educational devices as the big myths.

There is a long tradition of using stories as educational implements in a far more deliberate way than Plato seems to propose. Steiner has a great deal to say about the method. In his many publications of Sufi literature, Idries Shah indicates how central to the training of the sages and saints of Islam are the traditional tales. Sometimes no more than small anecdotes, sometimes lengthy and involved adventures such as were collected into *The Arabian Nights*.

As I pointed out, using the example of the Christ story, the first step is to learn the story, as if it were laying down the foundation. The next phase rests with the natural process of the imagination.

The story is, as it were, a kit. Apart from its own major subject – obvious enough in the case of the Christ story – it contains two separable elements: its pattern and its images. Together they make that story and no other. Separately they set out on new lives of their own.

The roads they travel are determined by the brain's fundamental genius for metaphor. Automatically, it uses the pattern of one set of images to organise quite a different set. It uses one image, with slight variations, as an image for related and yet different and otherwise imageless meanings.

In this way, the simple tale of the beggar and the princess begins to transmit intuitions of psychological, perhaps spiritual, states and relationships. What began as an idle reading of a fairy tale ends, by simple natural activity of the imagination, as a rich perception of values of feeling, emotion and spirit which would otherwise have remained unconscious and languageless. The inner struggle of worlds, which is not necessarily a violent and terrible affair, though at bottom it often is, is suddenly given the perfect formula for the terms of a truce. A simple tale, told at the right moment, transforms a person's life with the order its pattern brings to incoherent energies.

And while its pattern proliferates in every direction through all levels of consciousness, its images are working too. The image of Lazarus is not easily detached by a child from its striking place in the story of Christ. But once it begins to migrate, there is no limiting its importance. In all Dostoevsky's searching adventures, the basic image, radiating energies that he seems never able to exhaust, is Lazarus.

The image does not need to be so central to a prestigious religion for it to become so important. At the heart of *King Lear* is a very simple Fairy Tale King in a very simple little tale – the Story of Salt. In both these we see how a simple image in a simple story has somehow focused all the pressures of an age – collisions of spirit and nature and good and evil and a majesty of existence that seemed uncontainable. But it has brought all that into a human pattern, and made it part of our understanding.

From *Children's Literature in Education* No. 1, 1970

Old Tales, New Listeners

Perry Nodelman

Perry Nodelman is a Professor of English at the University of Winnipeg. He writes '"What Makes a Fairy Tale Good" was my first attempt at writing about children's literature, and I look back on it with nostalgic fondness. I've since learned more, particularly about literary theory; in the process, I have produced about eighty-five articles about various aspects of children's literature and, also, two books: *Words about Pictures: the Narrative Art of Children's Picture Books* and *The Pleasures of Children's Literature*.' He has recently written two novels for young readers.

WHAT MAKES A FAIRY TALE GOOD: THE QUEER KINDNESS OF 'THE GOLDEN BIRD'

Once upon a time may have been a very good time, but as Joseph Jacobs (1890) said in 'The Well of the World's End', 'it wasn't in my time, nor in your time, nor anyone else's time'. The difference between the magical world of fairy tales and the world we actually live in is so striking, that to some the difference is their most important quality. J. R. R. Tolkien (1964) says that the tales 'open a door on Other Time, and if we pass through, though only for a moment, we stand outside our own time, outside Time itself, maybe'. Even Bruno Bettelheim (1976), who believes the main virtue of fairy tales to be their psychological usefulness, implies that the tales are beneficial simply because, on the overt level at least, they 'teach little about the specific conditions of life in modern mass society; these tales were created long before it came into being'.

While there is truth in these observations, it is not the whole truth about fairy tales. Fairy tales as we know them are literature, no longer part of the oral tradition that engendered them, but stories in books. They deserve the respect and the close attention we accord other works of literature. Bettelheim, for all his emphasis on the inner content of the tales, says that 'the delight we experience when we allow ourselves to respond to a fairy tale, the enchantment we feel, comes not from the psychological meaning of the tale (although this contributes to it) but from its literary qualities – the tale itself as a work of art'.

It is interesting that most commentators ignore the literary qualities of fairy tales; they do not seem easy to discuss. Unlike the other literature children are exposed to, they predate the literary conventions modern criticism was designed to accommodate and seem to confound contemporary techniques of analysis and evaluation.

Nevertheless, those techniques are surprisingly helpful in defining the special qualities of fairy tales. It should be possible to investigate the 'literary qualities' mentioned by Bettelheim and to discover what the artistry of fairy tales consists of. To do this, I have chosen to investigate a tale typical of the genre, 'The Golden Bird', one of the stories collected by the Brothers Grimm, Jakob and Wilhelm). It is not a tale that has seeped into the popular consciousness to the point that everybody knows it, but it is not an obscure or unusual tale either.

A literary analysis of 'The Golden Bird' suggests that it has few of the virtues of good stories and most of the vices of bad ones. But the ways in which it fails to satisfy the demands of criticism turn out to be the key to its distinctiveness.

In 'The Golden Bird', a king sends first one and then the other of his elder sons to find a golden bird that has been stealing his golden apples. Ignoring the good advice offered them by a fox, the elder sons give up their quest for the pleasures of a tavern. The king then sends his youngest son, who listens to the fox, avoids the tavern, and finds the bird.

But in attempting to steal the bird away, the youngest son rejects the fox's advice about not putting it in a golden cage. The bird cries out, and the son is caught. He is told that his life will be spared if he finds a golden horse. Again the fox helps him, and again he rejects the fox's advice, and puts the golden horse in a golden bridle. Captured again, the son must find a beautiful princess in order to save his life. Yet again the fox helps him, yet again he rejects the fox's advice, and yet again he is captured. This time the son is asked to move a mountain; the helpful fox does away with the mountain while the son sleeps. Joyful and obedient at last, the son now listens to the fox; as a result, he wins the princess, the horse, and the bird.

But the story is not over yet. On his way home, the youngest son discovers his brothers on the gallows and ignores the fox's advice by saving their lives. They turn against him, steal his prizes, and leave him for dead. Rescued once more by the fox, the youngest son regains his possessions; the older brothers are put to death, and the fox turns out to be the princess's brother, who had been under a spell. 'And now there was nothing lacking to their happiness, so long as they all lived.'

For all its complications, 'The Golden Bird' is not much longer than my synopsis of it. That is because it is nearly all plot; the success of the story depends almost totally on our interest in the events it describes; the language it uses to communicate those events is noticeable only because it is so perfunctory.

Critical analysis thrives on linguistic subtlety; we like writing that is complex enough to require explanation. But even in the graceful version of 'The Golden Bird' by Randall Jarrell (1973), the only noticeable descriptive word is 'golden'; the few other adjectives in the story merely communicate factual information. In fact, the specific words in which fairy tales are told do not seem to have much effect on our enjoyment of them. We experience the tales in translation, and at that, a translation of something that was once not written at all. And the tales seem to survive the inadequacies of all but the worst of their translators.

Furthermore, and contrary to the prejudices of criticism, the lack of stylistic ornamentation in 'The Golden Bird' may be one of the sources of our enjoyment. Our delight in the mysterious otherworldliness of 'once upon a time' would be spoiled if we knew that the hero's hair was auburn or that the princess's dress was an Empire-line tufted organza with a fichu and raglan sleeves. By drawing so little attention to itself, the language of 'The Golden Bird' focuses our interest on the events it describes.

But those events do not seem to warrant much attention. While wonderful things happen in 'The Golden Bird', anyone with even a minimal knowledge of fairy tales must admit that none of the events it describes is particularly unusual; they are clichés of the genre and not particularly entertaining in themselves. They might, however, become entertaining because of the way they are related to each other; perhaps it is the plot of the story that interests us.

Criticism asserts that a well-constructed plot is suspenseful; the way it joins events together creates interest in how they will turn out. But a perceptive reader knows soon after beginning 'The Golden Bird' how the story will end. The only real question is how long it will take. After the hero has made his first wrong choice and placed the golden bird in the golden cage, the story could finish at the end of any of its episodes, without damage to its meaning or our interest in it. The story establishes a pattern, one that could be repeated indefinitely; and there is no suspense unless a pattern is broken. If 'The Golden Bird' is entertaining it is not because of the excellence of its plot; that the story is little more than a plot and that it still entertains us only frustrates the manipulations of criticism.

An analysis of character as the story presents it is just as frustrating. We believe that good fiction describes complex personalities in a subtle way, and the characters in 'The Golden Bird' are not complicated. The king is kingly, his sons stupid; but we learn nothing of their inner lives. In fact, the little personality the youngest son displays turns out to be a liability. The only decisions he makes for himself are bad ones, and his luck improves only when he stops acting for himself and trusts the fox.

Our critical assumptions also tell us that well-drawn characters grow and change in response to their experiences. The characters in 'The Golden Bird' are static. They cannot grow because they do not change. In fact, they find it hard to respond to experience at all. At the beginning of the story, the king is convinced that his youngest son is worthless, and he does not want to send him into the garden to discover who has been stealing apples. But when the youngest son betters his brothers by discovering the thief, the king refuses to respond to experience – he sends first one, and then the other of the two brothers who have already shown their incompetence to find the golden bird.

The hero himself is just as inflexible as his father. It takes him a long time to learn his lesson and do what the fox tells him to do. And the fox, who appears to be the only wise being in the story, is just as inflexible in his unchanging evaluation of and commitment to the hero, who disappoints him continually.

Analysis suggests that the characters in 'The Golden Bird' are too simple and too static to engage our interest. But that may be a virtue; since we do not have to worry about motivation or development, we can simply enjoy what happens.

In fact some commentators suggest that the simplicity of fairy tales is their main virtue, particularly because it allows the tales to make uncomplicated moral statements. Joan E. Cass (1967) says that 'many of the old folk and fairy tales provide simple, clear-cut patterns, where wrongdoing is punished and goodness justified'. But investigation of 'The Golden Bird' shows that its apparently clear-cut morality is not so clear-cut after all.

While 'The Golden Bird' appears to be a story in which virtue triumphs, a closer look reveals that it praises vice; in particular, thievery.

The hero is a successful thief, and is rewarded not only with his booty, but also with a kingdom. His brothers, who are unsuccessful thieves, are punished with death. Success seems to be more important than adherence to the Ten Commandments.

Furthermore, the story provides no evidence to justify our faith that the hero is good enough to deserve his rewards; in fact, it does the opposite. The elder brothers lose our trust when they are too proud to listen to the fox; the youngest does listen to the fox, and gains our respect. But he does so only once. On four consecutive occasions he is just as obtuse and as self-confident as his brothers were. Nevertheless, he is young, he is helped by a supernatural figure, and he does win out in the end; these things demand our faith in his goodness, and no matter what he actually does, we continue to think of him as good. In 'The Golden Bird' good and evil are static, unchanging categories, quite separate from the evidence of actual behaviour.

Ironically, however, its refusal to consider the implications of conduct seems to allow 'The Golden Bird' to give us one of the things we want from it – a happy ending. As any student of moral philosophy knows, attempts to investigate the nature of goodness only lead to confusion. Better to ignore the subtleties, take goodness for granted, and let it triumph. 'The Golden Bird' does that; but we certainly cannot admire either the clear-cut simplicity or the consistency of its morality.

The theme of the story, which seems just as simple and clear-cut as its morality, is just as inconsistent. The main idea of 'The Golden Bird' is easy to discern: things are not what they seem. The king assumes his youngest son is less capable than his older brother; but things are not what they seem. The older brothers choose a pleasant-looking inn over an unpleasant one; but things are not what they seem. The youngest brother assumes that a golden bird deserves a golden cage, and a golden horse a golden bridle; that beheading a fox is wrong; and that his brothers can be trusted. In each case, things are not what they seem.

But things are not what they seem in 'The Golden Bird' as a whole either. The fox insists that the hero does not trust appearances, against all the demands of logic. But he *must* trust the fox, which is the most illogical thing of all. And the story itself demands our trust as readers; if we stopped to question the existence of a golden bird or the disappearance of a mountain, the story would lose its power over us. It works only if we refuse to act on the idea it expresses.

In sum, then, critical analysis suggests that 'The Golden Bird' is inadequate, its language unsubtle, its plot without suspense, its characters static, its morality and theme inconsistent. None of its literary components withstands the close attention of criticism.

But continuing the analysis does make one thing clear; the apparent failure of each of its components results from the story's refusal to engage the intelligence of its readers. The bias of criticism is that reading literature is an act of understanding – understanding events by responding to a writer's ability to describe them (style), understanding how events are tied together (plot), understanding personality (character), understanding what goodness consists of (morality), understanding ideas (theme). 'The Golden Bird' does not require its readers to understand anything more than that some wonderful things happened.

Even if we have heard of similar occurrences in other fairy tales, the events described in 'The Golden Bird' are beyond the pale of ordinary experience, and their magical otherworldliness is their most important quality. But the story itself expresses no excitement about the events it describes. When the fox talks to the oldest son, his reaction is, 'How can a foolish animal possibly give me reasonable advice?' He might well have asked how the foolish animal could talk to him at all. But he doesn't. The story asks none of the obvious questions about the wondrous events it describes, and makes no attempt to explain them.

This lack of astonishment at the astonishing, the most surprising thing about 'The Golden Bird', seems to be the key to its effect on us. If unusual occurrences are not explained, if they are not even worth getting excited about, then they seem inevitable. Things merely happen. If the story does not question them, we must accept them also.

But 'The Golden Bird' does not simply suggest that unblinking acceptance is the proper attitude to the astonishing irrationality of the world it describes; it also implies that, seen properly, that world is not so irrational after all. There *is* a pattern, even if the logic of its operations is unfathomable. One will get the bird if one can get the horse. One can get the horse if one can get the princess; and so on. Once having accepted what appears to be frighteningly illogical, one learns to discern the logic in it, and to trust its operations.

In fact, that seems to be what 'The Golden Bird' is all about. The hero has his happy ending when he stops thinking for himself and simply lets things happen to him. Up to that point he has only worked himself deeper into trouble. But like the characters in many fairy tales, he is rewarded as soon as he becomes passive. Just as Snow White and Sleeping Beauty triumph by going to sleep, the hero of 'The Golden Bird' triumphs by sleeping while the fox removes the mountain, and by thereafter doing what he is told to do.

Furthermore, the story creates in us an urgent need for the hero to be passive. As he continues to make the same mistake again and again, the pressure builds to have him stop trying to act independently, to give in to the pattern of the mystery and accept it. Our interest in his character is created by our desire to have him be without character. Suspense is created, not by the events themselves or by their relationship to each other, but by our need to have them end the right way, and by the numerous times the story thwarts us by not yet ending the right way. Our satisfaction reaches its height when they do end that way. And our moral awareness is aroused by our understanding that it is not a rule we are dealing with, but an attitude; the point is not whether or not one is a thief, but whether or not one can be sensible enough to take the world for granted. The person who takes it most for granted is granted most of its gifts.

This profound praise of placidity runs counter to our most deeply held contemporary convictions about existence. It is no wonder that the world of fairy tales seems strikingly different from, in Bettelheim's phrase, 'the specific conditions of life in modern mass society'.

But it may not be so different after all. Speaking of his own childhood, G. K. Chesterton (1908) once said that 'the fairy tales founded in me two convictions; first that this world is a wild and startling place, which might have been quite different, but which is quite delightful; second, that before this wildness and delight one may well be modest and submit to the queerest limitations of so queer a kindness'. Chesterton believed that the 'wild and startling place' described in fairy tales was actually the world he lived in. He may have been right.

The world we inhabit *is* mysterious to us. If it were not, we would have no interest in reading about it. The common assumption that 'literature . . . gives order and form to experience and shows life's unity and meaning' (Rebecca J. Lukens, 1976) is undeniably true; but its corollary is that we spend much of our lives not understanding life's meaning. Trying to understand it is one way of coping with the mystery. In describing its own wondrous world so matter-of-factly, 'The Golden Bird' may in fact imply another, equally satisfying response to the wonders of the real world: 'before this wildness and delight one may well be modest and submit'. I suspect our pleasure in fairy tales like 'The Golden Bird' stems from our enjoyment of their placid acceptance of existence.

For children, the 'wild and startling place' described in 'The Golden Bird' may seem no more unusual than it did to Chesterton. All of us must cope with the mysterious inexplicability of the world we live in, but as any parent knows who has tried to explain to a child why the grass is green or why Cleveland isn't called Chicago, children confront it in an especially intense way. As neophytes in a complex world, children are constantly exposed to new facts and new mysteries; their cheerful willingness to broaden their horizons in order to accommodate whatever new information comes along is admirably echoed by the matter-of-fact attitude of 'The Golden Bird'. If a child's view of the world is always shifting in response to new, strange things, then he will find the world described in fairy tales very satisfying indeed; particularly when fairy tales insist by their very lack of astonishment that acceptance is possible, and that being shocked by experience and not understanding it can be enjoyable. Paul Hazard (1944) once said that fairy tales 'date from the primeval ages of humanity . . . in listening to them, we link ourselves to the most remote members of our race'. If we do, then the theories of the psychologist Jean Piaget, who thought his investigations suggested 'possible resemblances between the thought of the child and that of primitive man', are especially relevant. For children, the world of fairy tales may be an accurate image of their real world.

If this is so, then tales like 'The Golden Bird' ought to be particularly entertaining for children. In fact, a calm acceptance of what ought to be astonishing, so profoundly expressed by fairy tales, may be a quality of all good literature for children; perhaps of all good literature. For if literature 'gives form and order to experience', its content is the unwieldy and bewildering substance of life itself; and the order literature imposes on that bewildering substance allows us to accept and delight in it. Perhaps fairy tales accept bewildering events more complacently than most literature does; but the order any work of literature imposes on existence is more significant for the satisfaction it offers than for what it specifically consists of. The queer kindness of 'The Golden Bird' is only a little queerer than the queer kindness of all good literature.

From *Children's Literature in Education* No. 26, 1977

Ann Trousdale

Ann Trousdale teaches courses in children's literature, language arts and storytelling at Louisiana State University. She holds a Master's degree from Tulane University and a Doctorate in Language Education from the University of Georgia. Her research interests include social and political issues in children's books; storytelling and the oral interpretation of literature; and children's responses to traditional tales.

WHO'S AFRAID OF THE BIG BAD WOLF?

'Let's read this one,' said two-and-a-half-year-old Christie, as she pulled Walt Disney's read-along version of 'The Three Little Pigs' from her bookshelf. 'Here's this,' she continued, handing me the tape player. I could see that the Three Little Pigs cassette was already in place – the last story she had listened to. I was visiting Christie and her mother for the weekend, and Christie had asked me to read her bedtime story to her. We sat next to each other on her mother's bed. I started the tape recorder, and Christie opened the book and gave it to me to hold as we read along. It was my first exposure to Walt Disney's version of 'The Three Little Pigs'.

As we made our way through the story, I was not surprised to discover that the first two pigs were not eaten by the wolf but rather escaped to the house of the third little pig: a number of contemporary versions soften the story in this way, allowing the first two pigs to survive. I noticed that Christie seemed preoccupied with the wolf; every time we turned the page to a new picture of him, she pointed him out to me and said, 'There's the Big Bad Wolf.'

Eventually the wolf emerged from the woods for the third time to try to blow down the third little pig's house of brick. He failed, and resolved to come down the chimney. We turned the page. The Big Bad Wolf did come down the chimney into a kettle of hot water placed there by the third little pig – but, to my surprise, rather than being cooked and eaten for dinner, he screamed, 'Yeeeooow!' and scurried back up the chimney and escaped back into the woods.

Christie turned to me. 'He's gonna come back,' she announced. I tried to reassure her that the wolf was so scared he wouldn't ever come back, but she seemed unconvinced. 'Let's read it again,' she said, and we did. Again, the wolf escaped up the chimney and into the woods, and Christie turned to me and said, 'He's gonna come right back'. The next morning Christie wanted to read the story again. We did – twice more. Both times Christie made the same prediction of the wolf's return. As we put the story away, Christie asked me, 'Does the Big Bad Wolf come to *your* house?' I assured her that he did not, but she did not seem much comforted.

I discussed Christie's reaction with her mother, who told me that Christie had been asking for that story often, and that she also frequently initiated dramatic play involving the Big Bad Wolf at her pre-school. She had had several nightmares in which she saw the Big Bad Wolf, or the Big Bad Wolf had come to her house. She also told me that Christie had another version of 'The Three Little Pigs' which they sometimes read. In that version the wolf is killed in the end, but she had been substituting the Walt Disney ending to 'shield' Christie from the wolf's death.

As I considered Christie's responses to this version of the story, I began to wonder whether a terrible irony had not occurred – whether attempts to make the story less frightening had not resulted in making the story far *more* frightening to her. Is it possible that when the wolf is allowed to survive and roam free, children are left with the sense that, indeed, he may certainly come back at any time? An element of gruesomeness has been deleted from the story, but along with it has been lost the security of knowing that in the end the danger is resolved for good.

How adults have viewed fearful elements in fairy tales

The effects on children of the violence and brutality found in many fairy tales has been the source of considerable debate. Many adults consider the brutality in the tales harmful to children; there have been concerted efforts to remove fairy tales from the shelves of children's sections of public libraries for this reason. A number of parents have told me that, in choosing reading matter for their children, they have 'protected' their children from the tales because of the violence and fearful elements contained in them. I know of parents who actually have returned gifts of fairy tales to bookstores, not wanting the stories in their homes. Some parents, not wishing to frighten their children, choose the softer, rewritten versions, which omit any mention of death or brutality.

A quite different point of view is taken by other adults, however. They see the tales as not only suitable for young children but actually beneficial to them. F. Andre Favat (1977) maintains that there is a 'fit' between characteristics of the young child and characteristics of the fairy tale, allowing children to relate particularly well to the tales. Favat points out that the retributive justice contained in the tales is compatible with the young child's morality of constraint. According to Bruno Bettelheim (1976) the certainty of the punishment of the villain is a necessary element in the tales for children; it has a salutary effect on their psyches as well as on their moral development. Linda Dégh (1979) goes even farther to maintain that exposure to the tales is so essential for young children's healthy development that being deprived of them will result in negative effects in adult life. C. S. Lewis (1966) points out that, while the tales may indeed occasion fear they do not *cause* fear. What the tales do teach children, says Lewis, is the courage that wars against such fear.

According to Carl G. Jung (1959) the characters and situations in fairy tales are archetypal forms, representatives of the contents of the collective unconscious present in all human beings, regardless of age. That is, the dangerous or threatening forces in fairy tales may not represent only danger that comes to us from without but also danger or evil that is present within. Kay Stone (1981) however, has suggested that adults and children may respond very differently to the tales. In an informal series of interviews with adults and children about their memories of fairy tales, she found that adults remembered gruesome elements as more frightening or offensive than children did.

How children have responded to fearful elements in fairy tales

It seemed to me that if we are to discover how fairy tales affect children, it might be a good idea to begin some systematic studies of children's actual responses to fairy tale texts. Accordingly, in 1986 I set about to study young children's responses to selected fairy tales. Christie's responses to the ending of the Walt Disney version of 'The Three Little Pigs' served both to illuminate and to substantiate findings from those earlier studies.

Constructing the inner text

In times past, children were introduced to the tales through hearing them told or read aloud. Many contemporary American children are introduced to the tales through such media as television, film or audiotape. I wanted to include contemporary media in considering response; consequently my studies have included versions of the tales presented through oral telling, reading aloud and television.

These studies have indicated that there were varying interactions between children and media, but that regardless of the medium of presentation, the children were actively constructing their own inner text for the tales.[1] This inner text, as represented in their own tellings of the stories, was influenced by the version or versions they had had exposure to as well as by their own active, selective, imaginative and interpretive mental processes. It is the inner text that seemed to be the key to the children's responses to the dangerous or evil elements in the tales.

When I analysed the children's tellings of the stories, I found that the only plot elements that were consistently present in all of their stories were those elements that dealt with danger and escape from danger – with one exception. One child, Rebecca, did not remember the ending of 'The Sleeping Beauty'. She asked that we use 'The Sleeping Beauty' as one of the tales in the study, which I had planned to do in any case. Her telling of the story after seeing the Faerie Tale Theatre version[2] did contain the element of resolution. On the level of plot, then, the children's stories indicate that for them the tales are tales of danger and escape from danger. Many other elements were seemingly negotiable, but a safe and secure happy ending was not.

Rebecca

In 1986 I asked seven-year-old Rebecca to participate in a study of two fairy tales, 'The Three Little Pigs' and 'The Sleeping Beauty.' With each story, I asked Rebecca first to tell me the story in order to discover what her concept of the story was at the outset. Then we watched the Faerie Tale Theatre television adaptation. I interviewed her at the end of the viewing. A week later I met with her again to ask her to tell me the story once more to determine whether or how the television version had affected her concept of the story. The sessions were relaxed and informal; Rebecca seemed to feel free to express her reactions freely, even during the viewing of the videotape.

Rebecca and 'The Three Little Pigs'

Rebecca knew the story of 'The Three Little Pigs' quite well. She told me that she had it by her bedside and that she read it often.

Rebecca's telling of the story reflected a traditional version in which the first two pigs are eaten by the wolf. The wolf subsequently falls down the chimney of the third little pig's house and is himself eaten for dinner.

The Faerie Tale Theatre adaptation of 'The Three Little Pigs' is quite humorous. In this version, the first two pigs escape the wolf's attempt on their lives. When he gets to the third little pig's house and is unable to blow the house down, he climbs onto the roof and falls down the chimney into a kettle of hot water, is hit over the head with a frying pan, trussed like a roast suckling pig and delivered on a garnished platter to the cave he shares with his nagging wife Nadine. There he is left to her inevitable rage.

Rebecca enjoyed the film, laughing outright in many places. She did not seem to be disturbed by the ending, which left the wolf alive. A week later, when I asked her to tell me the story, she very seriously told me again the traditional version in which the first two pigs are eaten and the wolf is cooked and eaten for dinner. It appears that within the framework of what she considered to be the 'real story', she was able to tolerate and enjoy a playful parody in which the dangerous wolf is not eliminated in the end. She knew what the 'real story' was – one which has an ending that takes care of the dangerous wolf.

Rebecca and 'The Sleeping Beauty'

Rebecca was not as familiar with 'The Sleeping Beauty' as she had been with 'The Three Little Pigs'. All that she recalled of the story was that a 'witch' had not been invited to a party after Sleeping Beauty was born and that she cast a spell that the princess would prick her finger on a spinning wheel. She did not remember how the story ended, and was eager to start the videotape.

In the traditional Grimm brothers' tale, the fairy who is not invited to the christening appears once in the story. She comes to the feast, utters her curse and disappears. The danger to the heroine becomes the spell that she has cast. The role of the evil fairy is greatly expanded in the television adaptation. She appears throughout the film, working her magic to make sure that her vengeful ends are accomplished. During the film, Rebecca told me that Henbane, the evil fairy, was her favourite character. She said that she liked Henbane because she could 'do all those things'.

At the end of the film, however, Henbane becomes a far more threatening figure. As the prince is attempting to get to the castle, Henbane transforms herself into a monstrous giant and tries to kill the prince in order to keep him from the sleeping princess. As this scene progressed, I noticed that Rebecca became quite tense. She gasped aloud several times during that scene. Later, she told me that the one time that she had been afraid during the film was 'when the witch turned into a giant'. I asked her how she felt when the prince killed Henbane (her-up-to-then favourite character). With a little sigh of relief, she said that she was 'glad'.

Rebecca seemed to be drawn to the powerful, manipulative and vindictive Henbane until the fairy's desire for revenge got out of hand and turned her into an evil monster. When the evil became uncontrollable, Rebecca was frightened – and relieved when the monstrous Henbane was destroyed.

Rebecca's responses to the dangerous figure in 'The Sleeping Beauty' indicate that the figures in fairy tales do provide children with the opportunity to objectify inner conflicts, as Bruno Bettelheim (1976) and Jane Yolen (1977) have suggested. As I was attempting to understand Rebecca's responses to Henbane, I asked her father whether Rebecca had recently had the experience herself of not being invited to a party. He told me that several months previously a little girl in the neighbourhood had had a birthday party and had not invited Rebecca, who had been very much upset. Rebecca seemed to use the figure of the evil fairy to explore angry impulses within herself, within the safety of a story form. Her reaction to the battle between the fairy and the prince suggests that she had a strong need to see these dangerous impulses brought under control at the end of the story.

Carey, Kim and Peg: the happy ending and the punishment of the villain

Following my study with Rebecca, I asked three eight-year-old girls – Carey, Kim and Peg – to participate with me in a study of 'Snow White' and 'The Sleeping Beauty'. In this investigation, I read to the children the Grimm brothers' version of the tale after their initial telling of the story. A week later they told the story again and we watched the Faerie Tale Theatre adaptations. A week later they told the story a third time.[3]

Their responses to interview questions and their own tellings of the tales indicate that for them the stories were also essentially stories of danger and escape from danger. It was of utmost importance to them that the danger be resolved. When I asked Kim what was most important about 'The Sleeping Beauty', she replied, 'That Sleeping Beauty wakes up!' For Peg what was most important about the story was 'that it has a happy ending'. (Carey included the resolution of danger in all of her stories, but for her what was most important about each story was the heroine herself, because 'she has the most lines'.)

The children's responses to the Grimm and Faerie Tale Theatre versions indicated that they tolerated and approved of the punishment of the villain – if it made sense to them. If the resolution of the danger did not require the punishment of the villain, however, the story could be brought to a satisfying conclusion without it.

The form of the punishment of the queen in the Grimm brothers' 'Snow White' did not make sense to them. In the end of that story, at the wedding of Snow White and the prince, the queen is forced to put on red-hot iron shoes and to dance until she drops dead. All three children asked me to reread that section, and commented variously that 'That part never made sense to me', or 'How could they make her do *that*?' or 'What happened if they didn't fit?' They understood and approved of the punishment at the end of the Faerie Tale Theatre version, however. In that version, all of the vain queen's mirrors are turned black by the magic of the prince's court magician; the queen is never again to be able to admire her beautiful face. She is so overcome she falls to the floor in a screaming fit. The children said that that was a 'good punishment' for her. Yet the tendency in their own tellings of the tale was to end the story with the breaking of the spell. Neither Carey nor Peg included any punishment of the queen in any of their three tellings of 'Snow White', despite its appearance in both the Grimm and Faerie Tale Theatre versions, and despite our discussions about it.

Kim did not include a punishment in her first telling of the story. After hearing the Grimm tale, she did mention the queen's punishment, but in a rather vague and offhand way. She concluded her story saying, 'and these men did something with her shoes or something'. After seeing the Faerie Tale Theatre adaptation, she told of the queen's going to Snow White's wedding, but then she ran into a bit of a maze as to the punishment:

> And then she went to the wedding and they made her, um, and she was invited, and then she met . . . and there was Snow White and she didn't know . . . . And so he said, Each one of your mirrors when you look in it, they'll turn black and that's the end.

In including the punishment as a plot element, Kim had to choose between two possibilities and chose the one that was most salient for her. Her telling of it, however, did not indicate that it carried a great deal of significance for her; it seemed simply to be tacked on to the end of the story.

In the Grimm brothers' version of 'The Sleeping Beauty', the evil fairy disappears from the story after she pronounces her curse. In the Faerie Tale Theatre adaptation, she reappears throughout. The prince must fight her in order to get into the castle to rescue the princess. Finally he throws an axe at her and she disappears, apparently destroyed by the magical properties of the axe. Carey, Kim and Peg said that they found this punishment a good one.

Neither Kim nor Carey mentioned the punishment of the evil fairy in any of their tellings of 'The Sleeping Beauty'. Peg's treatment of that element indicates the impact of the known text or texts – and illustrates the possibilities which an alternative text provides.

Peg was familiar with both the Walt Disney and Faerie Tale Theatre versions of 'The Sleeping Beauty'. Her first telling of the tale followed the Walt Disney version, in which the uninvited fairy becomes an embodiment of evil, bent on destruction. In the end of Peg's story, as in the Disney and Faerie Tale Theatre versions, the prince fought the fairy and defeated her. So strong a part of the story was this battle and defeat for her that when I subsequently read to her the Grimm version in which the prince simply passes through the hedge into the castle, Peg cried out, '*That's* not true!' Then she added, 'That's not how most of 'em are.'

A week later, just prior to watching the Faerie Tale Theatre adaptation, Peg's story conformed to the Faerie Tale Theatre version because, she explained, 'That's the one we're gonna watch.' Her story concluded with the prince's defeating the fairy in battle, then going on to awaken the sleeping princess with a kiss. When she told the story a week later, however, she omitted the struggle and defeat of the fairy. In this third version, she allowed the prince simply to enter the castle, find the princess and break the spell by kissing her.

Once she had found a way to establish the happy ending without the punishment of the villain, she was apparently content to do so.

Such a tendency on the part of children to omit gratuitous violence from the inner text suggests that the violence found in the stories does not provoke in children an unhealthy interest in brutality or turn them into little sadists, as W. H. Auden (1943) has insisted they will not. Robbing them of the means of gaining control over danger, however, may arouse fears that could threaten to become pathological.[4]

A happy ending

The story of Christie and 'The Three Little Pigs' does have a happy ending. When I returned to my home from my visit with Christie and her mother, I sent her a traditional unmollified version of 'The Three Little Pigs'. In this version, the two foolish pigs are eaten by the wolf, but he comes down the chimney of the third little pig's house and is made into stew and eaten for dinner by the third little pig. A couple of weeks later, I received the following message from Christie's mother: 'Well, we put the Big Bad Wolf to rest. When asked, she says he's not going to come back – but retells the story without the [first two] pigs getting eaten – which supports your research'.

Conclusions and implications

Fairy tales, like most good fiction, deal with a struggle between good and evil on some level. This struggle may range from such life-threatening matters as battles with evil forces bent on destroying the protagonist to the performing of difficult tasks set to block the way to the desired goal.

Fairy tales possess a dimension of wonder or magic as well, whether that dimension be achieved through talking animals, magic helpers or evil witches. Whereas adults may be able to maintain a detached view of the particular manifestation of evil presented in the tale, young children do not easily discern the boundaries between reality and fantasy, between the fictional and the real. And when those evil forces take an uncanny or supernatural dimension, and when they are not conquered in the end of a story, their ability to arouse fear can be overwhelming.

If indeed the figures and situations in fairy tales are archetypal figures as Carl Jung maintained, the lack of resolution to a danger which has been presented may be frightening to a child on a level far deeper than that of the threat of external danger alone. Christie's nightmares about the Big Bad Wolf indicate that the fear was quite powerful on the unconscious level, while in her conscious, waking life she was also struggling to gain control over the fearful wolf. But as long as the only story she knew allowed the wolf to run free in the end, she could not resolve the struggle.

The implications of these studies are not, I think, to deprive children of fairy tales. It seems, rather, that adults should question the value of attempting to soften the fairy tales by removing any violence from them. The punishment of the villain in the tales does not seem to have a pathological effect upon children – but it is quite possible that a lack of resolution of the danger that is presented may have such an effect. The children whom I have studied do not seem to be drawn to gratuitous violence, but they do need to have any danger that is presented firmly resolved in the end. If the danger is the threat of a big bad wolf, he must be done away with. If the danger is an evil spell, it must be broken. As long as the story provides the 'consolation of the happy ending' that J. R. R. Tolkien (1966) points to, the children seem to be able to find ways to cope with the fearful elements. Indeed, as C. S. Lewis (1966) maintains, the tales may teach children means of struggling against and overcoming such fears.

Within the framework of such a tale, children may discover ways of dealing with their own fears, of objectifying inner conflicts, of confronting danger through vicarious means, knowing that in the end the danger will be safely resolved.

Notes

1 The results are presented in Ann M. Trousdale (1986, 1987, 1989).

2 Faerie Tale Theatre is a twenty-six-part television series of dramatisations of fairy tales and other familiar tales. It was produced by Shelley Duvall and such actors as Robin Williams, Vanessa Redgrave and Ben Vereen have appeared in the series, which has gained critical acclaim and won numerous media awards.

3 Data were collected through audiotaped sessions with the children, interviews with their parents and field notes. The children's stories as

well as the Grimm and Faerie Tale Theatre texts were analysed comparatively and according to Propp's Functions. I chose children of the same age, gender and socio-economic status because I wanted to control possible differences in response due to differences in these factors.

4 As I was discussing this research with a friend, she agreed with my hypothesis. She told me that she had sought psychological counselling for her own feelings of general ineffectiveness, compounded by the fear that no one could help her. Her therapist had asked her whether there was a fairy tale or nursery rhyme that had recurrent interest for her. 'Yes,' she said, 'Humpty Dumpty.' She told me that through counselling she had come to realise that she had so internalised that nursery rhyme and identified with Humpty Dumpty that she herself felt broken apart and beyond help. I am happy to report that counselling was able to help my friend significantly.

From *Children's Literature in Education* No. 73, 1989

P. Gila Reinstein

P. Gila Reinstein's interests are in the history of children's literature, Victorian studies, folklore, and the relationship between art, literature and popular culture. She has served on the editorial boards of professional journals and has presented papers on children's literature at national meetings. At the time of writing this article (1983), she was teaching at Rhode Island College.

AESOP AND GRIMM: CONTRAST IN ETHICAL CODES AND CONTEMPORARY VALUES

People often think of Aesop's fables and the folk tales of the brothers Grimm together, since both are collections of traditional folklore, classics of children's literature and important sources of American popular culture. Both are retold in elementary school readers; both are regularly selected by artists for reinterpretation and reissue as picture books. Political cartoonists and advertising campaign designers take advantage of the public's familiarity with Aesop and Grimm for purposes of their own. Aesop and Grimm appear to have been adopted by and incorporated into our culture, to the degree that few children grow up today without somewhere along the way absorbing the plight of Cinderella and the fate of the tortoise and the hare. Sometimes these stories are first encountered in library books or school texts, but more often they are introduced through the popular culture, by way of animated cartoons, Sesame Street or Walt Disney adaptations, mass marketed books like those published by The Golden Press, and in the most traditional manner, by word of mouth.

Although the popular culture tends to link the stories of Aesop and Grimm together, actually the fables and folk tales are profoundly different and provoke very different responses from their readers. It is these differences in origin, in content, and in reader response which I propose to examine.

Neither fable nor folk tale originated as children's literature. Little is known of Aesop himself, but legend has it, according to Ben Edwin Perry (1965), that he was a Greek slave of the sixth century B.C., and the fables attributed to him were originally designed as political criticism in an age of repression. The fables are not simplistic children's stories, but highly intellectual exercises which take abstract ideas and translate them into formalised dramatic encounters. Jakob and Wilhelm Grimm, in contrast, were nineteenth-century philologists and students of German regional culture. They gathered the tales which bear their names from diverse sources, and their interest in the stories was not primarily child orientated; they were studying folklore and the history of words in the spoken German language.[1] Over the years, both Aesop's fables and the Grimms' folk tales became the property of all the people, not only intellectual orators, not only scholars of language and folk literature; and both have become the special property of children.

As early as the first century A.D., the Roman writer, Quintilian, recommended that children study the fables to help them develop skill in reading and writing.[2] William Caxton produced an edition of Aesop in 1484, making it one of the first books ever printed in English. During the Renaissance, educators such as Sir Thomas Elyot, in his *Boke named the Governour* (1531) recommended that the fables be a child's first reading. Such notables as Sir Philip Sidney, Francis Bacon and John Locke endorsed the teaching of Aesop to children. Since the first edition of Aesop that was designed specifically for children, in 1692, there have been many versions of the fables for children, with and without morals, illustrated and elaborated, almost without number.

The first collection of folk tales by the brothers Grimm was released in 1812, entitled *Kinder und Hausmarchen,* and although the Grimms intended the book to be read to children, they saw children only as a 'secondary audience'[3], coming after adult scholars. The first English edition was published in 1823 and has been available ever since. There was some opposition to children's reading these fairy stories when they first appeared, because they violated the doctrines of rationalism, but Charles Dickens, Juliana H. Ewing and others defended the folk tales as vehicles for the teaching of morality. In the October 1, 1853, edition of *Household Words,* Dickens wrote,

> It would be hard to estimate the amount of gentleness and mercy that has made its way among us [through fairy tales]. Forbearance, courtesy, consideration for the poor and aged, kind treatment of animals, the love of nature . . .

all are absorbed by young readers of these stories.

The fables and the fairy tales both convey values which our society respects. Each collection of Aesop's fables presents a fairly consistent world view, a philosophy, a prescription for right behaviour. It is the same with the brothers Grimm. Despite Bruno Bettelheim's (1976) assertion in *The Uses of Enchantment* that the folk tales do not prescribe behaviour, the Grimm stories present a rather clear ethical code based on an unstated philosophy that recommends certain behaviours and warns against others. It is perplexing that the ethical code of Aesop's fables is dramatically different from that of the Grimms' folk tales, and yet both are highly influential sources for the teaching of values to young people in our society. Each collection of folklore embodies a sense of what the world is like and how one must live to succeed in that world.

Some examples will help to demonstrate their differences. First, from Lloyd W. Daly's *Aesop Without Morals* (1961):

> A lion fell in love with a farmer's daughter and asked for her hand. The farmer couldn't bear to give his daughter to the beast, but since he was also too much afraid to refuse, he struck on this scheme. When the lion kept pressing his suit, the farmer said he found him quite worthy to marry his daughter, but that he couldn't give her to him unless he pulled out his teeth and cut off his claws, for his daughter was afraid of them. The lion was so much in love that he readily submitted to both, but the farmer was now contemptuous of him and chased him off with a club when he came back. (p. 152)

This fable clearly suggests that love leads one to be foolish; one must, therefore, beware of it. Love produces weakness, not strength. The farmer's manipulative duplicity is rewarded, for this story takes place in a world in which the weak must use cleverness to survive when the strong seek to dominate them. The following fable further demonstrates that respect comes from power: surrender the means to power and you lose what you might otherwise have kept:

> A lion, an ass and a fox reached an agreement with one another and went out to hunt. When they had made a big catch, the lion told the ass to divide it for them. When the ass divided it into three parts and told him to take his choice, the lion flew into a rage, jumped onto him, and ate him up. Then he told the fox to divide it. The fox left only a little for himself, put everything else in one portion, and urged the lion to take it. When the lion asked the fox who had taught him to divide things that way, he said, 'The fate of the ass'. (p. 155)

This fable teaches the reader to learn from the misfortunes of others, and if there is a lion in your midst, you had better respect his power. The clever but weak fox cannot hope for equality. Mercy is out of the question; justice is not to be expected. The fox is lucky to escape from the lion with his life. Another moral is illustrated here:

> A fox slipped in climbing a fence. To save himself from falling he clutched at a brier-bush. The thorns made his paws bleed, and in his pain he cried out: 'Oh dear! I turned to you for help and you have made me worse off than I was before.' 'Yes, my friend!' said the brier. 'You made a bad mistake when you tried to lay hold of me. I lay hold of everyone myself.' (p. 4)

Faithfulness and cooperation are meaningless here. In the world view presented by Aesop's fables, each individual must defend his own.

The familiar fable of 'The Town Mouse and the Country Mouse', and the less widely known parallel story, 'The Thorn Bush and the Oak Tree', teach the value of obscurity: safety comes before luxury or glory. Consider 'The Grasshopper and the Ant' in all its variations: diligent toil is admired; the pleasure principle is a dangerous one to follow. The fable of 'The Wayfarer and the Frozen Snake' suggests that a good deed is often not returned, and since some people are inherently evil, no kindness, no charity can change them.

Although there are some exceptions, taken all together, the fables teach pragmatic lessons: they recognise that the world is a dangerous place, full of exploiters, bullies and false friends. Love counts for little; it exposes you and foolishly allows you to relax your defences. The fables teach self-protection and the value of hard work. Goodness is rarely rewarded, but evil is often revenged. The fables recognise that in the real world, might does make its own right – unfair, perhaps, but true, nonetheless.

To put it mildly, Aesop's fables are not idealistic. They do not recognise miracles. The world is what it is: the enemies, the people in power, are tyrannical lions, tricky foxes, vindictive snakes; the victims, the little people, are vain crows, foolish donkeys, self-important rabbits, and ill-advised lambs. No one is perfect – neither oppressor nor oppressed – and no one can change who he is. The best you can do, according to the fables, is to stand up for yourself, selfishly, if need be, since you can expect no one else to stand up for you; trust only yourself; expect to be attacked and have the sense to lie low when threatened;

and, if you are lucky, take your revenge when you get the chance.

The world of the folk tales collected by the Grimms recognises enemies and dangers, but unlike the world of the fables, it also allows for perfect goodness and the possibility of coming through a trial unscathed, and resting on that one victory happily ever after. Aesop's fables present no ideal characters, no heroes, no heroines. The fairy tales, in contrast, offer many models of perfection. The perfect female is a Cinderella, a Snow White, a Rapunzel: young, beautiful, gentle, passive and obedient. She must suffer patiently, until she is rescued by fate, usually in the form of a marriageable young man. The perfect male is young, handsome, kind, brave, generous, gentle and lucky. He is the one who shares his crust with a fox who just happens to be endowed with magic powers, in 'The Golden Bird'; he is the one who arrives, by good fortune, at the castle of the sleeping Briar Rose just when the one hundred years' spell is up. Often he is the simple, unsophisticated youngest son, mocked by his clever elder brothers. In the Grimms' world, intelligence and cunning are frequently signs of character weakness.[4] In their folk tales, forethought seems inferior to blind action; common sense is less valued than simple faith. While Aesop's fables urge watchful cleverness, the fairy tales suggest trust and patience as the better way: after all, miracles can happen. Cinderella can go to the ball in a dress that rains down on her from a tree. Sleeping Beauty may have to wait for a century, but ultimately she awakens to love at first sight. Straw can be spun into gold; brothers can be turned into swans or ravens, and a sister's sacrifice can redeem them. And, most significantly, what is dead can be made alive again.

According to the values promoted by the fairy tales, it is better to be self-sacrificing than to look out for your own interests. To go out and aggressively seek wealth and power pretty nearly guarantees a bad end: the gentle sister, in 'The Three Little Men in the Wood' is sent to gather strawberries in the snow, clothed only in a paper dress. Her willing helpfulness to the three little old men wins her the dubious reward of having a golden coin fall from her mouth every time she speaks. When her assertive stepsister sensibly bundles up to go out and claim the same, she is cursed for her forwardness by having a toad jump from her mouth every time she opens it. And later, in the same tale, after the good sister has married a king, born him a son, and been transformed by her stepmother into a duck, she returns to care for her infant, not to seek vengeance against the stepsister who has taken her place in the royal bed. It is the evil stepmother who suggests her own awful punishment: 'to be put into a cask with iron nails in it, and to be rolled in it down the hill into the water'. Once the wicked stepmother and the false queen are punished, the innocently murdered queen is restored to life and happiness.

The prevailing message of the folk tales reads: if you are happily poor, and neither complain nor take active steps to secure your fortune, you may be rewarded with wealth; if you are passively self-effacing and let others mock you, mistreat you, and enslave you, you may end up with both power and fame. Self-sacrifice becomes the prudent course of action. There is a puzzling irony here. The tales imply that it is wrong to set greater value on wealth than on goodness, yet material rewards are given to those who set the least store by them.

The Aesopic fables suggest that evil is commonplace. The Germanic folk tales present evil in more terrible guises, but also show that the virtuous victims are ultimately better off for having tangled with the evil.[5] Whatever curses or privations the innocent victims must endure, they are never embittered, never discouraged from their steadfast goodness. Cinderella doesn't whine to her stepmother about how unfair it is that she has to pick lentils from the ashes in order to win the right to attend the prince's ball; the girl in 'Rumpelstiltskin' doesn't curse her father for putting her life on the line, saying she can spin rooms full of straw into gold when she hasn't got a notion how to do it. It is as if there is a shatterproof bubble around these characters, so that they are never tainted by their contact with evil, never permanently damaged. Even if they seem to die, like Red Riding Hood or the little brother in 'The Juniper Tree', they are wonderfully restored to life. Magic helps them accomplish impossible tasks, and because of their flawless virtue, in the end, their burdens are lifted, their enemies are punished (brutally, as often as not), and they find themselves elevated to new planes of material success and emotional satisfaction.

Folklore does not exist apart from people; it rises from and expresses the beliefs, needs and hopes of those people who created it and kept it alive. Aesop's and the Grimms' stories, although not native to America, have nonetheless been absorbed into the American folk and popular culture and can, therefore, be presumed to express ideas and values important to our culture. Because of the all-but-universal familiarity of American children with many of the fables and fairy tales, I have taught Aesop and Grimm to students in children's literature courses at two different colleges, to give them adult perspectives on material which they 'have always known'. The students in one group attended a four-year state college in New England; those in the other group were enrolled at a two-year community college, a branch of the City University of New York. Interesting as the differences between Aesop and Grimm are, almost as interesting are the different reactions of the students to the fables and the fairy tales.

Their response seems to vary with their own socio-economic background. Students in children's literature classes at the New England college were predominantly young, single, white and middle to lower-middle class. The students in comparable classes in New York City were predominantly older (30–60 years old), married and raising children, black or Hispanic, and working class or on welfare. The four-year college students were mostly straight out of high school, often idealistic and relatively innocent of the ways of the world. The community college students, in contrast, had lived in the world – a particularly rough, urban world.

Many of the state college students found Aesop's fables unpleasantly cynical and felt that they were inappropriate reading for small children, but made interesting intellectual exercises for children of ten or older. These students believed that it was wrong to take from small children their sense of safety, their trust in loving adults who would shelter them from danger. On the other hand, these same students felt that the folk tales of Grimm fostered kindliness, loyalty and love, qualities they highly prized. They felt that children should be exposed to the fairy tales early, starting as young as three or four years old, to encourage imaginative and moral development, and they felt that the exposure should continue lifelong.

The community college students did not share these views at all. The city-wise older students discovered in Aesop much of the wisdom they felt their children needed to help them cope with the life of the streets, and they agreed among themselves that Aesop was the very book to read to small children of about four or five years old, before sending them out of the house alone to play or walk to school. As for the fairy tales of the Grimms, the City University of New York students enjoyed studying them, but reacted with cynical laughter to some of the idealistic and, to them, totally unlikely behaviour of the protagonists. These students felt that the Grimms' stories ignored reality and taught lessons appropriate for Sunday school but not for weekday use. Since most of them were churchgoers and believers, they felt uncomfortable about this inconsistency, but they couldn't avoid it: they did not want their children victimised. They could not afford to teach their children to be sweet, passive and trusting when the world was so clearly Aesopic to them, so full of predatory lions, wolves and foxes ready to swallow their children up and, once swallowed, chewed and digested, not magically restored to life unharmed. They saw themselves and their children as the lambs, the reeds and the ants of Aesop's fables, the powerless creatures who must lie low, use their wits when threatened, and work hard the rest of the time. These students felt that the Grimms' idealised world was appropriate reading for older children of about eight to twelve, for by that time the children could distinguish reality from wishful thinking. Beyond this, they raised some angry sociopolitical questions reflecting their radicalised perception of the fairy tales as an attempt by the 'power élite' to keep the masses passively hopeful, rather than rebellious over their lot. Among the more protected and upwardly mobile New England college students, these political issues did not arise.

And of course, the more you think about it, the more sense it makes. The fables and folk tales perform different functions. The former teach self-preservation, acknowledging the difficulties of life for ordinary people in the real world today – and, apparently, in every era of the past twenty-five centuries, if the continuous manuscript and publication history of Aesop's fables is any indication. Survival cannot be taken for granted; loved ones cannot always protect each other from harm. There are no apparent rewards for goodness, no assurances that justice will triumph. Fables are, and have always been, useful for the presentation of cautionary lessons to the underdogs in Western civilisation. The folk tales also recognise that the world can be dangerous, but the rules governing existence are profoundly different. The folk tales create an overtly idealised world in which evil is confronted, fearful situations are mastered, wickedness is punished and virtue is rewarded. Selflessness seems the sensible course, because it brings great rewards eventually. The lowly, if good enough, can therefore hope to be raised up. This is not the world we know, but the world we might wish to live in.

The students' reactions to Aesop and Grimm were strong and, I think, provocative. It is too often assumed that both fables and folk tales are interchangeably representative conveyors of the morality and values of our culture. Although both are examples of traditional folklore, still alive and meaningful, as well as entertaining and emotionally satisfying, they speak to different kinds of lives, reflect different needs, foster different dreams. Both are good and right, when they fit the lives, the needs, and the dreams of their readers.

Notes

1 Eliot, Charles W., ed. *Folklore and Fable* (New York, 1909), p. 48.
2 See Daly, Lloyd W. *Aesop Without Morals*, p. 15.
3 Peppard, Murray B. *Paths Through the Forest* (New York, 1971), p. 41.
4 Some of the stories run counter to this trend and urge a little self-help. Gretel must push the witch into the oven and slam the door; Rapunzel must jump from the tower to her beloved. Some of the stories, notably the animal tales such as 'Cat and Mouse in Partnership' show the triumph of wit over simplicity. Other tales, including 'Hans in Luck' and 'Fred and Kate', mock stupidity. But in the main, the most memorable of the Grimms' tales focus on the passively good characters who stumble upon their rewards without any goal-directed behaviour.
5 Bruno Bettelheim has persuasively argued that satisfying psychological messages run beneath the surface of the folk tales. The protagonist's confrontation with danger and evil, most often emanating from mother and father figures, is necessary to the process of dealing symbolically with strongly felt, but unacknowledged emotions. See *The Uses of Enchantment* for amplification of these ideas.

From *Children's Literature in Education* No. 48, 1983

What If . . . ? A Range of Fictions

Geoffrey Trease

In 1994, Geoffrey Trease celebrated his 85th birthday and the 60th anniversary of his book, *Bows Against the Barons*. A few months later he published two new books, *Bring Out the Banners* (about suffragettes) and *No Horn at Midnight* (the end of the stage-coach) and delivered another new book, his 105th, to his publishers. He has been revising, where necessary, old stories for re-issue, notably his *Trumpets in the West* (1947) for Purcell's tercentenary. After many years living in the Malvern Hills, he is now settled in Bath.

THE HISTORICAL NOVELIST AT WORK

When I began writing historical fiction, right back in 1933, I think the common attitude of the reader was expressed by a schoolgirl called Gillian Hansard. She said, and I quote, because her comments appeared in print: 'Though the details of Scott's novels are not always correct they give one a very good idea of the period, and though they are rather painful to read they always give benefit.' The phrase 'the giving of benefit' – as understood all those years ago – has a rather depressing sound. At that time, children showed a stubborn and pardonable resistance to historical stories which had to be broken down before the storyteller could get anywhere. I would like to think that it is nothing like so strong or so widespread today.

The author has to be clear from the start what *kind* of historical fiction he is going to write. I am not thinking so much of the differences between the adult novel and what I like to call the junior novel rather than the children's story; apart from length, and the possible use of illustrations, those differences become fewer and fewer as the scope and depth of so-called juvenile fiction are enlarged. Those of us who write for both age groups know how little conscious we are of what Rosemary Sutcliff has called 'the quite small gear change' when we turn from one type of work to the other, and most of what I want to say applies to both. The distinction I have in mind concerns first of all the attitude one adopts to the past. I think that most readers of historical fiction – adult readers anyhow – tend to fall into one of two categories. They are concerned with, fascinated by, either the differences between bygone times and their own, or the similarities. Broadly speaking, the former category read to escape from real life; the latter to illuminate it by comparison and recognition of unchanging human characteristics.

The authors in their turn fall into the same two categories. If they belong to the first they are likely to produce the 'costume' novel as I prefer to call it to distinguish it from the true 'historical' novel. They may do an impressive amount of research. We can be pretty sure today that they will get all their dates right and that every button will be in the proper place, though not necessarily fastened, for of late years the old 'cloak and sword' school of fiction has rather given place to what we might term 'bed and bawd'. But as we were long ago taught by the Hollywood film producers, the greatest possible accuracy of isolated detail can still add up to a total effect of psychological falsehood, and that is what happens all too often with a novel conceived in this spirit. Everything has to be larger than life – more colourful, more violent, more passionate, more romantic. Wit, subtlety, understatement, have little place in such novels. They lower the temperature; the reader feels let down. That is why, I think, historical novels in general are intellectually suspect and despised by a sophisticated public which has not examined them closely enough to discern that quite another type exists.

This type is the product of the other category of writers. It is the true 'historical novel', seeking not only authenticity of fact but – so far as it is humanly discoverable – a faithful re-creation of minds and motives. In the last analysis a good historical novel is a good novel, neither more nor less, whose story happens to be laid outside the time limits of living memory. You can subdivide it again if you like. There is the novel which closely follows historical events and introduces famous characters. And there is the novel which we could distinguish as the 'period novel', in which every event and every character is as imaginary as in a contemporary story, but in which the author's aim is to re-create some historical period. But both subdivisions stem from the same approach to history, both can claim in turn the interest of the same writer.

In fact it is often a pleasant relief to turn from one method to another. My own motives in writing have sometimes impelled me towards some of the great subjects that I wanted to tell children about – the French Revolution, the Russian Revolution, Garibaldi. In such cases the chronology of well-known events imposes a ready-made framework on the fictitious plot – I found this particularly with my two Garibaldi stories. It is all very labour saving but can also be inhibiting. Although grateful for the splendid material history hands over ready-made – the colourful characters, the dramatic incidents – one sometimes experiences a wonderful sense of liberation when planning the next book as what I have called a 'period novel' in which one admittedly has to do all the work – all the invention of plot and character – but one also has complete liberty of action.

Whichever of these two kinds of novel an author is planning to write, I think it is important that he or she should be in love with the period. Some authors are so deeply, so inexhaustibly, in love with a single century that the affair goes on throughout their working lives and they never feel the need to look elsewhere for inspiration. I myself have to admit not perhaps to promiscuity but certainly to polygamy. So many aspects of history attract me that I have never been able to confine my attention to one. I have flitted widely between the Athens of Socrates, the fifth century B.C., and Saint Petersburg of A.D. 1917. But it would be quite easy to lay a finger on the single common factor occuring in every period I have chosen between these extremes in time – the period has to be *literate*, or at least someone in the story has to be literate. I once did a book about the Danes. I could not possibly have emulated the primitive gusto with which Henry Treece so splendidly handled that kind of subject. It's not the splitting of skulls with battle axes that inspires me; it's the opening of minds in a gentler sense. I could only bother with Guthrum because of Alfred.

That particular book, *Mist Over Athelney* (1958), will serve to illustrate another consideration that affects my choice of theme. I like sometimes to get two themes into the one story. It's not just economy of effort – two statements for the effort of one; it's not just the growing consciousness that I shan't have time to write all the books I'd like to. It is rather that the interplay of two themes, as in a piece of music, helps to give the story an extra depth and texture. Sometimes those two themes are conveniently embodied in the same historical period. Many years ago, waiting in India for my release from the army, I filled in my time writing a story about the Glorious Revolution which interested the political side of me. But just about that time I had been learning a little about Purcell, and John Blow, and Jeremiah Clarke, and I was full of another enthusiasm to tell English children that there had been a time in history when England had been the most musical country in Europe. Any fellow writer may imagine my glee when I discovered that dates coincided and would fuse my two story lines into one. William of Orange entered London in January 1689, and February saw the performance of the first English opera, Purcell's *Dido and Aeneas.* When I add that the performance took place at a girls' school in Chelsea – which meant that my fictitious heroine could sing in it – you will appreciate that it was truly, in a different sense from usual, 'a turn-up for the book'. *My* book, *Trumpets in the West* (1953), was quickly written in the East and posted home to my wife four foolscap pages at a time. That was as much as would go post-free by Forces Air Mail.

It is not often that two suitably interlacing themes emerge so neatly from the period itself. The second theme may be a general one. I wanted for years to write a story of the French Revolution to counteract the aristocratic bias of the romantic novelists. I also wanted to use a character who was to develop into a painter. *He* could have gone into a dozen other historical stories. As it happened, he went into *Thunder of Valmy* (1960). Sometimes the second theme can be modern and highly topical, but suitably transmuted and transferred to another period it helps to give the emotional vitality the story needs. To refer again to my story about the Danes, *Mist Over Athelney,* the first theme – the obvious initial inspiration – was the rich, underestimated civilisation of those who used to be dismissed as 'our rude Anglo-Saxon forefathers'. But the second theme came straight from the atmosphere of the time when it was written in 1957. We were then experiencing one of our monotonously recurrent economic crises. Each evening the newsreels showed us the queues of would-be emigrants outside Canada House and Australia House. The usual cry was going up, 'England's finished, there's no future here'. And I realised that in the winter of 878 people had been saying just the same – doubtless in the rudest Anglo-Saxon. People in Hampshire and Dorset actually *were* emigrating – packing into ships and crossing the Channel to settle on the other side. They thought it was all over; Alfred was dead, and it was just a matter of months before the Danes overran the last south-western corner of England. People had been wrong then, they could be wrong again. The emotion of 1957 came out in the story of 878.

So the author picks his period. He knows it or he couldn't love it, but the knowledge at this stage can be very superficial. You can fall in love with an unknown girl in a railway carriage, as my father did with my mother, but he had to put in a lot of patient study afterwards.

Authors today need to do a great deal of research. I suppose the standard of sheer accuracy attained by the average historical novelist today has never been equalled in earlier generations. He is writing, of course, for a much better educated public, alert for the slightest mistake. I believe that Victor Hugo once referred to James II of England as 'a jovial monarch', and in another passage somewhere appeared to imply that a 'wapentake' was a kind of Anglo-Saxon policeman. Such casualness would be inadvisable today. Some nineteenth-century writers were more conscientious. George Eliot tore up the first draft of *Romola* when she realised how many mistakes she had made, and writing that book is said to have 'changed her from a young woman into an old'. I sympathise with her, though I have never been in quite the same danger. When I look round my own study shelves, full of handy illustrated volumes on every aspect of everyday life in different historical periods, I wonder how on earth people like Scott and George Eliot managed to get as many details right as they did.

On the other hand sometimes I reflect that ignorance could be bliss. There are just too many books now. Somewhere, in some book, someone has recorded everything (if only one knew where to look) and that realisation is paralysing.

I recall a moment of utter despair one evening, walking down the Herefordshire lanes near my house. I was in the middle of *Thunder of Valmy.* I had read, or at least skimmed, about fifty books on the French Revolution. I thought I had got all my facts at my fingertips. I had just finished writing about that historic June morning in 1789 when the deputies were locked out of the hall at Versailles and had to move into the tennis court. I'd imagined a June morning at Versailles – sunshine, sparkle, splendour. And then in the public library I'd come across the fifty-first book, the one I hadn't seen before, the memories of the American ambassador at that time, and he'd noted what a miserable wet morning it had been. It changed the feeling so completely that I had to rewrite the whole passage. And I said to myself, if this is going to happen all through the story, I'm going to give it up. I'll switch to a period where there aren't so many damn documents.

Does it matter? Would anyone spot it? You never know. In *Mist Over Athelney,* when I realised that my adventurous young people would have to eat sooner or later, I let them encounter a hermit and share his campfire supper of rabbit stew. That detail passed my learned publishers without comment, it passed the *Times Literary Supplement* and a host of other reviewers. But it didn't pass an eleven-year-old boy in Aberdeen, who wrote to tell me that there were no rabbits in England before the Norman conquest.

Even if no one else is going to pounce on a mistake, one hates to make them. They're like a secret burning shame inside, if you only discover them in the published book and it's too late to do anything. But you can't go on researching and checking for ever. You have to ask yourself – as the girl in some historical novels should ask herself but too seldom does nowadays – 'How far ought I to go?' You do your best to get things right. You can do no more.

Now I have to admit, and I do so with some reluctance, that many a book with unsound history is far better literature than one in which the details are impeccably researched. What's worse, I could go further and concede that some old favourites of bygone ages which are no great shakes either as literature or as history have done far more to stimulate an enthusiasm for the past than many books which are their superiors in both respects. They are bad or mediocre books with, in general, good, lasting effects. I would put the works of Henty and Harrison Ainsworth into that category. But surely the success of those books lay not in their shortcomings but in their other virtues – they won their public in spite of their faults, not because of them. Falsifying history just to make a better story is to me a confession of artistic laziness and imaginative poverty. The elder Dumas justified it if it led to a good book, not otherwise. He expressed it in a characteristically earthy Gallic way: 'One can violate History only if one has a child by her'. I may be thought prudish and pedantic, but I still prefer my own literary offspring to be legitimate.

You have to work at it. Strict adherence to truth can present baffling problems. An example occurred in my own book about ancient Athens, *The Crown of Violet.* I had a boy character and a girl. For the plot to be possible the girl needed a certain freedom of movement to come and go in the city. This is an oft-recurring problem in historical fiction. In the Athens of that date I was up against the blunt fact that no respectable Athenian girl – no citizen's daughter that is – could possibly have gone around like my Corinna; she would have lived a life of almost Asiatic seclusion. I could overcome this difficulty quite simply by making her one of the numerous resident aliens, who were less fettered by conventions. But this solution merely created a new difficulty. I wished to imply, at the end of the story, that the boy and girl would later marry.

Yet the law of Athens forbade marriage between citizens and non-citizens. It seemed an insoluble problem. Of course it wasn't. Few problems are if you think long enough. A solution presented itself, and it was a solution supported, though not consciously suggested, by one of the traditional plot situations and dénouements of classical comedy. I think the book was improved by sticking to historical truth rather than by taking the quick and easy way out and falsifying it.

Of course none of us can say, with his hand on his heart, that he has never bent the documented record in some trivial detail, for example, by telescoping some period of time and combining two unimportant episodes into one in the interests of dramatic unity. But speaking for myself, I always make even the most minute adjustment of this kind with a feeling of reluctance. One would like to manage without it, but sometimes one just can't. The overall authenticity is what matters. Also the fiction writer has got to produce a picture which *looks* right as well as *being* right. Paradoxically, it can happen that the documented truth sounds false, and the fiction writer, unlike the straight historian, cannot slip in a footnote reference to justify himself. I remember once using the phrase 'What the dickens' in that story of the Glorious Revolution. My publishers challenged it. I replied that Shakespeare had used it in *The Merry Wives of Windsor.* Historically I was right. Artistically I was wrong. The average reader winced at what he thought was an anachronism. You shouldn't make your readers wince. There has to be a measure of compromise.

And there has to be compromise, I fear, on other and more important points. There is the question of what is acceptable to modern taste, and by that phrase I don't mean anything to do with sexual outspokenness, where indeed the 'modern taste' seems to be for highly spiced dishes. No, I mean quite simply how can the author hold his reader's sympathy, how can the reader identify wholeheartedly with the historical character – all of which is absolutely vital, especially when we are dealing with *young* readers – when so much that is authentic and unavoidable, or at least socially acceptable, in the period of the story repels the reader today?

One's Elizabethan heroine probably had black teeth and anything but a sweet breath. The one atmosphere which was probably authentic in most historical eras was of human bodies too little washed and too heavily clothed. It was not only the villains who smelled. Or take our changed attitude to cruelty. What happens to our readers' sympathy if our debonair Regency hero goes, as well he might, straight from partnering the heroine at an elegant ball to the enjoyment of a public execution at dawn? With the young public I should think that the treatment of animals would be one of the worst stumbling blocks, if we represented it with complete historical accuracy. The old squire dies. He may have included in his last wishes – I believe it was commonly done – that all his dogs should be hanged. It would be a foolhardy author who let his hero carry out that sort of instruction. One can think of countless such difficulties where the author is compelled to present something less than the complete historical picture.

Not every awkwardness is so charged with potential emotion and disgust. There are many little genuine period touches which merely seem odd and may distract the reader, again especially the young reader, such as the way seventeenth-century men sat about indoors with their immense hats on. Then there are the things which may strike a modern reader as ambiguous when at the time they were innocent and commonplace, such as the way men used to share a bed. Some of Pepys's most enjoyable conversations on music, careers and life in general seem to have been conducted in this setting, but it is open to misunderstanding if it is used by a novelist.

Psychological authenticity is the great problem. Anyone can find out what people wore and ate. We know how a portcullis worked, and a ballista, and a kitchen spit. But do we know how people's *minds* worked?

I remember as a very young man going up to Naomi Mitchison after a lecture and shyly telling her what her books about the ancient Greeks and Romans had meant to me, *Cloud Cuckoo Land* (1925), *The Conquered* (1923), *The Corn King and the Spring Queen* (1931), and I can still recall vividly my utter dismay when she told me she wasn't going to write any more books like that. She had come to the conclusion that she had got the ancient Greeks and Romans all wrong, they hadn't really been a bit like that. I still regret her decision, but I think now that I can understand why she made it. To imagine the *internal* and not just the *external* reality of historical characters is a most daunting enterprise.

Stop and imagine the simplest things. The significance of nightfall when there was no good artificial light; the misery of winter for the same reason, as well as many others; conversely the tremendous liberation of May Day and the lengthening days. Imagine the bodily sensation of cluttering clothes in wet weather before the invention of rubber and plastics. Think of the different sense of time before we had watches with minute hands. There was no really practicable watch, I believe, before Robert Hook invented the balance spring about 1675. Stop and consider how this affects our description of suspense. An officer might conceivably count the minutes before battle was joined at Blenheim; he couldn't really have done so at Naseby. So too with slow communications and consequent anxieties. The invaders might have landed days ago, a man's son might have been born to his wife on the other side of England, a new king might already be on the throne – and there was nothing faster than a galloping horse to bring you the news. It *must* have affected the way people thought and felt.

These, as I say, are the simplest things. Add a few of the complications – taboos, superstitions, religious certainty, medical ignorance. My lord collapses, writhing in agony, and is quickly dead. Today any doctor can tell us various natural conditions which, if not quickly treated with all our modern resources, could prove fatal in such a situation. Our historical characters have no notion of such things, any more than they know malaria is carried by mosquitoes and mental illness is not induced by evil spirits. How many hapless cooks and courtiers must have died horrible deaths for supposedly poisoning their masters who really died of, say, a burst appendix? Spells, astrology, hell fire and horoscopes – these were just some of the things that shaped the thoughts of our ancestors. On the other hand, they were spared the brain washing of the advertisers and they knew nothing of opinion polls.

Is it any wonder that sometimes the conscientious novelist despairs of being able to think himself inside the skin of someone living in an earlier century, when he wonders if he hasn't merely achieved the result he so much despises in other people's books – to create what are really only modern characters decked up in fancy dress? In such moments of depression it is salutary to turn to contemporary writings of some other age – to Byron's letters or the Pastons', Pepys's Diary or Evelyn's, Lucy Hutchinson's memoirs or Boswell's journals, even to some passages from Plato or Aristophanes, Pliny or Petronius or Martial. At once you sense their common humanity – what I meant when I emphasised at the beginning of this article the *similarities* in history, which to some of us make a deeper appeal than the differences, however picturesque. And sensing that common, continuing humanity you take heart again.

So you get your characters, you costume them correctly, you see them in action against a background as accurate as you can make it, you do your imaginative best to endue them with an authentic inner life of thought and feeling. All you have to do now is *write* the book!

Most of the problems now are those common to any kind of fiction. Most of the differences that emerge at this stage *are*, I think, those between the adult and the junior novel. Making every allowance for the great development in breadth of theme, in maturity, in sophistication, of the junior novel in recent years, and making every allowance for changes in the juvenile audience – their conditioning, for example, by television and other media to a quick-witted grasp of techniques, such as the flashback, which would have puzzled an older generation of children – making every allowance for all this, I think it is still fair to say that plot and incident retain all their old importance, and that the younger reader, unlike some of his elders, likes a story to have a beginning, a middle and an end – and in that order. And if the adult writer feels bored doing it this way, he might be wiser to work in another field.

We all know that a worthwhile children's book of any type has more than one level. Each reader penetrates as deeply as his years, his sensitivity, his emotional maturity allow. What really inspires the author may be what lies at the deepest level. But he must be prepared for many children to love his book for what he himself regards as the superficial qualities. What I think is vital is that he should never privately despise those superficial qualities and think of them as synthetic decoration – put on, in a calculating spirit, to make the book attractive to the young. It must be a genuine book at all levels. When he is choosing his theme and doing his research his standards can be as adult, indeed as academic, as he likes. When he is writing – when emotion and art begin to take over from intellect – then he must let the child in himself dictate much of the form. I say very deliberately 'the child in *himself*'. Some writers acknowledge the influence of their sons and daughters or other individual children they have specially studied to please. But on the whole a writer should please himself, and a children's writer should not worry and scheme to study children's interests and cater for their demands. He should be a children's writer because he still retains inside himself, perhaps more vividly than the average adult, the vestigial child he once was, and can still enjoy some of the same things that he did then. He may plan his book, as I planned *The Crown of Violet*, with an adult motive – indeed a didactic motive – to inform children about classical Athens and to communicate my own interest and enthusiasm. But in the telling he must, at another level, enjoy the action as genuinely as he wants his readers to enjoy it. To paddle up the shallow river in its gorge, to find a cave with a mysterious girl playing a flute, and then later to get caught up in a plot to overthrow the government – the author himself has got to love every minute of it himself. He is not 'putting it in because the children like it'. He is living it, in imagination, because it is a fantasy which after forty or fifty years still satisfies a hunger of his own.

There is one special problem for the historical novelist, and this applies whatever the age group he is primarily addressing. It is the problem of the vocabulary he should use for his dialogue.

When I came into this field of writing, right back in 1933, the historical adventure story for children was bogged down in tushery. People shouted, 'Quotha!' and 'Ha, we are beset!' and a quotation I specially cherish is ' "Yonder sight is enough to make a man eschew lance and sword for ever, and take to hot-cockles and cherry pit," exclaimed the Earl of Pembroke, adding an oath which the sacred character of the building did not in the least restrain.' One of the reasons why historical fiction was then in the doldrums was, I am sure, that even in the leisurely 1930s the child could not be bothered to fight his way through such verbiage.

Should dialogue attempt an authentic period flavour? It is of course possible to construct pastiche conversations for an English story that goes no further back than the eighteenth century and use no single word that has not contemporary authority. It is possible. It is debatable whether such an exercise is worth the effort, or whether it can fully convey what the characters mean, as well as what they are saying. For we can never afford to forget the way in which words have changed their meanings while preserving their appearance. Today, I imagine, a bishop welcomes any sign of 'enthusiasm' among his clergy. He would not have done so in the eighteenth century.

In any case, if we go back to earlier periods, we cannot attempt a faithful reproduction of speech without becoming almost unintelligible. And the effect is to push the characters further and further back into the past, to raise more and more barriers between them and ourselves.

From the moment I planned my very first book I was in no doubt as to my own way of dealing with the problem. The answer had really been given me (I didn't realise it consciously but it was there all right, submerged in my mind) about seven years earlier, when as a schoolboy I had read Naomi Mitchison's story of Caesar and the Gauls. It was only long afterwards, when I dipped into *The Conquered* again, and read Ernest Barker's introduction to my pocket edition, that I knew my debt to Naomi Mitchison. *I* had made Robin Hood speak modern English, without tushery or archaisms, because I felt it was the only way he could speak to the modern child. But it was Naomi Mitchison – even before Robert Graves with his *I Claudius* (1934) in the same style, which I had not heard of then – who blazed the trail. As Ernest Barker said in his introduction:

> If the novelist of classical times were to make the speech, dress and other appurtenances true to the text of a classical dictionary, he would hardly make his puppets live or his action move. These ancient figures must break into modern speech if they are to touch us.

They must indeed. Obviously they must not break into modern slang or jarring anachronisms. I believe there was once a Hollywood film showing Henry VIII at the Field of the Cloth of Gold, and one courtier was made to say to another, 'I do hate parties, don't you?' There must be artistic compromise. The ear must be the final judge. A line may be historically right and still sound wrong and if it sounds wrong, it must go as remorselessly as any other kind of blemish. At every moment of the story the reader has got to be simultaneously convinced of two separate things: first that these characters are alive and warm and tangible, as if they were in the room with him; second that they are *not* modern people in this room, but are in another time and place whose atmosphere they have thrown around him and themselves, like some magic pavilion. The achievement of that illusion is really the whole craft of the historical storyteller.

From *Children's Literature in Education* No. 7, 1972

Brian Earnshaw

Brian Earnshaw went straight from Cambridge to a housemastership in an 'enjoyably chaotic school run on Ruskinian principles' by an 80-year-old headmaster. After an optimistic year doing a certificate of education at Bristol, he says, he spent some lotus-eating years in Lyme Regis and some windswept years among the Welsh at St David's writing poetry and science fiction. Twenty years of teacher training in Cheltenham were terminated by a surfeit of reform and theory. Armed with a newly acquired doctorate in German Gothic horror, he retired early to publish scholarly architectural history and Heinemann Banana Books for young readers.

PLANETS OF AWFUL DREAD

When I looked through a current list of children's science fiction writers, I was rather piqued to find that while old warhorses like Arthur C. Clarke and Robert Heinlein were still featured, my name was nowhere. With seven of my Dragonfall Five titles still in print I thought I was safe, but apparently I've slipped off some spaceranger's Top Twenty. Consequently, I feel rather bogus to be writing this; but even if the computers have gone spiteful and turned me into a nonperson for giving them a bad write-up in *Dragonfall Five and the Mastermind* I'm still interested in the genre and I'll at least finish this article. If I sound rather sour, you know the reason.

Every now and then, I go around primary schools and children's libraries talking about what I write and why. My agent tells me it's a good thing to keep in touch; pressing the flesh, I suppose, like an ageing politician recharging his batteries. Usually, in fact, it turns out to be a disillusioning experience for the children. As a bachelor I can afford to stand on my principles and I refuse to tell lies to the children. So I always tell them that I make up all the science side of what I write and that several of them know more at nine-plus than I do. Then I slam in with the truth and tell them that the whole world of science fiction is phoney.

You can see the boys' faces fall. The girls take it more cheerfully. Men seem to need day dreams. We are trapped, I tell them, in the solar system forever. The Moon was a bore, Mars was an anti-climax, and the other planets will never be more than television robot images. The great universe outside may contain anything and everything, but we'll never reach the speed of light so we'll never get there, and E.T. never got here. Science fiction was just invented to satisfy a craving for what we will never reach.

Then I get rougher and more political. Science fiction is dangerous because it gives us an escape from reality, and reality desperately needs to be coped with, thought about, pushed around. You can see the boys' faces go sulky then. At question time they never pick the point up. There will always be a hyper drive or a photon jet to zap things up a bit. Or what about using those black holes as short cuts through to where the Galactic Empire is striking back?

The fact is that I believe the whole science fiction industry is spawned out of our frustration in knowing too much. There are no lost corners of the Amazon jungle left to contain the hidden redoubt of the Incas, and the Chinese made short work of Tibet some years ago. When I was young the stars were not necessary; now I churn out a new opiate for the youthful masses. I have no real feelings of guilt about it, however. Most lives have to be inadequate, and you can't stage a Falklands campaign on the media every year to keep us going. I read science fiction myself whenever I can find spare time from reading up the gothic novel in the late eighteenth century. The trouble is that I think the gothic pulp satisfied women's wishdreams and science fiction does the same for boys.

Because I lecture on English literature with a corner on Jean Piaget and genetic epistemology I have to have a conscience. Once upon a time, back in 1966, I was eavesdropping in a senior common room, and I picked up the snippet that there was a gap in science fiction for the eight and nine year old. I wanted some quick cash for an ambitious holiday so I went home the next week and slam bang! I knocked off three books in three weeks. They're still going the international rounds, and I handled their Portuguese translations a month ago.

My conscience saver is a genuine one. What really matters in children's fiction, science or any other kind, is not this delicately sensitive Guardian Award stuff. That can come later when children know they are being got at. What is essential is that they should read fast by the time they are eleven. If they don't consume a book an evening by that age then the whole reading thing will remain a slow chore to them forever. Books are still the way in to real knowing; the whole video thing is another opiate to keep people shallow. So what I wanted to do, and sometimes have done as an author, was to become addictive to children, usually boys I think, between seven and ten. Once they get into a series or an author and read for easy, shallow pleasure, I don't care if it's pony trekking, ballet mania, or garden manuals, then the word consumption rate per minute goes up and up, and by the time they are twelve the whole book world is open to them. Speed first; selectivity later.

That is why I have always had a warm corner for Enid Blyton. I know all the attack lines about xenophobia, class consciousness, and lesbian undertones. What mattered about that woman and her cottage industry churning out books in Hampshire was that children of every class consumed her like candy floss. You ask them when you meet them in schools! Despite the disapproval that teacher training colleges inspire, the children still read her. She is temporarily immortal, a kind of science fiction figure herself, still potent in the tomb. Which brings me to politics. Science fiction is in the thick of it.

The world is divided between the pessimists and the optimists, and children's science fiction writers weigh heavily in with the pessimists. I've been skimming through the shelves to write this and, name no names, but seven times out of ten a book will begin on a ruined world, sometimes this one, sometimes a version, and that world has usually been ruined by atomic war. Blood-crazed mutants or fascist space pirates run riot around the glowing radiation zones. Cowering human survivors shrink back into lead-sealed caverns; robots stomp through the ashes.

True, there is usually a gleam of light at the end. A symbolic door creaks open, a frail rose flowers, or a last rocket takes off for Novo Anglia. But what enrages me is the general level of morbid depression. We all know how children will write their way out of a difficult patch by: '. . . then I woke up and it was all a dream.' Well your average writer of children's science fiction writes her or himself into an easy book by:

> Kerron looked out across the desolate landscape. The only sign of life among the ruins was a furtive scurry of clawed feet in the shadowy places. Though he did not know it, red unblinking eyes were watching him.

The sum total of all this writing has to affect someone somewhere as someone grows up to take someone's place on Greenham Common. We may not have indulged in a single atomic conflict since 1945. Automobiles may be a thousand times more deadly than atomic power stations; but it does not matter. People know, because they read about it as children. The future is a waste land because the bombs did go off and the radiation did spread in a hundred easy pages of time gazing. This tendency I believe to be dangerous and mind warping.

Much science fiction for children puts them off science and puts them off the future; but let us be careful about warping young minds. We want evidence, not nine-toed Garuks lurking in the flaccid undergrowth.

Wait for the self praise which my grandmother always told me was no recommendation. My books are always optimistic. It is true that one of them, *Dragonfall Five and the Space Cowboys,* did feature a world that had blown itself to pieces. A little innocent fun at the expense of Lyndon Johnson and his Texas. But the cowboys still herded cows on floating pastures and the rival Indians came out on top with a superior and very aesthetic sculpture-carving civilisation.

The big trouble about science fiction, whether for children or for adults, is the monster, and, if not the monster, the robot. Once, the B.B.C. allowed me to adjudicate one of their science fiction writing competitions for children. It was a profoundly depressing experience. Not one of those entries, and I only saw the best, raised my spirits or my interest. Every one of them relied on some hideous tentacled piece of jelly or an ill-intentioned robot for its kicks. If I'd had my way no one would have had a prize.

The worrying conclusion is that children thrive on hate and fear. It is the beginning of the syndrome that ends with them as grey-faced grannies and grandads, afraid to step out into the suburban dark for dread of the mutant muggers lurking there. Children like to squash things, but we coax them into more positive behaviour. Monster writing does not help. In those schools I've just visited Darth Vader dominated the Star Wars posters. His was the helmet-kit they wanted for Christmas.

Nothing against Darth. He dresses with a sense of style and runs a trim battlestar. His creator kept William Blake in mind. We need the passive Good and the positive Evil; without contraries there is no progression. No science fiction works without some kind of villain, but the lesser writers are not following Blake to his conclusion. In the end there are no villains. To understand all is to comprehend all. Out with the jelly blobs and the mad machinery! The conclusion of a children's star epic must be understanding, so the opening chapters should not spring from chaos.

The implications of all this are endless. Where would the Reds be without the Blues? What an exhilarating star we tread that holds the

Russian Galactic Empire of the Frozen North and the American Democratic Republic of the Golden West! We have them so let us enjoy them both, and let our literature teach that all are human, that right and wrong are varying concepts, and that it is a joy to walk the tightrope.

My own experiences with American editors have been disturbing though comprehensible. The very dear lady who handled me over there – do not be deceived, she was not very dear, for when I sent her my photograph for a book jacket she said that I must frighten the children – anyway, this lady took exception to my plots. I polarised the races on my planet too often. My planets in deep space are always full of animals; that way I avoid monsters. But sea otters fight with walruses, white hares with black, and she did not like this.

On the other hand, the other side of the Atlantic hotted up my violence. 'Sanchez felt angry with him' got stepped up to 'Sanchez felt like plugging him'. So I felt that I had some understanding of the U.S. homicide rate. To be fair the Americans had infinitely higher standards stylistically. I hope they taught me much about sentence length.

As for monsters, the Americans must be given their due for E.T. That film surely proves my point. We do want to be optimistic about worlds up there and worlds down here. It was a brilliant visual poem to make that flabby tortoise loveable; and it was all achieved without making the police actually horrible. True that E.T. ended up behaving disturbingly like Jesus: being resurrected and mounting heavenwards, preaching vague good will. But that is only picking up the hopeful human paradigms of a second birth, so no harm to it.

My conclusion is that nothing in any book can profitably be invented. Anything that works in fiction must be based on the writer's experience of the real. The implications of this for science fiction are confining. The robot R2D2 only convinces by its human likeness. No writer has experienced another world, so all strange stars are mere versions of this. They must, therefore, be handled responsibly. Dislike, yes. Hatred, no. Caution, yes. Despair, out with it!

Swift had the answer back in George I's reign. Laputa and Brobdignag can usefully comment upon human folly; but those horses were robots, and they were what drove him mad. One of my Dragonfalls went into Women's Liberation. The women otters were heavier and longer than the men otters so every time the two sides played rugby under water, the men got beaten up and lost. Of course Sanchez, who was me, came along with a power jet up his trousers and snatched victory for the men, but that was just ingenuity and we needn't go into the Freudian implications.

Ingenuity I see no harm in. If children have to go through a fantasy phase to make them more resilient to the possibilities or emptiness of the adult world, then the writers who profit by it through writing science fiction should measure their responsibilities. States of mind which you satisfy sometimes turn into states of reality. Tenth-century Europe literally marked time because it was expecting the Second Coming of Christ in the year 1000!

All we have a right to do in children's science fiction is to lure them into thinking about the human condition from a detached viewpoint, and bring them back on the last page in a positive plane. Then, with affectionate and optimistic thinking, by the next century our rotund flying Earth saucer may not be quite the claustrophobic and doom-laden vessel some of us seem to find it today. It's all in the mind, and the mind's from the writing.

From *Children's Literature in Education* No. 51, 1983

Judith Armstrong

Judith Armstrong is a writer, teacher and mother of three children. She has worked in England and abroad, notably in Ethiopia, where she ran a school for young children, affiliated to the University of Addis Ababa. She took a Master's Degree with a thesis on the function of ghosts in children's literature (about which she wrote for *CLE*). She has written plays for radio and is currently working on a novel for children.

IN DEFENCE OF ADVENTURE STORIES

Adventure stories are a despised genre, especially those that come in a series involving the same characters. They are not often bought for school libraries or school bookshops, seldom used as class readers, and usually tolerated by parents as only just preferable to comics or television on the grounds that it is better the children read anything whatsoever than nothing at all. The child of sophisticated parents is often encouraged to grow out of reading them as soon as possible, and if he persists will have it pointed out to him that in these stories the characterisation is perfunctory, the dialogue unrealistic, the plots far-fetched and ludicrously contrived; and there are additional accusations against specific authors that, for example, their stories either condone or encourage fascist attitudes and class divisions.

So there would seem to be very little in their favour, yet the paperback market in adventure stories for children is buoyant. Between the ages of seven and thirteen or so, many children become addicted and will read only adventure stories, stating flatly that other books are 'boring'. Stories written in the 1940s and 1950s are constantly reprinted (Enid Blyton's 'Secret Seven' and 'Famous Five' series, Malcolm Saville's 'Lone Pine', Captain W. E. Johns's 'Biggles', Carolyn Keene's 'Nancy Drew', and 'The Hardy Boys' by Franklin W. Dixon are among the most successful): an implied accolade not accorded theoretically more worthy children's books of thirty years ago, and this despite many much ridiculed anachronisms such as the ubiquitous boarding school all children apparently attend. Yet pupils in the age of 'Grange Hill' stuff these paperbacks into jeans pockets and sports bags. The Hardy boys, who solved their first case more than half a century ago, and their companions have stood the test of time, and considering that this is one of the accepted literary criteria for assessing worth, perhaps adventure stories as a genre have more to recommend them despite their evident solecisms than has generally been acknowledged.

There is first the undeniably atavistic delight in narrative: events in succession linearly contingent. The logic of cause and effect has its fascination; the unfolding of a sequence with its balance of expectation and surprise is stimulating. This is the basic craft of the storyteller in which adventure stories excel. It is currently an undervalued skill in our fragmented culture, so it is disconcerting to note that more homogeneous societies considered it indicative of decline if they did not possess a living storytelling tradition. The status of the storyteller himself was high. The exploits of gods and heroes were the staple of storytelling in societies in which the members identified themselves with the fate of the group (in this respect, the society in Ancient Greece and that of many 'primitive' tribes is similar, in which the function of storytelling goes far beyond personal entertainment). Modern adventure stories are still preoccupied with daring deeds, though of a non-heroic scale, but the protagonists are 'ordinary' people. These characters purport to be representative individuals from our own society, which does not identify with the great so much as with the typical. We shall return to this point later, but for the moment it is important to recognise that an overriding interest in what-happens-next is a healthy one.

I went to discuss adventure stories with a group of twelve year olds at my son's comprehensive school. They had been forewarned of the purpose of my visit, and only those who wanted to participate and had experience of reading adventure stories for pleasure did so. The resulting group of seventeen children was fairly evenly divided between boys and girls. After general discussion and sharing of the books they had brought to show me and each other, I asked them to suggest titles they would find irresistible if they saw them on the shelves. The following brief list indicates that their expectations of the genre were narrow and therefore extremely precise. The zest with which they applied themselves is entirely masked by the banality of the titles, though each child in fact glowed with anticipation of the wonders behind the imaginary covers:

> The Mystery of the Man-Eating Tunnel
> In the Woods
> The Mystery of You-Know-What
> The Mystery of Skull Island
> Susie, Who Ran Away
> The Mystery of the Disappearing
> School Children

'Mystery' and 'adventure' seem to be synonymous terms, both more indicative of the expectation of excitement than, for example, the problem-solving intellectual exercise appropriate to a detective story. These titles, concocted on the spur of the moment, held a promise of adventure for these children, an expectation of real emotional experience. The titles also indicate that adventure stories make special requirements of the basic narrative what-happens-next. The use of the word 'mystery' suggests that successive events have to be ordered in such a way as to produce fear and anxiety, which is only pleasurable because of the certainty that release will follow, and everything will be all right in the end.

In order to test just how precise was their concept of the genre, I pursued some rather tongue-in-cheek arguments. I knew this group had read *Beowulf* recently in a modernised version as a class text. I suggested to them that *Beowulf* too was an adventure story. This they vehemently denied: it wasn't exciting at all, they said. What about *Sir Gawain and the Green Knight* then, I wondered, since they had just seen a film version? They admitted that this had been both exciting and mysterious, but it still wasn't an adventure story. One of the reasons for their denying these classic myths the status of adventure stories was plainly to do with the narrative pattern. A myth or legend assumes terror in its listeners, it does not set out to create it. Legends eschew empathy on a primary emotional level, the kind of empathy that is the *raison d'être* of adventure stories. There is an even more essential difference between the two forms which is in the nature of their respective protagonists, a point which I will return to later.

Children who read adventure stories avidly are addicted to that special sort of excitement which the very narrowness of the genre unfailingly provides. They return for more like animals to a salt lick, and in response authors like Enid Blyton, Malcolm Saville, and Carolyn Keene produce a series of such stories which may extend to as many as twenty or thirty – all concerning the same characters, all playing ingenious variations on very limited themes. The characters neither develop nor grow up; they do much the same things in a variety of places, and the outcome is always successful.

My other son, who is eight years old, has read all twenty-one of Enid Blyton's Famous Five stories. When he came to the end I teased him about the bleak life he was going to have without the Famous Five. He merely turned round and began at the beginning again. 'So you've forgotten what happens in the early ones, have you?' I asked. 'No,' he assured me, 'I remember everything, but it's better the second time.' Surprised, I argued that it could hardly be as exciting. 'Oh yes it is,' he said, 'I know now where the exciting bits are coming; I'm not so frightened so I like it better.' For him the diminution of the real terror of the first reading provides an entirely pleasurable level of excitement the second time round. So surprise and originality are not apparently essential to the nature of this excitement, at least not in young children. The group of twelve year olds thought they would not reread an adventure story unless they had forgotten it, but they were not very definite about this. I got the impression they were rationalising what they thought should be the case, rather than reporting from experience. It seemed they were really saying that it is more difficult at twelve to be entirely taken over by a story than it would be at eight. The emergent rational self which judges likelihood and scoffs at things which 'wouldn't really happen' precludes their empathising as much as they once did, and this is encouraged by their awareness that adventure stories seem to carry a low status with their parents and teachers.

Upon reflection it seemed to me that the eight-year-old response is at least as rational. The genre advertises itself as paradoxical in that it puts risk at a premium even though there is no doubt that the heroes will win. The twelve year old, opening an adventure story for the first time, knows that the heroes' jeopardy is only temporary; the eight year old, reading for the second time, has only reassured himself about this. The salt has lost none of its savour at a subsequent lick.

The reading of adventure stories is not of course confined to children. The adult best-seller lists are dominated by them; they are the stuff the majority of films are made of, though the characteristics of the genre alter slightly depending on the age of the readership. Characteristics such as technical detail, which are peripheral in stories intended for young children, become more pronounced in those written for teenagers and adults – to compensate for the adult inability to empathise as an eight-year-old child does. Adults and older children need to be beguiled by such things as the calibre of weapons, detailed maps, or the elaborate structure of spy hierarchies, for example, into suspending their scepticism. The occasion of the adventure tends to be one man's chance to sway the fate of nations rather than petty thieving in the school holidays, but essentially there is little difference. Adventure stories at whatever level are read for the excitement the genre promises and judged by how skilfully the author creates and concludes that tension.

Interestingly I have the impression among friends and acquaintances that those who now read adventure stories for adults did not read at all as children, and those who were hooked young on the Famous Five are now more likely to be reading Booker Prize winners or modern poetry. Yet the latter are often the same conscientious parents who distrust their own children's obsession with the very stories which served them so well. Surely, they argue, reading this stuff and nothing else, worse still rereading it, means the children are absorbing bad writing at a critical age, which will inhibit their ability to appreciate the good for the rest of their lives. Setting aside the fact that it did not, on their own evidence, damage their parents, it seems to me that the very triteness of plot, the undeveloped characterisation, the standard banality of most pulp adventure stories all work in the addict's favour. Stories which represent the same formula in different guises allow an appreciable gap between the words on the page and the experience of the child as he is reading. The printed words combined with his expectations become a complicated cipher directly analogous to the rules of certain playground games whose object is the generation of a similar excitement. There are stones which the ritual says you have to touch, just as there are the words which have to be read, but everything in between is up to you. Thus adventure stories leave the imagination freer the more banal they appear to be and the faults which any critical analysis cannot but reveal simply do not register with the young reader and so can do no harm.

By the time they are twelve years old, children are capable of being both within and without the fiction at the same time. They still lust after the excitement knowing full well that it is after all only a story. It is at this point that the influence of their reading on their own language development is interesting. They will use in their own writing phrases like 'little did he know that', 'one moment . . . and the next minute . . .', 'to his horror', 'unaware that . . .' These phrases are used with a self-conscious zest which is almost, but not quite, the parody they would have to be in 'respectable' writing.

This delight in the almost absurd, the beginning of a sense of irony – these are sophisticated skills. So too is the twelve-year-old's awareness of the craft of narration. The group I questioned all agreed that they read adventure stories faster than any other kind of story, and that they read fast to get to the exciting bit. I suggested that it would save them a lot of trouble to skip most of the narrative, especially at the beginning, and go straight into the adventure. Again their protest was unanimous: it wouldn't work, they all said, it wouldn't be exciting. One child commented ruefully that she'd tried that with a book she found particularly thrilling, had tried to get the same 'kick' by reading again just the 'best bits' but it wasn't successful. They were all very well aware that you have to work for your pleasure, that suspense is slow to accumulate, that apparently inessential and distracting detail will tell in the end – not as clues in a detective story, but as part of the build-up of emotion. At the same time they are quick to condemn a 'boring' book, and when asked to define 'boring' say it didn't get to the adventure fast enough. Evidently the writer of adventure stories is walking a tight-rope with reference to pace: either too quick or too slow and his work will be rejected. In their hasty approvals and condemnations these twelve year olds are applying sophisticated critical skills, even though they do so unconsciously. How do they know a story will be boring without reading it all the way through, which they certainly do not do? It is not a simple measurement of thrills before page twenty-five or else. . . . It is an elaborate decoding of the way the language is working, which indicates to them how much tolerance they will be required to show. They read, quite separately from narrative information, the ratio of description of character and place to incident; they are prepared to be distracted by humour in conversation, or by technical detail about map-reading, for example, or morse-signalling, but all the time they are monitoring their own tolerance and judging whether or not the game is worth the candle. These are the kinds of criteria they are unconsciously applying when they tell a friend with typical taciturnity: 'That's a good book, that is' or 'That's dead boring'. This tolerance factor is relevant when they decide whether or not to buy the next in the series. And the older they get the more tolerance they seem prepared to show: they have trained themselves through the reading of adventure stories to appreciate the craft of narration.

To return finally to the characters who people adventure stories. Julian, Dick, Anne, George and Timmy the dog are 'real' to my eight year old. Distinguished from each other only by age and sex, all intrepid even in the grip of fear, all friends of authority although they are always getting into trouble, all cleverer than the adults realise, they are collectively marvellous counterparts of his inner self, who is also underestimated but never given their opportunities to prove himself. He could be any one of them if only criminals frequented his doorstep and his friends didn't fall out in the school holidays. However similar, characters in the stories the twelve year olds read are not thought of as 'real' in the same way. 'They're not real,' said one, 'I mean, were not like that. They're typical.' The distinction was acknowledged as valid by the group although its constituent characteristics were not clear. So I asked them to give me some adjectives, first to describe their typical hero. 'Brave, happy, strong, big, just, wise, kind, helpful': there's not much else you can say about a typical hero. A typical villain is even more difficult since they recognised that 'strong' used before as a term of approbation now has to be used as a term of disapproval: 'strong, cruel, mean, vicious, nasty, selfish, wicked, sly, ruthless, unscrupulous and greedy'.

Thus the protagonists confront each other very much in the manner of a morality play. Again the writer of adventure stories is working within a tight compass. His craftmanship alone can tell him how much depth a character can take, and how much elaboration, particularly in terms of moral subtlety, the plot will bear. If he paints the villain in shades of grey the simple moral polarities are lost, and the story moves out of the adventure genre towards a broader novel. On the other hand, if the villain is too evil and powerful he also threatens the convention because he has moved from stereotype to archetype, and the adventure story will have changed into a myth or a legend. This was one of the bases for the twelve year olds' opinion that *Beowulf* should not be called an adventure story: its hero is not typical but its opposite in this context – impersonal. The Green Knight is not typical either, but an impersonal force and therefore does not belong to the adventure story genre. Characters in adventure stories are caricatures, not because their author is incapable of psychological subtlety, but because to elaborate beyond a finely judged point would wrench the story out of its own convention.

Adventure stories on the whole are free from didacticism; they do not preach, they demonstrate in action the virtues of good comradeship, truthfulness, championship of the weak, trust among friends, and self-reliance: most obviously they are metaphors of initiative. The genre does not allow for discussion of these virtues, which would inevitably involve modification; it simply assumes them. And old-fashioned though some of them now sound, more like a prospectus for an Outward Bound School than anything to do with literature, the concept of Adventure itself, of which all these are attributes, is an important one. The philosopher A. N. Whitehead (1933) asserts its importance in the history of civilisation: Adventure is 'the search for new perfections'. It is placed with Truth, Beauty, and Peace among his most fundamentally important ideas in the development of mankind. Adventure stories for children are a persuasive introduction to these moral concepts in an age characterised by cynicism. If they cannot, on the whole, be defended as models of good literature, we can at least acknowledge the pleasure they give to those children who are their enthusiastic readers, hooked on what Whitehead calls 'the freedom of enjoyment derived from the enjoyment of freedom'.

From *Children's Literature in Education* No. 46, 1982

Poets on Poetry

Brian Merrick

Until 1993, Brian Merrick taught at the School of Education, Exeter University, where his courses ranged from Shakespeare and Dickens to Language Work in the Primary School. In the early eighties, he devised poetry shows, performed by student teachers, which toured around local schools – the shows still play to some 3,000 children in a single week each summer. He is the author of the best-selling *Exploring Poetry: 8–13* (1991) and (with Jan Balaam) *Exploring Poetry: 5–8* (1987). In 1993, with Geoff Fox, he published an anthology, *Poems from Other Ages.*

WITH A STRAIGHT EYE: AN INTERVIEW WITH CHARLES CAUSLEY

Charles Causley is one of the most distinguished contemporary British poets. He was born in Launceston, Cornwall, where he still lives. During 1940–46 he served on the lower deck in the Royal Navy, an experience which still influences his writing. In 1967 he was awarded the Queen's Medal for Poetry. In 1977, he received an Honorary Doctorate from the University of Exeter and, in addition to awards for different collections of verse, he was further honoured (in 1986) by the Queen for his services to poetry. He is an experienced and very popular performer at poetry readings. Much of the following interview, recorded in December, 1987, grows out of his long experience as a teacher of young children in his home town.

BM Can you remember a point in your life when you began to think of yourself as a poet?

CC Oh no. No. I don't think that I do now, particularly. I think it's a kind of appellation that people should apply to themselves, maybe, not at all. It's for other people. Nothing is worse than a self-appointed poet.

Everybody thinks he can write poetry because it doesn't seem to require very many words and looks as if it can be done easily like the short story; but like the short story it is a profoundly difficult occupation. Who was it said to Mozart, 'too many notes'? Trouble with poetry, 'too many words'. One has to slice away words all the time. I always wanted to write a book. I loved reading from the time when I was a tiny boy, and always wanted to write a book. To me, somebody who'd written a book would be the most interesting person in the world. I knew that I would rather meet somebody who'd written a book than meet the King or the Pope or the Tzar of Russia, or anybody like that. It seemed to me a wonderful kind of magical trick to be able to do it. And all through my teens I had this urge to write, and tried all kinds of forms, I mean plays, the novel, poetry and the short story, absolutely everything. And I was hampered by the fact that nobody had ever said to me that the material for poetry is what lies under your nose – you don't go and search for it. I felt that my own life was too constricted and restricted ever to produce anything interesting enough to put into a book. So as a child, and when I was still in my teens, I was writing plays about London, and I'd never been to London. I was trying to write terribly sophisticated stuff. One has to work through all that.

And then I found myself in the Navy – the war came along – I was called up. I was six years in the Navy. And I found myself in this totally new world with its marvellously Elizabethan language. The slang. Wonderfully exotic. Travelled the world. And couldn't get it down as a novel or a play – you can't write novels and plays on the lower deck of a destroyer, but you can write poems in your head while you are doing other occupations. That was what channelled me into writing what I hoped were poems, and that's mainly what I've gone on doing ever since.

BM Had you had anything published by then?

CC Yes I had. Before the war, when I was still in my teens, I wrote some plays – one-act plays: there was a great market for one-act plays in those days and I published four, I think, and I wrote a radio play which was broadcast in about 1939. That was a tremendous boost.

BM Your fascination with the sea is very strong still isn't it?

CC Yes. Oh yes. It's very alarming. I mean, it's very frightening. Although I've lived all my life in Cornwall and knew from tradition and from reading what the sea could do, I'd no conception of just what kind of an element it was until I found myself on a destroyer in mid-Atlantic. This terrifying, unresting, sleepless element. I absolutely loathe it, and I wouldn't set myself on it unless there was absolutely no alternative, nowadays. Certainly, not since I came out of the navy in '46. I can remember reading an abridged version of *David Copperfield*, and there's a moment when young David is on the beach at Yarmouth with Little Em'ly – I think it must have been while Mrs. Copperfield is marrying the dreadful Mr. Murdstone, and David goes down to stay at Yarmouth – and David says, 'Oh, I love the sea. I think it's wonderful'. And Little Em'ly says, 'Oh I don't! It's cruel and sleepless and I've seen it tear a boat as big as our house all to pieces.' Something like that. That absolutely woke me up as to what the sea could do. And by God, Little Em'ly was right. So I find it very alarming. And it creeps into you. If you live in Cornwall you're never more than fifteen miles from the sea, wherever you live. I like looking at it – for limited periods – but it's in my consciousness quite enough without me wanting to add to it. The war was just an awful experience one had to get through. But the sea was much more alarming to me than the Germans or the Japanese in the Second World War. And now the very last thing I would do would be to hire a boat and put out from Boscastle to catch mackerel.

BM I would like to talk about how you see yourself as a poet. Does that sound like an impossible question?

CC Well. It's very difficult. I dislike being called a Cornish poet, for example. This is not because I don't want to be regionalised. Cornwall is very beautiful and is a great fund and fount of experience for me, but I don't see why one should be necessarily proud of an accident of birth. I don't think it matters where you were born or where you live – you simply make the most of wherever you are, what you see, and whatever your imagination prompts you into. I feel like a man who walks through a meadow in summer, perhaps, and you come out with all kinds of little things sticking to your clothes – little burrs, and little leaves, and little fragments of grass and all that – and that may be bits and pieces of Cornwall. But I'm unconscious of the fact that it's there. If I seem to write with a Cornish accent, fine, but I certainly don't want to go down the road of professional Cornishry, if you know what I mean.

BM The immediate locality, on the other hand, has been very important to you.

CC Oh yes. This goes back to the old business of teaching in a school: you write about what you know, or what you *think* you know. I've lived most of my life here in this town, where I was born, and I still try to write about it. But it's very difficult and dangerous because I have, all the time, to examine what I've written to make sure that I'm not writing about something, or an experience which I *think* looks like that, or *at one time* looked like that, but which maybe if I walked into the town or descended from Mars doesn't look or feel like that at all. Because places, like people, are organisms, and they change. So it's perpetually fascinating just to walk from one's own acre and try and identify just what's happening to the place, and just what's happening to me and the people who live here. But it's very difficult to keep a straight eye on it.

BM A long time ago I asked you how many of the poems you start get thrown away, and you said none, every poem that you start eventually gets finished. Would you say that's still true?

CC Yes. It's a kind of stubbornness in a way. I don't think that one should be defeated by one's material. I remember Roy Campbell – who is a great and very good friend of mine – saying to me once about writing poems that there's nothing more discouraging than seeing a poet in the grip of his material, rather like trying to wrestle with an octopus. You must always be the winner. But only just. Not ostentatiously. So you *have* to be in control of your material. . . . It takes me some time to embark on a poem – whether I really want to write it, how much I want to say it – but I think a lot of good poems haven't been written because poets have abandoned them for various reasons. Eliot said a poem is never finished but merely abandoned, and he was quite right. The great danger that I have always experienced is that I work too much on a poem. I beat the living daylights out of it. And one has to be very careful: you have to know when to stop, when the reader can exercise a kind of leap of imagination and intuition to grasp what it is that you're saying and what you're *not* saying, what you've missed out, and the reverberations and resonances that you've tried to exercise between the lines, the things unsaid. The reader has to do some work. It shouldn't be pap. But I would still struggle and finish it somehow or other.

BM Does that mean that you're not necessarily satisfied?

CC Absolutely. The poem as published, or as finished, would be the best I could make of it at the time. But I wouldn't care to go back over a lot of my early poems and rewrite them, do the sort of thing that Robert Graves, I think, did quite cheerfully. I think that a poem should represent you at a particular moment, saying whatever it is you want to say, as well as you can at that particular time. And instead of rewriting poems I think you should use that imaginative energy in writing something new, something fresh.

BM Do you sometimes write very quickly?

CC No. Never. Very, very slowly indeed. I always feel like a very inexperienced subaltern in the First World War given a map of enemy territory, and I see the enemy lines, those grey lines over there and those heads peering over the top. And I know that I've got to get over there, somehow or other. But it's getting into the poem – over the parapet and through the barbed wire, very conscious, through the minefield and all that. I can see the shape of the poem by that time, how many stanzas or how many sections the thing should be.

BM Are there occasions when, having worked a lot on the poem, you decide that the problem you are having is a problem of form? And you change it fundamentally?

CC Yes. That's perfectly possible. But that would usually happen quite early on, about a week or ten days in, though it might take me a month to get it right, or longer. I don't mean that I sit down for eight hours a day and just stare at a piece of paper, but it would always be exercising my mind. Another thing Campbell said to me was – he gave me a lot of good advice, Campbell – that lots of poems, particularly bad poems, were in fact two poems: there was another poem in the box. You have to disentangle it and simplify. I always admired Campbell's wonderful sense of form, and I said to him one day, 'How do you write such perfect poems, Roy?' – and he said, quite unselfconsciously, 'With an ordinary lead pencil, boy.' That's nice. I knew exactly what he meant.

BM What do *you* write with?

CC I like a pen that's got a felt tip. But not too thick.

BM You don't type and you don't use a word processor?

CC Oh, no! Never use anything like that. That's absolute death! If you type – this is even true of the difficult business of writing prose, which I do as little as possible – if you type something it looks too good too quickly. The manuscript should be an absolute mess, and then when you come to type it up and start correcting it from that, if it looks and if it *reads* pretty well in that awful mess, it is going to look O.K. when you put it in type.

BM All of your poetry has got a sharp edge to it, and with much of it, as used in schools, the sharp edge perhaps doesn't reach the child. Does that bother you?

CC No. It doesn't trouble me at all. I think that the wonderful thing about poetry is that you can read a poem all your life, and it is not until years later that it suddenly illuminates itself. Certainly that is true for me, and I am talking about my reading of the work of other poets, I'm not talking about my own. I think a poem should be a kind of magic stone that gives out signals . . . keeps on giving out signals. And because a poem is a living organism it is going to change. All the time. This is what makes a poem great. You can read it a thousand times and it gives out something different every time, no matter how familiar. So one just hopes that something will come through. I know what it is that I'm trying to do . . . I'm trying to say. So one just lives in hope. I don't really mind what works. Poetry is an enormous forest or garden, and nobody is going to like everything in the garden or everything in the forest. The great thing about it is that there is something there for everybody. Absolutely everybody. And what works for one doesn't work for others. It's an entirely personal thing.

BM To what extent do you see yourself as a children's poet separately from an adult poet?

CC Oh I don't see these separately at all. What happened was that I didn't write a book of children's poems, or so-called children's poems, until 1970: until *Figgie Hobbin*. I'd written what I considered purely adult poems all my life until then, and I noticed that a lot of the poems up to that point were used in children's anthologies – as well as in adult anthologies. I'd just published *Underneath the Water*, a collection of adult poems, in 1968. At that particular time my mother fell ill, with whom I was sharing this house, and she talked a lot about her childhood. I had to be here because she was virtually incapable of movement, and she talked a lot about her childhood. And I turned a lot of this into poems which I thought I'd make into a book of children's verse. I've always been very much influenced by the idea that the only difference between an adult poem and a children's poem is the *range* of the audience. I mean a children's poem is a poem that has to work for the adult and the child as well – at the same time – that's the only difference.

BM But there are poems which work for adults but not children?

CC Absolutely. A child's experience would be incapable of encompassing some particular things. What I'm really saying is that I try to look at the poems with an absolutely straight eye, and not write down to children. Only when I'm asked for a poem for children by a publisher would I think about whether it was for adults or whether it was for children. If I have an idea for a poem I write it and decide afterwards whether I should put it in a book for children or a book for adults. I keep two absolutely distinct files. Sometimes it's impossible to decide, so I put 'em in both!

BM At the time when you first produced *Figgie Hobbin*, had you read any of your poetry in school?

CC No. You know that I was a teacher for well over twenty-five years? No, I felt my audience was a captive one and that it would be very unfair of me to read my own stuff. There was so much else that I wanted to do with children as far as poetry went, that I thought with a bit of luck they might come on to mine later. But whether or not they did was of no great concern to me.

You see, when I began teaching, or rather when I began being employed by the education authority – which is how I would describe it – in '48, I had absolutely no idea what to do when it came to reading poems or talking about poetry to children. We were in the Stone Age as far as that kind of experience was concerned, and I tried all kinds of different poems – the sort of thing that *I* thought was children's poetry, like A. A. Milne – which personally I had no feeling for at all; and I very rapidly made the discovery that the children in my classes hadn't very much feeling for it either, because it spoke of a world which was almost entirely divorced from their own. I tried all kinds of ways of doing poetry, and all the so-called children's poems didn't seem to work.

But round about that time, I had a double class of boys on Thursday afternoons. All the girls did needlework: in those days girls were supposed to be the only ones interested in needlework. And so I had about eighty boys on a Thursday afternoon, and I used to read them a story. One day I was making off into the classroom, and I picked up the wrong set of books and I found myself in there with them, *not* with the books that I intended bringing. I daren't go out . . . you don't go out and leave a class of eighty boys in a primary school . . . and I had, as luck would have it, a book I had just bought. It was a selection by Robert Graves of English and Scottish traditional ballads, and I thought, 'God, I must do something', and I just opened the book.

It opened at a poem called 'Young Beichan', and I thought, well here goes, and I read:

> Young Beichan was a noble lord
> A lord of high degree
> He wente forth to Palestine
> Christes tomb for to see . . .

A little boy was sitting in the front row. I can see his face even now. I had to turn over – the first verse was at the bottom of the page – and I turned over two pages and was fumbling a bit, and this boy said, 'Go on then!' And I made what was for me a major discovery: that very young children are quite capable of taking poetry, or literature or anything else, whatever one has the courage to give them. They know all about betrayal, seduction, sudden death, marital infidelity, murder, and God knows what, and they simply lapped up those ballads. I discovered that young children were a kind of medieval people. For this reason, whenever we did a Christmas play I tried always to do the medieval plays, from the Mysteries. They seemed to understand what was going on on the surface *and* underneath the poems as well. That was how I started on a very long road of discovery as to how or what one should offer to children.

I think another thing is that one should never use the word 'poem'. I used always to say to the children, or to anybody else for that matter, 'What do you think of this?' or 'I like this story. What do you think of it?' and I avoided using that dread word, which I think is terribly off-putting.

There are another couple of points I would like to make. One is that my schooldays were made absolutely miserable because I had no feeling whatever for any kind of sporting activity except swimming – which I've always loved. And I came across some fairly unsympathetic people as a child. Not entirely. But some. And I always vowed that I'd never do the same things as far as English Literature or history were concerned. I was an English and a history specialist, so called, although in a primary school you had to teach everything from religious instruction to disorganised games. Everything. And if Miss Stansbury was away I had to take needlework – wonderful! That's all very good for someone who's trying to be a poet. But I hoped that I would never put anybody off poetry, or literature, or reading – and always had this in the back of my mind.

BM How regular a thing was reading in your normal teaching week? Would you read just when you felt like it?

CC Well the nice thing about being a primary teacher in those days, of course, was that nobody in the world except your little class, which was very like a little family, knew what was going on once the classroom door was closed. So if things weren't going very well in maths, which they very often weren't or some other boring activity, I used to pack it in and read. Or maybe, we'd sing. I became 'A Music Specialist' because I am a pianist, and so we were always able to sing. I mean, in the event of national disasters and things which invaded the normally quiet life of the school, the headmaster would say, 'I'll deal with this. Mr. Causley will take singing in the hall.' I was very popular with the rest of the staff because they all had an hour off.

No matter what inspectors said you were able to do it your own way.

And the children knew that. I'm jumping about in my experience now over the years, but I remember, not long before I left teaching, the children were writing poems. We published an anthology and I always used to give them lots of time to write their poem. I never said, 'I want it by twelve o'clock.' *I* couldn't write a poem by twelve o'clock. It might take me three months. So I didn't mind if *they* took three months as well.

BM How did you handle this? Did they have a notebook which was for poems?

CC No. I never set a subject, for example, unless they absolutely needed a bit of help: the general rule was that you wrote about something you loved or something you hated. There's no middle ground in poetry or in art at all, I don't think. You have to feel very strongly about it. And I discouraged writing about things they'd seen in a film or on television, but always tried to make them write about their own lives. Autobiographically. And write autobiographically they certainly did. With plenty of time for it. I always felt most people were capable of painting one picture or writing one poem in their journey through life. I painted a picture once and I've still got it here somewhere. I'm terribly proud of it. I was a mere forty-two at the time.

BM And never again?

CC No. Never again. I was encouraged. I went off on a course and I absolutely loved it. And I've found with children who are now adults here – they may only have written one poem, but it seems to have been something that they are very proud of doing. And I felt everybody was capable of doing it. I mean we've always had classes of around forty children. This happened when I began teaching with the fourth year and it was still the case when I left. It was one of the reasons that encouraged me to pull out. You can keep order but you can't teach.

But about writing the poems. We'd occasionally publish a class anthology say, once a year, and we wouldn't publish it until everybody had made a contribution. So some children wouldn't produce anything maybe for the whole year, but in the end, produce a poem they would. And I found children had the most wonderful eye for the architecture of a poem. I don't think enough work has been done on the visual effect of poems. I mean, I don't know about you, but when I think of a poem I can see it on the page even before I can conjure up the actual words.

And I found children have a very, very, good eye for just how a poem should look and just how long it should be and whether it should be a short thick one, as some of my children used to say, or a long thin one, which was their marvellous description of a ballad. But I was very, very careful not to interfere but just to make suggestions. And to encourage them. I never worried about misspelling. I think the only thing that the teacher, so-called, in this particular activity should do is get the spelling right if the thing is going to be printed and distributed amongst other people. Otherwise the poem becomes comic, and people are amused . . . especially semi-illiterates who are more interested in bad spelling than the feeling and the impulse in the poem itself. So I used to get the spelling right before the poem was printed, but apart from that, I interfered as little as possible.

And the other thing to be wary of was that literate children – such as I was, and such as most teachers are – tended to have that kind of facility, that kind of slickness in writing which made them produce poems which on the surface seemed good. But the most interesting poems for me were almost always written by children who could scarcely put two words together. But they had feeling, the real personal feeling: they hadn't read it in a book and they weren't trying to imitate something which they'd seen or read somewhere else. It was something which came absolutely from the well, the deep well, of their own experience. I think one should beware of fluency. It's the same danger that adult writers have. You can be so fluent that eveything bowls along easily, but there's no substance, there's no gristle in it: the thing has no guts to keep it going.

BM Did you ever consciously use poems as models?

CC No I didn't. I simply used to read them poems that I enjoyed. I remember one little girl. I was trying to get her to do something and to write, and she was very, very good. And I said,'Why don't you write as well for Miss X when you are with her?' (Miss X had said to me, you know . . . 'I can't get anything out of her.') And this kid, she looked up and she said, 'Ah, she doesn't write poems like you do.' Which is very shrewd. To me this lines up with the fact that the enthusiastic child footballer has some sort of model in the adult who *really does it for love,* and not the kind of make-believe thing for a lesson. I think that if one hasn't any feeling for poetry at all, hasn't any feeling for literature, it's a terribly dangerous thing to try and teach children.

BM When there's an anthology in the air that you're going to put together with a class, would you increase the amount of poetry that you read to them?

CC No. We only had something like two poetry sessions a week of about thirty minutes, with the great mass of other things we had to get through. Oh no. But I found the children responded like anything to the request for a poem from them all. They had this extra-sensory thing: they knew when you were patronising them or when you were genuinely encouraging them, and it was marvellous when they felt that you really meant it, and weren't just saying 'Oh, that's very good' and all that stuff. They spotted phoney encouragement.

BM When a child had finished a stage of their poem, or thought they'd finished the poem completely, did you ever interfere?

CC No. I would ask them if they thought it was finished ... and they usually knew. My only contribution to the anthology was to write an introduction just to make it clear what I thought a poem was – what it might be. Anything else was quite unnecessary. The thrilling thing was that everybody, but everybody, had something in the book. Nobody was missed out. My view wasn't a charitable one: it wasn't based on the fact that all parents must have something from their child. Not at all. Everybody was *capable* of rising to the occasion and by God, they did! I went to the butcher's the other day and there was a young lady at the cash desk and she said, 'Young Fred here says he's written a poem and had it in a book. It's all a lot of rubbish, isn't it?' There was Fred, standing there, blushing brightly. I said, 'Oh yes, he certainly did. And it was a very good poem.' It was wonderful: he's still proud of it!

There is a book by a Russian, whose name I can never remember. He was the one who said things like, 'Alas. Most good children's poetry gets thrown in the waste-paper basket by teachers who can't recognise the good from the bad.' It's so dangerous if you don't know what you're doing.

BM Did you write poetry at school?

CC We did have a very enthusiastic and very standards-demanding Welsh teacher, who would occasionally set us a poem to write for homework. And write the poems we did. I think those were the first poems that ever I wrote. I would have been about twelve or thirteen I suppose. And this chap was very demanding. Never gave high marks for anything. My social standing and all that was absolutely zero at grammar school, with all my wild inefficiency at everything. But I produced this poem, and I got ten out of ten. And I remember the attitudes of my contemporaries changed, not because they thought it was a very good poem, but because the chap had given me all these marks for it. And I was quite pleased myself. It was terrible stuff of course, but that was how I began.

From *Children's Literature in Education* No. 70, 1988

Vernon Scannell

Vernon Scannell has written novels and criticism as well as the poetry for which he is best known. Born in 1922, he served in the Middle East and took part in the D-Day landings in 1944. His work is frequently anthologised in collections for young readers. His most recent publications include *Collected Poems 1950–93* and two volumes of autobiography, *Arguments of Kings* and *Drums of Morning*, all published by Robson Books.

POETRY FOR CHILDREN

During the past thirty years or so I have visited hundreds of schools from state primary to independent public schools to talk about and to read poetry and to encourage and guide the children in the writing of their own. I have also written a good deal of verse for younger readers, and at the time of writing this article, I am in the last stages of completing a new collection for children which is provisionally entitled *The Clever Potato and Other Poems.* I propose, in the pages that follow, to set down those beliefs, which I feel reasonably confident are valid, regarding the best ways of guiding children towards and into a real enjoyment of poetry. You may well feel that I should be more specific about the age range I have in mind when I speak of children, but while adjustments of vocabulary and terms of reference have to be made according to the maturity of the pupils, the essence of what I have to say remains constant whether I am speaking to eight or eighteen year olds. So my initial job on confronting a group of students for the first time is to find out what prejudices and misconceptions they already hold and to attempt painlessly to dislodge them.

First, the most common misconception – especially, though by no means exclusively, among younger children – is the belief that any form of words which employs metre and rhyme is poetry. Doggerel, whether sentimental or facetious, is not inferior poetry: it is the antithesis of poetry. When we use language in such a way that any change in the order of the words or of the words themselves destroys the artefact that has been created, we are using language poetically. In other words, a poem is a verbal construction that cannot be tampered with or paraphrased without the loss of everything that makes it valuable. Take a tiny poem by Edward Thomas, 'Thaw':

> Over the land freckled with snow half-thawed
> The speculating rooks at their nests cawed
> And saw from elm-tops, delicate as flowers of grass,
> What we below could not see, Winter pass.

It should be obvious that any attempt to paraphrase the poem would reduce it to invisibility just as it would brook no interference with its vocabulary. Perhaps we could point out a few of its felicities: the way in which the poet in the first two lines views the landscape through the eyes of the rooks so that the patches of earth and grass revealed by the melting snow are *freckles* on the body of the fields and that *freckled* chimes phonetically with *speculating* and the harsh 'K' sounds echoed in *rooks* and *cawed* imitate the sound of the birds. *Speculating* carries a hint of speckle, which relates it visually to *freckled* as well as the double meaning of looking out and considering. Then, with the elm-tops seen as 'delicate as flowers of grass' the reader is brought down to earth and is looking up at the trees. Mankind is too close to the ground to witness the thaw as it affects the countryside and, as the poem implies, we need to distance ourselves from what we are contemplating so that we can see it whole.

Now let us look at a piece of doggerel:

> There was a boy named Johnny Lee
> Who claimed he had more strength than me.
> We had a wrestling match to see
> Who would gain the victory.
> The verdict was a draw, so we
> Agreed I was as strong as he.

We find that, although it uses metre and rhyme, it is in fact prose. We could paraphrase it, alter the order of words and change the words themselves. What we would be left with would be the same unambiguous, flat series of statements. Nothing *happens* in this piece of writing. The reader is given information; he is not implicated. This, I believe, is the first thing for the young student to grasp: poetry, or at any rate the poetry of the last hundred years or so, is not primarily concerned with telling us *about* events; its aim is to enact events or make something happen. A poem is not a report on experience; it is a re-creation of the experience itself. It is an event in language and, like non-verbal events, it will elicit different responses and interpretations.

This leads naturally on to the next popular misconception about the nature of poetry: that it offers, or should offer, its readers great truths about the human condition, edifying or consolatory messages, or moral and spiritual guidance. There are, of course, excellent poems which might do one or more of these things, but it is not the primary purpose of their authors to achieve this end. T. S. Eliot has written: 'The chief use of the "meaning" of a poem, in the ordinary sense, may be . . . to satisfy one habit of the reader, to keep his mind diverted and quiet, while the poem does its work upon him: much as the imaginary burglar is always provided with a bit of nice meat for the house-dog.' I do not believe that 'meaning' can be regarded separately from the other elements of the poem in the way that Eliot seems to suggest, though I am in complete agreement with the implied belief that poetry which offers little or nothing in the way of paraphrasable statement can still be enjoyable.

The third heresy to correct involves the language of poetry. That children, in their own attempts at writing poems, should use inversions and archaisms in the belief that they are writing 'poetically' is surprising but not all that uncommon. This, however, is quite easily put right. What is much less easy to remedy is the conviction, which has almost certainly been implanted and fostered by their teachers, that the prodigal use of adjectives and adverbs will result in 'poetic' description. The following piece by an eleven year old was entered for a Children's Poetry Competition of which I was one of the adjudicators:

Stormy Seas

Violent waves crash on the rocks,
Swirling wildly around,
Plunging on to the shore,
Raging wildly never seeming to stop.
The leaping waves dance carelessly
Pouring over the shore.
The howling winds angrily growl.

> The mighty force rocks the boat
> Savagely, furious as an enemy,
> Raging madly and dreadfully . . .

and so on. Simply by cutting out a few of the repetitions and removing all of the seven adverbs and all but one of the five adjectives it can be shown how much more effective the lines become:

> Waves crash on the rocks
> And plunge on to the shores;
> The wind howls;
> Seas rock the boat,
> Furious as an enemy.

I think the physicality of language should be emphasised, and a useful analogy might be drawn between its nature and the human body. The verb and the noun (or noun equivalent) are the muscle and bone of language. Prepositions, conjunctions and articles are the ligaments and sinews, and the qualifying words, the adjectives and adverbs, are the flesh. These last are necessary for health, for life itself, but laid on too extravagantly the result is corpulence, flabbiness. The young writer, whether in verse or prose, should learn to cast a critical eye on his own use of qualifying words and ask himself if each one is totally necessary and fully earning its keep.

That children should be encouraged to write their own poems is not only valuable for the satisfaction that the young authors will derive from the activity, but it can also lead to a deeper understanding of, and response to, the poetry they read. Incidentally I have found that, in most schools, far too little importance is attached to reading poetry aloud and to listening to it being well spoken. By being 'well spoken' I do *not* mean declaimed in the accents of the B.B.C. repertory or the Royal Shakespeare Company though some radio and stage actors do, in fact, speak verse well. Nor, when I refer to the usefulness of children becoming practised in the speaking of poetry, do I mean that they should be encouraged in that dreadful, histrionic performance of verse with 'perfect' elocution and 'appropriate' gestures and facial expressions that I have witnessed with horrified embarrassment in one or two schools, but to speak slowly, audibly, and with intelligent regard to meaning, stress, cadence and tone.

Roy Fuller, in his Sidney Robbins Memorial Fund Lecture (*see*

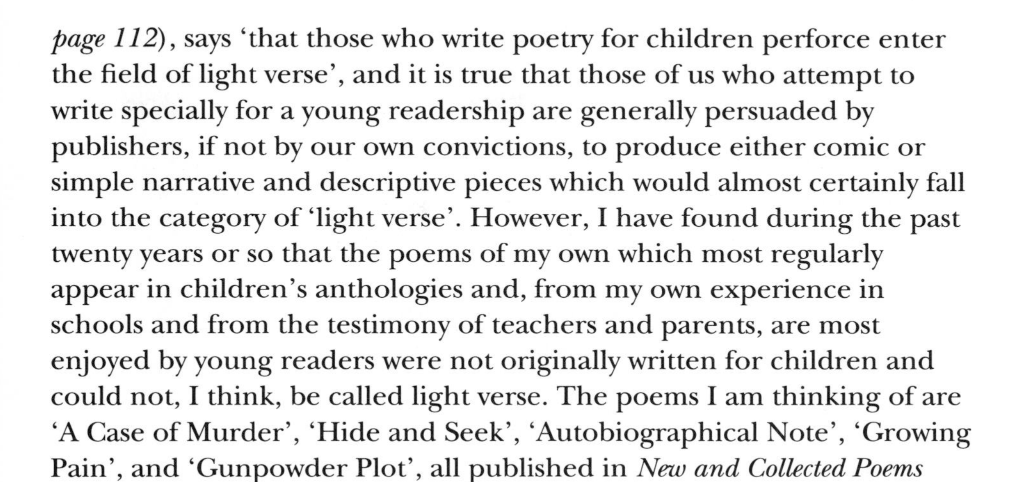

page 112), says 'that those who write poetry for children perforce enter the field of light verse', and it is true that those of us who attempt to write specially for a young readership are generally persuaded by publishers, if not by our own convictions, to produce either comic or simple narrative and descriptive pieces which would almost certainly fall into the category of 'light verse'. However, I have found during the past twenty years or so that the poems of my own which most regularly appear in children's anthologies and, from my own experience in schools and from the testimony of teachers and parents, are most enjoyed by young readers were not originally written for children and could not, I think, be called light verse. The poems I am thinking of are 'A Case of Murder', 'Hide and Seek', 'Autobiographical Note', 'Growing Pain', and 'Gunpowder Plot', all published in *New and Collected Poems 1950–1980* (Robson Books).

W. H. Auden, in his Introduction to *A Choice of de la Mare's Verse* (Faber, 1963), wrote these truthful and important words: 'while there are some good poems which are only for adults, because they presuppose adult experience in their readers, there are no good poems which are only for children'. This is a chastening thought for the author who is about to write for the young. In my recent verses in *The Clever Potato,* all dealing with some aspect of food, or eating, I have tried to write nothing that an adult reader would find trivial, boring, or patronising, and I have employed a considerable variety of metrical forms as well as a wide range of moods, from near nonsense verse to the deeply serious. I give two examples at the end of this article, entitled 'Eyes and Stomach' and 'The Porcupie' (p. 97).

My hope is that verses of this kind would elicit some response from most children aged around twelve and over, and for readers of more robust tastes who might need something more obviously funny than 'The Porcupie' and more vigorously narrative than 'Eyes and Stomach', I have included a few, almost surrealistic, comic pieces like 'The Olympic Eating Game' (p. 98).

What a teacher must never do is apologise for poetry or attempt to engage the sympathies and interest of children by offering them inferior but instantly 'accessible' verse on the grounds that the third-rate can be used as stepping-stones towards the excellent. By all means present a wide range of mood, style, subject matter and genre but never anything that you know is shoddy, inferior of its kind. The poetry itself should be trusted. Remember that it can give pleasure before it is rationally understood. One of the very first poems I read voluntarily and with real excitement and pleasure was a lyric by the little-known Victorian poet, Charles Dalmon, which I came across in Walter de la Mare's splendid anthology *Come Hither* when I was about fourteen. About twenty-five years later I read it one evening to my daughters, Jane and Nancy, who were then about twelve and ten years old. They loved the poem and were able after a few re-readings or listenings to recite it by heart. Here it is:

> O what if the fowler my blackbird has taken?
>   The roses of dawn blossom over the sea;
> Awaken, my blackbird, awaken, awaken,
>   And sing to me out of my red fuchsia tree!
>
> O what if the fowler my blackbird has taken?
>   The sun lifts his head from the lip of the sea –
> Awaken, my blackbird, awaken, awaken,
>   And sing to me out of my red fuchsia tree!
>
> O what if the fowler my blackbird has taken?
>   The mountain grows white with the birds of the sea;
> But down in my garden, forsaken, forsaken,
>   I'll weep all the day by my red fuchsia tree!

When I asked Jane what she thought the poem was about she said, 'Well . . . it's about somebody who's lost a blackbird'. Her enjoyment of the poem had little to do with conscious understanding: I am sure she enjoyed and comprehended instinctively the way in which those rhythms reflected the undulations of the sea, the contrasting rich colours, the glossy black plumage of the bird, the mist-veiled roses and the dramatic red fuchsia, and I guess that the whole thing communicated the sense of loss, of inconsolable sadness. I suppose I could have talked about the possibility of the blackbird representing the poet's mysterious gift of song and the fowler being a symbol of the hostile forces of materialism, the predator, the killer; on the other hand, it could be a love poem, the blackbird being an emblem of the poet's love and the fowler representing mortality or the inevitable ending of passion. None of this, I am sure, would have been of more than passing interest to my daughters. They had swallowed the poem whole and loved its flavour.

I believe that quite a lot of the poetry written especially for children would be better jettisoned in favour of poems, like Dalmon's, written for people of any age. I am thinking here of the kind of children's writing that is patronising either through whimsy or an ingratiating and sniggering vernacular 'free verse' that is in fact not verse at all. What is I believe valuable and perhaps indispensable is the kind of children's poetry which, as Auden demanded, is good poetry by anybody's standards. (In our own century in Britain I can think off-hand of de la Mare, Belloc, Causley and John Fuller.) But I would like to see poetry presented in schools, more courageously, poetry of all kinds and from all periods, presented with passionate conviction, with love, for, if this great art is neglected or grossly misrepresented, humanity will be diminished and the barbarians will have won yet another, perhaps the final, victory.

Eyes and Stomach

When, as a child, I asked for more –
Not hungry like poor Oliver Twist,
But simply greedy – Grannie swore
That I should learn how to resist
Temptation to eat up too much.
'Your eyes,' she always said, 'are bigger
Than your stomach.' She would touch
Her own eyes and her ample figure,
Smiling gently. I recall
Her words as now, so many years
Later on, I see this small
And solemn child through splintered tears;
This little African with eyes
Big indeed, but not beside
That pathetic belly's size,
Huge as pain and genocide;
Each eye, dark signal of distress,
The belly vast with emptiness.

The Porcupie

I should not try, if I were you,
To eat the porcupie;
Although the crust is brown and crisp
And packed with meat, you'll die.
Those little spikes will pierce your throat,
Those quills will make you ill,
And you will find no antidote,

No medicine or pill.
So let the little porcupie
Go quietly to its lair
And satisfy your appetite
With apple, plum or pear;
So porcupies may occupy
A world made safe for porcupies
Here and everywhere.

The Olympic Eating Game

My dear old schoolfriend, Pendleby Reid,
Could eat up his grub at incredible speed;
Savoury, sweet, seasoned and sour
All disappeared in well under the hour.
He could eat all the day and all the night too,
You wouldn't believe what that man could get through.
So when the Olympic Committee's report
Announced that the Games would include a new sport,
A race to find out who could swallow the most –
Believe it or not – mud pies and burnt toast,
Who was the Briton most sure to succeed?
The champion of chomping old Pendleby Reid!
The contest took place in the great Eating Ring
And everyone cheered and started to sing
As Pendleby swallowed his toast and mud pies
With speed and with relish, amazing all eyes.
His rivals surrendered, all except one,
The Chinese competitor, Choo Ing Flan Phun.
At last it seemed certain that Pendleby must
Defeat Choo Ing Flan, who looked certain to bust.
But then to the horror of Pendleby's faction
He suddenly lost his smooth-eating action
And flung down his shovel-sized spoon with a cry,
'I cannot go on, there's a hair in my pie!'
He lost by a whisker, and my story's told
Of how my friend Pendleby failed to win Gold.

From *Children's Literature in Education* No. 67, 1987

IN ESSENCE

Extracts from Articles

Edward Blishen

Edward Blishen is a broadcaster, reviewer, anthologist, writer, lecturer and the author of several autobiographies, some of which record his experiences as a schoolteacher. He was invited to bring to an end the 1970 Exeter Children's Literature Conference, from which *CLE* grew. In the course of his 'summing up', he recalled how he himself was drawn into the habit of reading.

A teacher who profoundly affected the relations of children and books in the school where I was taught myself was an Irishman appointed to teach mathematics on the grounds that he was an international lawn tennis player. He was actually a mathematical defective. He taught us in the first form and is certainly one of the reasons (along with some natural causes) why I am a mathematical defective myself. He taught us by an extraordinary method; he used to ask us what he called 'batches of five', and these 'batches of five' were intended to be mental arithmetic questions; but they degenerated very quickly throughout a lesson, becoming general questions about life, letters and so on. The school secretary would come in and he would say when she left, 'What is the colour of Mrs Hibbard's eyes?' I remember that (curiously, because we were all deeply in love with Mrs Hibbard) none of us knew the answer. There he was, mathematically defective but with a great natural passion for literature, which of course he was accordingly never invited to teach. He used to give us free use of his private library at home. He used to bring us books in a perfectly natural way. He talked about books with joy and pleasure, and also when it was necessary – and it turned out to be often necessary – talked abusively about books. He had a lovely habit as he came ungowned into Assembly – because, as you know, lawn tennis and a profound passion for literature don't earn you gowns – he had a habit, as he passed between the rows of boys, of tossing a book into your lap as he went by with some murmur of: 'Sh – you'll love this,' or 'Sh – you'll hate this,' or best of all, 'Don't let anybody see that! Keep it quiet!' I remember one of the books he told me to keep quiet about was *Tess of the D'Urbervilles*, and I am eternally grateful, though it was already half a century too late to keep quiet about that. But what a sense of conspiracy he knew how to generate! Pedagogically he was an immensely ingenious man, though in fact in pedagogy he might have rated very low indeed.

How simple was all that he did, and how good it was to be made part of his life as a reader! How influential to have this utterly natural exhibition by a grown-up, with whom you were constantly in contact, of the quality of a true reader who displayed before us, quite naturally, all the responses to books, rage as well as deep appreciation. How simple! Because indeed, *that's all.*

If the habit of reading does not grow, it seems to me that this is not due to some ineptitude of literature, but rather because, by being too teacherly (perhaps, as a teacher, I may use that term), we have allowed the excitement to disperse, the delight and humour and so on that are all important.

'That's all'
From *Children's Literature in Education* No. 2, 1970

Alan Garner

Alan Garner won the Carnegie Medal in 1967 with *The Owl Service*, which drew on a legend from *The Mabinogion*. In a review of the 1970 Medal winner, *The God Beneath the Sea*, a reworking of Greek myth by Leon Garfield and Edward Blishen, Garner considered the challenge of presenting myths to young readers.

Yet myth is no escapist entertainment. It is distilled and violent truth. Anyone who reads it is handling spiritual gelignite. Should children be let loose among the stuff, or are they at risk? The question may seem idiotic to the adult who has forgotten childhood. My own answer is clear. Children should indeed know myth, but it must be presented with the greatest skill.

There are three basic ways of handling the material. The writer may re-absorb and transmute (often subconsciously) the elements of the myth; or he may translate existing texts; or he may re-tell. Re-telling is the form most practised, since any competent literate can crib from a translation, although a few writers do have genuine ability in this narrow field, and can read both text and translation and retrieve what the scholar has lost. Translation is normally an accurate text from which the essence has gone. It is workable slag, which some steal and one or two build on.

Hardest of all is the absorption of myth, not the shape but the spirit, and making it relevant to the present moment. This absorption, if it works, is the most positive form for the myth to take, because the life of the myth is handed forward. It doesn't matter if the story changes, since what we take to be the original story is no more than the earliest form that we have. When it works, the writer is a transmitter, not an archivist.

There is another question. How has it come about that children are given explosive materials and left alone to play? The answer may be that myth has been defused. The worth's been taken out. For what we usually think of as myth is Classical Greek and Roman in form, and it's dead. It must have lived once, but by the time the foundations of our culture were established cynicism was weakening it: marble bled it, and the eighteenth and nineteenth centuries emasculated it as efficiently as Cronos set about Uranus.

'The death of myth'
From *Children's Literature in Education* No. 3, 1970

Peter Dickinson

At a conference on children's literature in Exeter in 1970, Peter Dickinson made what he thought would be a few ephemeral 'remarks about literary rubbish'. His own talk seemed to be ephemeral in itself, for as he finished reading each sheet of his text, he allowed it to drift down to the audience below him in the stalls of the St Luke's College Theatre. His words are still regularly quoted, not least because they are so quotable ('Nobody who has not written comic strips can really understand the phrase 'economy of words'. It's like trying to write *Paradise Lost* in haiku'). Peter Dickinson later wrote of this talk, 'If I'd realised then what a powder-keg I was throwing my fag-end of thought into, I would have kept my trap shut'. He advanced half-a-dozen reasons 'in defence of rubbish' – the last three are reprinted here.

Fourth comes a psychological point. Children have a very varying need of security, but almost all children feel the need of security and reassurance sometime. For instance, in those families where boys are sent away to boarding school it is often very noticeable that, in the first week of the holidays, the boys do not read just the books they read last holidays, but books off their younger brother's bookshelves. One can often tell how happy or insecure a child is feeling simply by what he is reading. And sometimes he may need to reread something well known but which makes absolutely no intellectual or emotional demand. Rubbish has this negative virtue, and I would be very chary of interfering with a child who felt an obvious need of rubbish.

My fifth point is more nebulous. There is no proof, or even arguing about it. But I am fairly sure in my own mind that a diet of plums is bad for you, and that any rational reading system needs to include a considerable amount of pap or roughage – call it what you will. I know very few adults who do not have some secret cultural vice, and they are all the better for it. I would instantly suspect an adult all of whose cultural activities were high, remote and perfect.

Sixth, it may not be rubbish after all. The adult eye is not necessarily a perfect instrument for discerning certain sorts of values. Elements – and this particularly applies to science fiction, about which I was talking at the conference – may be so obviously rubbishy that one is tempted to dismiss the whole product as rubbish. But among those elements there may be something new and strange to which one is not accustomed, and which one may not be able to assimilate oneself, as an adult, because of the sheer awfulness of the rest of the stuff; but the innocence – I suppose there is no other word – of the child's eye can take or leave in a way that I feel an adult cannot, and can acquire valuable stimuli from things which appear otherwise overgrown with a mass of weeds and nonsense.

'A defence of rubbish'
From *Children's Literature in Education* No. 3, 1970

Fred Inglis

Fred Inglis, now Professor of Education at Warwick University, argued that Rosemary Sutcliff's historical novels were not merely an evocation of time past; they were also a political statement about time present. She spoke, his article concluded, 'in the present-day accents of that unkillable member of our society since 1800, the Liberal intellectual woman'.

To understand the situation of a present-day, liberal-spirited teacher with a training in the humanities and a struggling sense of history is to understand the genesis of Rosemary Sutcliff's novels. It is also to draw in the heavily political overtones of any literary study. For such an imaginary teacher finds in these novels the grander chords which seem to have been extinguished in the universe of adult novels – to have been absent indeed in modern literature since the death of Yeats. But there is a need still to hear those notes struck which have gone mute in the rest of literature, to find a prose which moves with ceremony and amplitude, with a portly courtesy and forgotten grace. I cannot help it if this analysis comes near the complaints of letters to the *Daily Telegraph* – 'The age of chivalry is dead'; Rosemary Sutcliff is the best of a mixed group of writers who register objection to a gaunt and toneless language, inept as to rhetoric, graceless as to manner. These writers have no academy to sustain them, and their only set of beliefs is that pale, anxious and rinsed-out liberalism which is the best most of us can do by way of a contemporary world picture. What therefore comes through as the strongest impulse to feelings is often an intensity of loss and regret, not bitter but intensely nostalgic for the sweetness of a youth and a landscape intolerably vanished.

'Reading children's novels; notes on the politics of literature'
From *Children's Literature in Education* No. 5, 1971

Ursula Le Guin

Ursula Le Guin's *A Wizard of Earthsea* was a popular novel in schools in the 1970s. *CLE* gathered several examples of lively classroom experiences with the book; and we also asked some twelve-year-old boys for their reactions – a precursor to the many articles the journal has published based on close attention to young readers' responses to novels, poems and picture books.

On Star Trek once I saw that Captain Kirk, who's in charge of the ship itself, he went into this world, and his evil departed from his good and they both fought. You know, evil was fighting good and they all parted from his body. You know, you're like that – you've got evil in you and good. . . .

He walked up to the Shadow, when he started the battle and when the real Ged, our Ged, said that was his name, I was taken aback and the Shadow said to him, 'Ged,' I didn't know what to do, and they, they started to fight and they both had a hold over each other because they had the name. . . .

Last night, I thought, crikey! what's the time? Six o'clock and I looked through it – quite good this. Maybe I'll do the fourth, maybe I'll do the fifth, sixth, seventh, eighth, ninth, I finished the book that night.

I read all of *Narnia* – fantastic books; if you compare them with this you say, 'Oh, looks like a book for people of about fifteen' you know, you look in there and the first word you see is probably one you've never heard of before. Every other line is a word there's never been heard of – like in Narnia you've got 'lion' and you compare that with 'otak' which I've never heard of before in my life, and you say cor! this is even more mysterious!

'Notes on teaching a Wizard of Earthsea'
From *Children's Literature in Education* No. 11, 1973

Nina Bawden

Some questions recur in the journal – Nina Bawden touches on two of them here. Do children's writers write for themselves, the child within themselves, specific children, for children in general – or for no one in particular? And do they show adults as complex characters, no more 'fixed' than children, or do they settle for the stereotypes?

The only real difference – or so it seems to me – between writing for children and writing for adults is a difference of viewpoints. When I wrote my first children's novel I just became eleven years old again.

And that wasn't so difficult. Time travel is not simply a device dreamed up by science fiction writers. We can all travel backwards, whenever we fancy, inside our own heads. You remember the physical sensation of, say, a stocking stuck on the blood of a grazed knee, the smell of dog dirt on the path by the railway line, and the emotional memories follow at once . . .

Writing for children I remembered, too, the kind of books I had enjoyed as a child. Adventure stories, of course. All children like adventure, and not just for the excitement of what happens next. You don't have to read Anna Freud to know that children enjoy Jack killing the giant. But more important than that basic fantasy is the fact that children are, by and large, singularly helpless. In real life they can't make anything happen. All they can do is stand by and watch. In adventure stories they can see themselves taking part in the action and not only that. They can also test themselves, measure themselves against the characters in the book. Would *they* be brave in such a situation, or would they run away? Would they be honest, or would they lie?

Remembering what I had enjoyed when I was young, I remembered what I had missed in children's books, too. The grown-ups, apart from a wicked stepmother or uncle, were always flat, peripheral figures with no emotions and no function. The books offered to me in my childhood left out the adult world, and even when they didn't, entirely, they never presented adults as children really see them. Parents and teachers were usually shown as kind, loving, distant figures – emotionally hygienic, you might say. Not only were they never beastly to children except in a stereotyped, fairy tale way, but they were never beastly to anyone. They were never the uncertain, awkward, quirky, *dangerous* creatures that I knew adults to be. Since it was the adults who had written these books, it was reasonable to assume that they didn't want to give themselves away; show themselves to us children, to their *enemies*, as they really were. I think, when I started writing for children, I wanted to put this right. To include the grown-ups as solid characters whose roles were as important in a child's life as I knew them to be, and also to *expose* them.

'A dead pig and my father'
From *Children's Literature in Education* No. 14, 1974

A. E. Day

Squadron Leader James Bigglesworth ('Biggles') is familiar to generations of young readers, for W. E. Johns's series is still reprinting in the 1990s, almost forty years after the last title appeared. In an affectionate account of Biggles's career, A. E. Day, a lecturer in librarianship, drew attention to a moment when the lemonade-swigging flying ace almost stumbled in the course of winning the First World War.

If the demon drink was not permitted Biggles, it is a little surprising that he was ever allowed even the purest of romantic encounters with a member of the opposite sex, but in '*Affaire de Coeur*' (*Biggles Pioneer Air Fighter*) he falls in love with Marie Janis, 'a vision of blonde loveliness, wrapped in blue silk'. Biggles's gallantry is rather stiff and formal but after all he was a British officer and gentleman, and British officers and gentlemen can hardly be expected to rival their Gallic allies in such matters:

> For a moment he stared as if he had never seen a woman before. He closed his eyes, shook his head, and opened them again. The vision was still there, dimpling.
>
> 'You were looking for me, perhaps?' said the girl again.
>
> Biggles saluted like a man sleepwalking.
>
> 'Mademoiselle,' he said earnestly, 'I've been looking for you all my life. I didn't think I'd ever find you.'

Tragically Mlle Janis turns out to be a German spy who leaves Biggles's life as quickly as she entered it but not before she writes him a farewell letter proclaiming her undying love for him. Biggles 'kissed the letter tenderly, then held it up to the candle and watched it burn away'.

'Biggles: anatomy of a hero'
From *Children's Literature in Education* No. 15, 1974

Roy Fuller

Roy Fuller was Professor of Poetry at Oxford University from 1968–73. He gave the annual lecture in memory of Sidney Robbins, the founder of *CLE*, in 1975. His talk was based upon his own novels and his poetry for children; his concluding paragraphs are reprinted here.

Many writers and anthologists for children, notably Walter de la Mare, have laid stress on a quality they believed children sought and were fascinated by in literature. I mean the quality of mystery, both as a feature of plot and characterisation and also as residing, particularly in poetry, in words and images themselves. Of course, the quality is important, perhaps overwhelmingly so. I don't mean that the poet should deliberately assume the magician's robes; rather the craft itself, the effort of trying to master it, leads him to shapes and colours and meanings he never imagined were in him. Moreover, poetic imagery is perhaps best when it is most daring; and poetic vision is akin to the fulfilment of primal human wishes; in such things we must be reminded of the strange, the outrageous and the memorable in the sayings and play of children themselves. I would like children always to be told that poets are ordinary men and women who put the experiences of their lives into extraordinary form; that poems can be 'understood' but that if there were a prose equivalent of a poem the poet wouldn't have troubled to write in verse.

Poets, when actually writing, don't bother about an audience, but *ex post facto* they may be rather rueful about their lack of readers. Some faith was no doubt pinned, apropos of this, in the postwar educational expansion and what were thought to be improved teaching methods. It would be interesting to talk about the still more or less static adult audience for poetry, but that is another story. A tiny recent poem of mine – for children, I hope! – puts the point at its starkest. It's called 'A Poet's Public'.

> I wrote a book for girls and boys –
> *Seen Grandpa Lately?*
> I doubt if any child enjoys
> It greatly.

But several grown-ups said to me:
'It's rather good –
The first lot of your poetry
We've understood.'

'The influence of children on books'
From *Children's Literature in Education* No. 20, 1976

Robert Leeson

Few authors have had such an understanding of children and young people of all social backgrounds as Robert Leeson. Much of that understanding (reflected in such books as *It's My Life* and the Grange Hill series) stems from the time he has spent visiting schools. His radical historical perspective is evident in *Reading and Righting* (Collins, 1985). For *CLE* he wrote about his 1970s *Maroon Boy* trilogy, which touched on such issues as slavery, women's rights and the class struggle embedded in the Civil War.

A century before the Civil War, ministers of Henry VIII and Edward VI were stringing up penniless Englishmen, Welsh, Irish and Scots by the hundred every year, simply because they were 'masterless'. For kings to kill commoners is unremarkable. For commoners to kill a King (even if many lesser ranking men died for similar actions) is considered to be unbearable. Yet why kill the King? What was it for? What had he to lose that he was ready to bring in troops from nations hostile to his own rather than come to terms with Parliament? To face such questions is a real challenge for a modern writer.

But there are other questions. In Cromwell's regicidal army rode the Levellers, the Agitators who were the troopers' and soldiers' spokesmen. These men who came from the loom and the plough, planned to remodel the state, to have equality before the law, end conscription, have regular Parliaments, extend the Franchise, make education more widely available, have freedom of speech and worship. Their pamphlets and speeches have so modern a ring that only by an effort of will can one remember the distance between them and us.

They were 'defeated' in their 'time'. Yet as fast as time seems to carry them away from us, their strivings bear them towards us, and they call out to us in voices which we recognise. Can we believe that we would today enjoy those things they strove for if their defeated struggle had not taken place?

Thus, when we see the present in the past, it is not by an act of hindsight, or of imposition, but of discovery. It is no coincidence but a quite logical thing, that the more we uncover of the neglected and undervalued of the past, working men and women, blacks and other oppressed people, the more we know about how they lived and thought and felt, the stronger a sense of community we feel between past and present. As we see them more nearly we know them more truly.

'The spirit of what age? The interpretation of history from a radical stand point'
From *Children's Literature in Education* No. 23, 1976

Michael Benton

Poetry had a poor time of it in many schools – and in the pages of *CLE* – in the 1970s. Even the liberally inclined Bullock Report gave only three and a half pages out of six hundred to the subject. In what was the journal's first piece to focus exclusively on poetry, Michael Benton, now Reader in Education at Southampton University, alerted readers to the dangers of neglect.

The cultural commonplace that poetry is a minority art is a useful cover phrase when we wish to avoid the question of who makes up this minority. I suspect that only a small proportion of English teachers are paid-up members. Along with the rest of society, most English teachers find reading fiction, watching film and television, or going to the theatre, more entertaining pursuits than reading verse. Poetry survives in the gaps, if at all. The other truism about poetry is that generally it requires more effort from the reader. It is harder work to remake a poem in the imagination simply because poetry is the most condensed form of language that we have. By the same token, a child's knowledge of what language is and does will become deeper and more subtle through poetry than through any other form of literature. To deprive children of poems is to deny them the society of clear, single voices and an irreplaceable range of feeling. We neglect poetry at our own peril.

'Poetry for children: a neglected art'
From *Children's Literature in Education* No. 30, 1978

Reinbert Tabbert

The editors of *CLE* hosted the Fourth Symposium of the International Research Society for Children's Literature at Exeter University in 1978. In a brilliantly lucid paper, Reinbert Tabbert of the Reutlingen College of Education, West Germany, outlined the relevance of Reception Theory to children's books. He included a discussion of Wolfgang Iser's concept of the 'telling gaps' which readers must fill as they bring a text alive. Here, Professor Tabbert writes about telling gaps and picture books.

The mediating function of illustrations is also appropriate in this context. An interesting example is *Where the Wild Things Are.* When I had the occasion once to talk to its author and illustrator, I asked him why he had not included a picture of the young hero's mother. 'Because,' Sendak said, 'you should only *imagine* what she looks like. It would be very wrong to show her. Because for some children she would look more scaring than the wild things. And for some children she is fine. I leave the mother to the imagination.' 'What about her reaction at the end of the story?' I asked. 'But you feel her there. By her absence she is more available.'

I think the last sentence could be taken as an appreciation of telling gaps in general. Illustrators do not always seem to be aware of the truth it conveys. Edward Lear's nonsense ballad 'The Quangle Wangle's Hat' has been turned into a beautiful picture book that was awarded the Kate Greenaway Medal. But alas, all the telling gaps of Lear's verses were filled in by the illustrator, Helen Oxenbury, leaving to the children's imagination nothing but speechless admiration. Take the main character, for example, whose identity is unknown for two reasons: he is hidden under an enormous hat, and we do not know what a Quangle Wangle is in the first place. A five-year-old boy to whom I had read the verses and later shown the pictures told me: 'Oh, the Quangle Wangle is a man with arms and legs. I thought he was some kind of monster.' Thus a puzzling creature of fantasy is cut down to human size.

'The impact of children's books: cases and concepts'
From *Children's Literature in Education* No. 33, 1979

Madeleine L'Engle and Jack Prelutsky

Betty Miles, then a U.S. Editor of *CLE*, invited various authors to write about their experiences when visiting schools. Madeleine L'Engle, famous for her *A Wrinkle In Time* (a Newbery Medal winner in 1963) described her response to a frequent question.

I like going to schools because kids still like to ask questions. Too many adults, if they ask at all, want a finite answer. But kids never stop asking, and they're open to unexpected answers.

Kids' questions are wonderfully uninhibited. They always want to know how old I am, and I give them my mother's answer: 'As old as my tongue and a little older than my teeth'. They want to know how much money I make, and I tell them lots, but that I work very hard for it. They want to know how long it takes to write a book. I give them three answers: it takes from the time I was born until the last page of the book; from the moment the idea comes into my head until two or three or four years, and perhaps one or two books, later; and, from the time I actually sit down to write, about eighteen months. I want them to know that years of thinking have gone into each book. And, in these days of instant everything, I want them to know that you don't just sit down and write a book through. You have to write and rewrite and rewrite. I think kids like to hear this.

... and Jack Prelutsky wrote about the value of children realising 'that books are written by people not unlike themselves, only taller'.

'You're weird,' offers a sixth-grade boy. I quickly respond, 'Thank you!' I've learned that this is probably a compliment.

Once, on a break between programmes, I was sitting in a school library, jotting down a few items in my notebook, when two very small second-grade girls strolled in. They hovered over me, apparently fascinated. 'Is that the man who writes the books?' asked the first. Her friend put her index finger to her lips and replied very softly, 'Shhhhhhhh! He's writing one now.'

'When writers visit schools: a symposium'
From *Children's Literature in Education* No. 38, 1980

Rhonda Bunbury and Russell Hoban

Rhonda Bunbury is a distinguished Australian teacher and writer in the field of children's books. When she interviewed Russell Hoban, author of many stories and novels for children and adults, including *The Mouse and His Child*, the conversation ranged widely. This exchange concerned Hoban's views on the teaching of writing and the study of children's literature.

Bunbury How then should teachers set about teaching literature? *Can* they teach literature? I know you're the writer so perhaps it's unfair to ask you but you might have a point of view.

Hoban From time to time I've done writing workshops, and I have found that university students who had studied 'English Literature' seemed very often to be handicapped in their writing because they were burdened with ideas about interpretation and analysis. Because they were overwhelmed by a need for structure they felt that there had to be a beginning, a middle, and an end, and they were not able, naturally, to take hold of the thing, wherever it offered a grip. So a natural story-making process – what I think of as a natural mythopoeic process – had been interfered with. It was no longer a natural capability. The natural resource had been atrophied, and a laid-on, an imposed thing had taken its place.

Bunbury There's one of your characters in *Turtle Diary*, Madera. At one point she says, 'I was thinking that possibly the biggest tragedy in children's literature is that people won't stop writing it.'

Hoban I said it, yes.

Bunbury *She* said it. Is it your point of view?

Hoban Well you know, I have to be honest. I make my living more from novels now, but for a long time children's books were my economic base, so I'm biting the hand that feeds me, but the fact is that now there are not only books for children, there are books about books for children, there are books about books about books for children, there are courses where one learns about the books about the books for children; there's this tremendous tottering edifice, piled upon the sagging and beaten down back of the child at the end of the chain, and I must say that I question it.

' "Always a dance going on in the stone" an interview with Russell Hoban'
From *Children's Literature in Education* No. 62, 1986

Bruce Carrington and Martyn Denscombe

The Reverend W. Awdry published his first Thomas the Tank Engine book in 1945, and in the 80s, backed by shrewd and diverse marketing, Thomas achieved a kind of superstar status. Bruce Carrington and Martyn Denscombe, both university teachers, suggested that the surge in Thomas's popularity was no coincidence.

In so far as the Railway Series can be shown to embody elements of both traditional and radical conservatism, one might ask: is it merely coincidental that the rise to superstardom of Thomas the Tank Engine and his friends has taken place at this, rather than an earlier juncture, in Britain's postwar history? In common with Thatcherism, Awdry's stories emphasise the importance of individual responsibility, discipline, order and respect for authority. The Series also celebrates the work ethic, enterprise, utilitarianism, patriotism and meritocratic values. Moreover, along with traditional forms of conservatism, his work may be read as a polemic against modernisation, technological change and bureaucracy. Certainly, the series presents a romantic vision of the way things were in the 'good old days'. Life on the well-ordered Island of Sodor, where everyone (irrespective of their position in society) has a use, place, and purpose, contrasts sharply with conflict-ridden contemporary Britain with its spiralling unemployment, uncertainty and alienation.

'Doubting Thomas: Reading between the lines'
From *Children's Literature in Education* No. 64, 1987

Virginia Hamilton

The American author, Virginia Hamilton, has received many awards, including the Newbery Medal for *M. C. Higgins The Great* in 1975. 'What I am compelled to write,' she has said, 'can best be described as some essence of dreams, lies, myths and disasters which befell a clan of my blood relatives.' Such memories found expression in her *The People Could Fly: American Black Folktales*. Here, she writes of the origins of that collection.

I am a tale-teller, a storyteller who writes her stories down. But my ability grew from a similar source, that of family gossip which took the form many times of what I call the 'near folktale'. The near folktale can be thought of as family history parcelled into segments, embellished by straight out-and-out lying, truths and half-truths, and polished over time from one time to another into a kind of true folk telling composed of the elements mentioned before, of the Known, the Remembered, and the Imagined.

My own family history is a tale of my grandfather, Levi Perry, escaping, crossing the Ohio River, and coming up through southern Ohio – from who knows where? – to the abolitionist John Rankin's house in Ripley, Ohio, along the Underground Railroad system to Jamestown, Ohio, and ultimately, to my hometown of Yellow Springs, Ohio. Five generations of my family have lived in Yellow Springs. Levi Perry was accompanied by his mother, name unknown, who having delivered him to friends in Jamestown, promptly disappeared forever. It has taken me twenty to thirty years to gather this basic tale of my own history. And it is still largely a tale. Actually, there are as many variations on the tale as there are days of the week. Levi Perry kept his own counsel. I assume his mother's name was never spoken. They, the fugitives, were so used to secrecy, that secrecy became a form of storytelling in itself. Once a year, Levi Perry set his children down, all ten of them, saying, 'Listen, children, and I will tell you why I ran.' Told to me by my mother when she was in her eighties. She is now 'going on' she likes to say, ninety-four.

But trying even now to get family members to tell the tale of Levi Perry's life has to it elements of mystery, myth and folklore and of the Known, the Remembered, and the Imagined. Yet, I believe it is from these tales that I became a student of American folklore in general and a collector of American black folktales in particular. The result of my studies and research and my collecting is the volume entitled *The People Could Fly: American Black Folktales.* There are twenty-four tales of all kinds in this collection.

Those former Africans brought here had no power and no weapons. Therefore, they used the folklore they created here to comment on their lives of servitude, to give them comfort and solace and strength through hard times. Some of these folktales are absolutely unique in the entire American folktale genre. The animal tales show the slave adopting various animals in the stories to represent personalities on the plantation. It was not unusual for the lowly and powerless rabbit to represent the slave in many of the tales. Rabbit was small and weak but he had big eyes, he could see all around, he could run very fast. Sometimes it looked like he might be actually flying as he ran. Rabbit was clever enough not to get caught in a snare. So the slave called him Brother. He was Bruh Rabbit and he knew how to do what had to get done, so the tale goes.

'The known, the remembered, and the imagined; celebrating Afro-American folk tales'
From *Children's Literature in Education* No. 65, 1987

Laina Ho and Bernard Ashley

The international basis of *CLE* has thrown up numerous insights, and some surprises. Here, Laina Ho, a Chinese contributor who teaches in Singapore (with a doctorate from Wales), notes the particular value to her students of a writer, Bernard Ashley, whose work is normally very much grounded in the city streets of England. The novels, she argues, emphasise Confucian rules and principles designed 'to preserve a social unity starting with the family and extending to the state and monarch'. The editors invited a brief comment from Bernard Ashley in reply.

Bernard Ashley himself perhaps did not intend to endow his protagonists with Confucian virtues (I could be wrong), but the virtue of parental love is again reworked in *Bad Blood*, a story about a teenage boy who overcomes family prejudice and who suffers rejection and humiliation in order to save his leukaemia-stricken father. But I can be sure that Chinese ESL readers will interpret these four novels as stories which highlight filial piety and family concern, without which the protagonists would not have acted in this way, and that this cultural identification will evoke a stronger empathy in us and a keener reading interest in Ashley's novels. The 'appeal' of Bernard Ashley's teenage novels is that they make a refreshing change from the stereotyped, realistic-problem teen fiction that comes from the United States and that shows a set formula whereby teenagers are too much preoccupied by the problems of growing pains in adolescence, aggravated by social problems of living in a modern urban place. Most common among these is the rejection of children by adults and parents. The slapstick humour and the friendly, quirky conversational style of the narrative, no matter how attractive and appealing, can become less appealing when readers are given an overdose. In Western adolescent literature, Bernard Ashley's teenage fiction is the most outstanding in coming closest to those values that we esteem.

Bernard Ashley writes: Dr. Ho is right in that any 'values' threading through my teenage fiction are there instinctively and not because I have sought to weave them in for teaching purposes. Individual development occurs not only through formal education but from experience, and these experiences in filial terms are of two kinds: of endorsement or reaction. My mother and father gave to my brother and me the happiest of homes because she had had a secure if poor childhood, and he had had a miserable one. He was going to be the father to us that he had wanted for himself, and our home was going to be the place he had never lived in. I suppose it was inevitable that endorsement of all that my childhood meant to me should become a steeped-in-value. It's not a merit, it's just a fact.

'Confucian values in the teenage fiction of Bernard Ashley'
From *Children's Literature in Education* No. 75, 1989

Elizabeth Jennings

Since 1953, Elizabeth Jennings has published widely admired poetry and criticism. *CLE* invited her to contribute to its series in which distinguished writers look back on a favourite book from childhood. She chose *What Katy Did*, the second of more than twenty books for children by 'Susan Coolidge', the pen name of Sarah Chauncey Woolsey (1835–1905). Elizabeth Jennings here considers the value of the classics for herself as a girl, and perhaps for other young readers.

It is remarkable how some children's books seem to defy time and to possess an enduring popularity. *What Katy Did* and its companions, *What Katy Did at School* and *What Katy Did Next*, are very much, in their values and manners, of their own time. Perhaps it is, paradoxically, this period charm which appeals most. It gives the book in question a haunting, mysterious quality. There was no cinema, radio or TV for Susan Coolidge's people; they made their own games and entertainments. However, it is not only the Carr family at play which has delighted children for so long, it is also the book's detail, its totally convincing tangible quality which satisfies us on a deep level, creates its own world, and invites us to enter it. In *What Katy Did* there is pain and sickness. I read about these with the same delight and curiosity which were aroused by Christmas and other happy anticipations. It is possible that children's classics prepare us, when we are very young, for the real tragedies which we meet as adults. We are quite unaware of this, of course, at the time. Adults often make the mistake of thinking children are morbid if they enjoy reading about death. They are wrong; good descriptions of death have almost a magic about them. What is spell-like in childhood becomes the reality of later years. But I also read *What Katy Did* with a deep gratitude for the variety of its characters and the range of their experience. I was learning important lessons but I was learning them in the best possible way – with pleasure.

'*What Katy did*'
From *Children's Literature in Education* No. 76, 1990

Natalie Babbitt

Teachers of literature may expect that at some point in the school year someone will raise the old question, 'Yes, but how do we know what the author meant?' (Experienced students understand that it's good for at least fifteen minutes of teacher provocation, if handled skilfully.) Here, the American writer, Natalie Babbitt, recalls some comments (which took her by surprise) about her own novel, *Tuck Everlasting*.

Unless they get it from the horse's mouth, the fact is that critics and other analytical thinkers can only *assume* that writers are saying what they mean. And another fact is that, based on what I know about my own stories, writers often say things the meaning of which is either totally obscure to them – or utterly devoid of meaning in the first place.

For instance. People sometimes look at me narrowly and say, 'All right. Come clean. What is the actual meaning of the fact that the villain in *Tuck Everlasting* wears a yellow suit? You're saying he's a coward, right?' Now, it's true that the word *yellow* suggests a number of things, some disagreeable and some not. But that's not why I chose it. I chose it simply because I needed a two-syllable colour, and *purple* was out of the question. I had to have a two-syllable colour because the phrase 'man in the yellow suit' is repeated quite often and needed the rhythm that two syllables gives it. It makes much better music with *yellow* than it would have with *black* or *grey*. And in addition, in those days – and even now, in the summer – men do sometimes wear cream-coloured, yellowish suits. But they never wear purple. Not if they have any sense. So the fact is that the term *yellow* is utterly devoid, here, of any symbolism whatever. People are often disappointed to hear this, but I cannot tell a lie just to please an analytical mind.

A man named Michael Tunnell, who is an assistant professor at Arkansas State University, wrote a highly complimentary essay about *Tuck Everlasting*. In it he says that I recognise, and I quote, 'the universal subconscious fear adolescents harbour concerning parental domination and their inability to achieve independence'. This came as happy news to me. I had no idea that I recognised such things. Actually, as a child, I basked in parental domination and had no desire at all to achieve independence. Or so my conscious memory tells me. Even now, as I approach my dotage, I still view independence as a decidedly mixed blessing. And yet, in reading what Michael Tunnell had to say, I could see that I *was* saying what he says I was saying. In other words, I was saying what I didn't know I meant.

In thinking it all over, though, it seems to me that in the final analysis, it doesn't matter in the least to the average reader what a writer thinks he has said. A book, once it's published, takes on a sort of chameleon-like character. It becomes something different for each person who reads it, and who's to say one of these interpretations is more valid than another? Once, at a school visit, I was asked what the message in *Tuck Everlasting* is. I said, as I always do, that I didn't mean it to have any message at all. But a boy stood up and declared with some heat that he didn't care *what* I said, *Tuck* had a message for *him,* and the message was that you have to pay a price for what you do. A stern message indeed! And a message it wouldn't occur to me to write a book about. Still, that's what *Tuck* meant to this fifth-grader.

He was doing what all of us do who are not real critics. He was applying his own filters to a story and taking from it what seemed to him to be true and useful.

'The mad tea party maxim: or how books don't always mean what the writer intended'
From *Children's Literature in Education* No. 81, 1991

Catherine Storr

Catherine Storr chose H. Rider Haggard's *SHE* when accepting the journal's invitation to revisit a childhood favourite. She contributed to the first issue of the journal in 1970, writing on 'Fear and Evil in Children's Books' and has written more than thirty books for children.

Perhaps what strikes me most, on this rereading, is that this book exemplifies what I've often suspected: it is the writers with relatively uncomplicated minds who are able to originate figures who outlive their creators and become part of our folk history. I don't mean to sound patronising to Haggard or to Conan Doyle, to Bram Stoker or Edgar Rice Burroughs, if I say that I think they were able to retain a link with the unconscious which is often lost or disregarded after childhood; by drawing on this, they stir to life something with great power but largely unrecognised in the minds of their readers.

Jung quotes Ayesha as an example of the anima, the personification of the eternal feminine principle, archetypal womanhood. Ayesha is elemental; she is ageless and fundamentally amoral. She knows no rules but those she makes for herself. Perhaps it was Haggard's naïvete which made it possible for him to write about her; I have read somewhere, though I now can't remember where, that Haggard was once accused of betraying, in one of his novels, the intimate family secrets of a local Yorkshire squire, though in fact the similarity between Haggard's plot and the real events was fortuitous. This sounds to me very probable; in his more domestic novels, Haggard often introduces elemental passions which, though they certainly existed in the Victorian age, would not have been publicly acknowledged. A writer who drew so effectively on what Jung calls the 'collective unconscious' would have been likely to hit on some of the hidden dramas of domestic life. He wrote freely about hereditary curses, illicit passions, and bitter hostility within the family, as well as of savage, undying women; ageless, malevolent witches; incredibly evil monarchs; tractless deserts; Solomon's diamond mines; secret caves; and eternal fires. I'm not surprised now, looking back sixty plus years, that I was entranced by what he wrote. It is what we all keep forever in our childish dreams. It is the stuff of myth.

'H. Rider Haggard's *SHE*'
From *Children's Literature in Education* No. 82, 1991

Julia MacRae

The publishers' angle on the children's book world is rarely made public – yet their decisions are crucially influential. For more than thirty years one of the most courageous publishers in the field has been Julia MacRae. *CLE* invited her to recount her story to date, and with disarming modesty she describes her work, early in her career, with one of her authors.

On the home front, the Collins years brought me into contact with Alan Garner, the most influential and controversial children's writer at that time in the United Kingdom. The 'teenage novel' had for some while been a feature of American publishing but was less developed as a genre in Britain. Alan Garner's *The Owl Service* came as a stunning, ground-breaking thunderbolt of a book. The manuscript came in to Collins, and I recall sitting up in bed all night, reading without stopping until I'd reached the end. I was not at all sure that I understood the book, but I was totally sure that it was a mesmeric and important piece of writing. Alan later asked me for my interpretation of the ending; I gave him my version, and he simply shook his head. 'Oh, you chocolate box,' he said, from which I gathered that I'd missed the point! The editorial conversations with Alan Garner rank as some of the most exciting and enlightening that I've ever had. He helped me to mature as an editor, and probably as a person as well. Another of his wonderful backhanders I rather treasure: he once told me that I was an intellectual nincompoop, but he knew when I had laughed or cried over a manuscript and that was all he needed to know. A useful lesson, for surely an editor's first responsibility is to *react*, to respond emotionally to what the author or artist has done? Academic or other critical nitpicking can come later – laugh or cry first, and let the author know at once how you *feel*, how your emotions have been engaged.

'The story so far'
From *Children's Literature in Education* No. 83, 1991

Philip Pullman

Philip Pullman's excellent *Ruby in the Smoke* trilogy has won recognition on both sides of the Atlantic. He touches in this extract on both the crafting and the subject matter of the trilogy; and unlike most teachers-turned-writers, he is willing to admit that he is still concerned to educate. His concerns about present-day society, he says, led him to explore the same concerns in the nineteenth century.

We make too much of this quality called originality: I think that we learn by imitation. Everything is an imitation of something else, in a way; and literary theory comes up with nice words like intertextuality to account for it. Writing is about writing as well as about life, and if you sincerely imitate the models that are congenial to you, you can't help but improve your command of the material. The danger comes, I suppose, when you begin to imitate yourself. So I read and imitate the writers I admire, and many of them – by chance – happen to have flourished around the turn of the century.

However, we can't avoid displaying an ideology of some sort, whether veiled or naked, so the best we can do is to be intelligent about it. What I write is art of a sort, I hope; it has to work in terms of story and pattern, but nothing is unmixed, thank God; everything is confused and impure, and there's a sense in which I would have chosen to write about the late nineteenth century even if the other considerations hadn't brought me to it. Because I've got another purpose in mind as well. That was a time when the seeds of the present day were germinating. Feminism, to take an obvious example. I didn't set out to write a trilogy with a female protagonist and give her exciting and interesting things to do: the story chose me. But I was glad to find a medium in which I could show how feminism didn't spring fully armed from the head of Germaine Greer but was being discussed, and was influencing people, a hundred or more years ago. The drug trade has a past as well; it didn't begin with *Miami Vice*; it's intimately entwined with our economic history. Terrorism – the modern sense of that very word first appeared then, and one of the characters in *The Tiger in the Well* learns it.

And finally, in the same book, I wanted to talk about socialism. It's had a bad press in the past few years; it's been depicted as the dreary source of every kind of repression, misery and failure. I wanted to show that it has a better history than that, that there was a time when it was the best response of the best people to the conditions around them. I wanted to celebrate a little: to celebrate the efforts of working people to educate themselves: the Workingmen's Literary and Philosophical Institute, in *The Shadow in the North;* the efforts of middle-class philanthropists to alleviate suffering among the poor; the Spitalfields Social Mission in *The Tiger in the Well.* (Here, as in many other places, I owe a great debt to William J. Fishman's *East End 1888* (Duckworth, 1988) – a book full of horror and darkness, laid out with enormous learning and lit with a steady, unflinching compassion. Reading and re-reading it is an experience more like life than like research.) So my ideology is educational. I was a teacher for too many years to stop teaching just because I'm no longer paid to do it; and as teachers used to know long before the National Curriculum gave them other things to think about, stories are a pretty good way to teach.

'*Daddy*, or Serendipity'
From *Children's Literature in Education* No. 86, 1992

Noriko Shimoda Netley

Noriko Shimoda Netley took an M.A. in children's literature at Reading University, and has worked as a translator. She was well placed, therefore, to consider what happens as a children's book passes from one language – and from one culture – into another. In exploring how radically a text can change, she took as her example Roald Dahl's *Matilda*.

In Britain, Roald Dahl's books are considered to be 'popular' fiction – something the critics and academics do not take seriously. Moreover, there are a number of hostile criticisms of his books. John Rowe Townsend has identified sadism, misogyny, the identification of women with villainous magic, obsession with the excremental, and the encouragement of children's vengeful and aggressive impulses as charges that have been laid against Dahl. David Rees disapproves of Dahl's books because 'it is to the gleeful, spiteful aspects of a child's nature that Dahl all too often appeals' (in *CLE* No. 70).

In Japan, however, Dahl seems to be highly praised because of his 'morality'. The translator of *Matilda* emphasises Dahl's moral message in his postscript: 'In this story, Dahl also expresses his belief in the importance of reading, his criticism of coercive, uniform education and his claim that books for children should be funny.' The translator also praises Dahl as a man who 'always wrote from the children's point of view, although cynically . . . consistently protesting against ostentation, hypocrisy and oppression'. The war of 'oppressed children against the oppressor adult' as the translator summarises this story, is generally approved of by liberal Japanese intellectuals, contrary to the attitudes of many British critics. Dahl's contradictory attitude towards children and the black-and-white simplicity of his morality do not seem to be noticed by the critics in Japan.

'The difficulty of translation: decoding cultural signs in other languages'
From *Children's Literature in Education* No. 87, 1992

Robert Westall

Robert Westall's choice in our 'Books Remembered from Childhood' series was Jack London's *White Fang*. Westall's first novel was published in 1975, and he produced a book a year whilst teaching full-time until he retired in 1985. Thereafter his output increased to four or five books each year. Sadly, he died shortly after the publication of his article in the journal in April, 1993; *CLE* published a critical appreciation of his work by Peter Hollindale in the Autumn of 1994. Here, at the outset of his essay on *White Fang*, Westall recalls his early experiences as a reader and writer in North-East England, the setting of much of his best work, including the Carnegie Medal-winning *The Machine-Gunners* (1975).

As a working-class lad, I never read a children's book. I came to my first, *Winnie-the-Pooh*, when I read it to my son. By then I was thirty-four, a teacher, and had wandered almost by accident into the middle class.

Yet I learned to read early. When I was four, my father used to take me on his knee and read to me from a comic called *Puck*. Like the board-school boy he was, he ran his finger under each word as he read. One day, to his utter amazement, he discovered I was three paragraphs ahead of him. No stress, no tension, no adult anxiety; reading has always seemed to me as natural as breathing.

Like that of most working-class boys, my reading was comics – not the sort with lots of pictures, but good solid wodges of print like the *Adventure* or *Wizard*. The interesting thing about these was that they dealt almost entirely with the doings of grown men. My hero was the great athlete Wilson, who ran a three-minute mile in a fictional Berlin Olympics, because he lived on a strict diet of wild herbs, learned from a hermit on the Yorkshire moors. Wilson had no use for this world's goods; he ran barefoot. He was also excessively modest, vanishing the moment he had won his three-minute mile. It was only later that people learnt he was over a hundred years old at the time.

Another great hero of mine was the Wolf of Kabul, an ex-public-school boy who lounged in flea-laden rags round the Northwest Frontier, saving the British Empire in ways that reduced the British top brass to apoplexy – a strange mixture of Kim and Lawrence of Arabia.

Their adventures are long forgotten, but their characters stay with me. My ideal hero is still the scruffy outsider with inside knowledge and a contempt for all establishments, the man who wearily defends his country, while seeing all its faults, because the way the British do things is the least of all evils. I love Le Carré now, and I feel the Wolf of Kabul and George Smiley would have understood each other.

Did I miss the boat with children's literature? Sadly, I feel not. I was not that sort of child. I was never aware of any magic of childhood. From the moment I first entered the school gates and saw one gang of giants charging another under a shower of stones, calling their battle-cry 'Chawooh', I wanted to be as big as possible, as quickly as possible. But I was not such a fool as to think mere size was enough. In adults were all mysteries, all powers; adults whispered secret messages above your head.

I became a model child in adult company, as I went around with my parents, in those days before baby-sitters invaded from America. I was as silent and well-mannered as the furniture. I could be fobbed off with the most unsuitable books to keep me quiet; the Bible and that *Home Doctor* that showed curiously sexless nudes spewing out masses of pink entrail. But I wasn't really reading, I was listening. As they came to regard me as no more than a bit of furniture, as they forgot I was there at all, the most delicious secrets tumbled indiscreetly from adult lips. I was becoming a most knowledgeable little monster, or perhaps an embryonic novelist.

I remember, when I was seven, we had to create our own newspaper in infant school. My banner headline read:

HUMAN TORSO FOUND IN CABIN TRUNK

The headmistress was discreetly summoned, pursed her lips, and shook her head at my teacher. A feeling of wonder and power surged through me. I had delivered my first shock as a writer.

'Jack London's *White Fang*'
From *Children's Literature in Education* No. 88, 1993

On Close Examination: Perspectives on Picture Books

Peter F. Neumeyer

Peter F. Neumeyer has taught in elementary and secondary schools and at several universities including Harvard, San Diego State and the University of Wales. He is the author of five books for children (three with Edward Gorey) and his scholarly publications include subjects as various as Shakespeare, Kafka, Ed Doctorow and Chris Van Allsburg. He writes frequently about children's books in popular newspapers and magazines. His *The Annotated Charlotte's Web* was published by HarperCollins in 1994.

We Are All in the Dumps with Jack and Guy: Two Nursery Rhymes with Pictures by Maurice Sendak

Can I see another's woe,
And not be in sorrow too?
William Blake

Clearly, Maurice Sendak is outraged. Outraged by the plight of the children. By their homelessness, their hunger, by the plague of AIDS visited upon the innocents, and by the prejudice to which the children, too, are subjected.

In his latest book – with the title, *We Are All in the Dumps with Jack and Guy*, placed curiously on the *back* cover – Sendak is more serious, perhaps less introspective, than he has ever been. The book is an exhortation to humankind, a cry to heaven for justice. And most important, it is a document of reconciliation and of hope. That's what needs to be said in the light of the attacks that surely will be heaped upon the book. And that's why the book will take some explanation.

Jack and Guy is not a fast read. In the guise of a children's picture book, it is a work of extraordinary complexity. Even the title has a double meaning: either there are the two nursery rhymes, 'We are all in the Dumps' and 'Jack and Guy' or 'we, *along with* Jack and Guy, live in the dumps'.

The book is clearly 'Sendak', harking back, stylistically, to earlier volumes such as *In the Night Kitchen* and *Hector Protector.* The illustrations are bold and broadly outlined, reminiscent somewhat of Sendak's 'comic book' genre. The printed text is spread very thin across fifty-five pages and the back and front covers. Many pages have no words. And within the illustrations, characters speak in yellow balloons of the comic strip variety, commenting with telling irony, even if only with a question mark, on the situations illustrated.

The book is structured around two traditional nursery rhymes, both recorded in only slightly different form by the Opies.[1] In order for us to understand how remarkably Sendak's picture book transforms these seemingly innocuous verses, I give them to you here first (Opie version):

In The Dumps

We are all in the dumps,
For diamonds are trumps,
The kittens are gone to St. Paul's.
The babies are bit,
The moon's in a fit,
And the houses are built without walls.

The second half of the book gives a larger role to the two urchins, Jack and Guy, or as the Opies spell it,

Jack And Gye

Jack and Gye
  Went out in the rye,
And they found a little boy
  With one black eye,
Come, says Jack,
  Let's knock him on the head.
No, says Gye,
  Let's buy him some bread;
You buy one loaf
  And I'll buy two,
And we'll bring him up
  As other folks do.

Looking at those rhymes after contemplating the book, one is struck by how many words there actually are. And if one knows that the 'normal' nursery picture book is thirty-two pages, one is astonished that these two verses are here stretched through fifty-two, plus title pages and cover. Attending to the disposition of the printed text and the intervals of illustration in the textless spreads, one may be amazed that Sendak has made so much of these words – even before one knows *what* that 'much' is.

If one knows Sendak's work even slightly, one knows, too, that his is a very special universe: a world of music, a world of art, and, more recently, a world haunted by memories of the European Holocaust. One knows that whatever Sendak has to say will be said in good part by allusions to these 'worlds'.

The book's cover is baffling at first, and we'll return to it later, when we know how.

The main character throughout is a little black child pictured naked except for a torn white cloth, howling in misery on the first page as we open the book. He (although the child represents either sex, I'll refer to it as a 'he', first, because it's not an 'it'; second, for convenience; and, third, for a reason that becomes clear later) stands under the title 'WE ARE ALL IN THE DUMPS'. The howling child is an apt emblem for the book.

'In the Dumps'

The double spread title page sets the tone and introduces the cast of human characters: homeless, bald urchins sleeping in boxes and barrels; a strange monk-like figure, bearing some resemblance to Thomas Merton, sitting under a blanket tent[2]; Jack and Guy stagefront; three alert kittens; a sad human-faced full moon in a dark and starry sky; a city of skyscrapers in the background; and the little black child, apprehensive in the left corner behind another child's box home, uttering the yellow speech ballon, 'Help?'

This question mark, which will recur, is astonishing, and its meaning deserves careful contemplation. Appropriately, a rough sign on the left-hand (first) page bears the instruction, 'Open on this side only.' As we'll see later, in this book that's very important. Sendak's elaboration of the first rhyme, 'In the Dumps', suggests how enormously an author–illustrator may create around the merest germ of an idea.

In the course of the next twenty pages, the little black child, holding out his begging hands, appeals ('Help?' again) to Jack and Guy. These two first brush him off. Against a backdrop of homeless, sometimes naked, always distressed children, two vile, yellow-eyed rats carry off the little black child. When Jack and Guy attempt to rescue him, the rats challenge the boys to a game of bridge, in which, of course, diamonds are trumps. With illustrative panache, Sendak shows us only a portion of the bridge players' hands before (next page) rat number 1 springs the ten of diamonds (trumps) on us, and rat number 2 makes off with the little black child. As the cast of dismayed waifs watches, the rats haul off the little black child in a wagon full of kittens; the black child breaks away, reaching again to the other children for help. The shark-toothed rat grasps the little black child, outlined against the huge and pitch-black gaping maw of the full moon. The enraged moon ('in a fit'), grabs up (rescues?) Jack and Guy as the other children flee in terror and as, heading for offstage right, the rat runs off clutching the little black child, who howls in pain and terror. The children wave newspapers in farewell, in grief, in sympathy, to the quickly ascending Jack and Guy. In the first 'book's' final spread, Jack and Guy, huddling in the face of the moon (who is already looking off to story number 2), clutch each other for solace as, on the facing page, the six waifs hold up their 'houses . . . built without walls': torn and ragged newspapers.

Strange plot

But of course the plot is only half the story, for in a good picture book, and as we learned early from *Where the Wild Things Are*, in a Sendak picture book especially, much – perhaps most – that is essential is not in the plot at all. The words are prompts merely, invitations to invent whole pictorial universes of allusion and reference and commentary and ironies that *use* the plot as a springboard to present a complex, intricate story in which, at times for example, the illustrations editorialise on, or even contradict, the words of the text.[3]

In 'In the Dumps', the little black child is kidnapped, and Jack and Guy, too, are snatched away. But the larger story is (threefold) in the spoken balloons, in the words we can read in the children's newspapers, and in the scenes pictured, and in the allusions within them.

The words in the balloons are sparse, but clear. 'Beat it!' say Jack and Guy when the little black child says (exclaims? asks? pleads?), 'Help?' 'Look what they did!' shouts a homeless child, perhaps about the rat carrying off the baby, perhaps about the squalor which surrounds them all. 'Rascal!' 'Thief,' shout Jack and Guy as the rats force the bridge game for the little black child's fate. And when the children lose, the waifs shout, 'Lost,' 'Tricked,' 'Trumped,' and 'Dumped'.

As for the text we can read in the ragged newspapers that make shelter or clothing for the waifs, the words function as a choral commentary on the scenes of urban waste, squalor and desolation in which the action takes place. Sometimes the words serve as captions confirming what we see. At other times, they are bitter contradictions, language of a consumer-indulgent society oblivious of the misery of the dispossessed.

'You can afford your own house – 50,000,000,' reads one text: 'very smart living! 79%,' reads the visible portion of another held up by the urchins who, themselves, live in torn and broken cardboard boxes (which sport their own significant labels and legends, such as 'private property' or 'uneeda biscuit').

'Homeless shelter system,' says another, and 'leaner times,' and 'Banks p[ost] . . . Big Gains,' scream the headlines in the pages in which Sendak shows a little black baby in the rat's evil grasp. As Jack and Guy are lifted into the sky, the papers (the 'news from planet earth,' as it were) tell of 'Famine in the world' – *but also* of 'Mozart and Schubert,' and, on another page waved by a child, we see the words:

Oct. 17, 1992
Jim goes home

Those last two legends, in fact, contrast to all the others. That 'Mozart' is Sendak's muse, that he stands for all that is good, genial, constructive in the world, we all know well. The 'Jim goes home' refers to the death of the children's illustrator James Marshall, who 'went home' on that date, and who was a friend to Sendak and, in the view of many of us, a champion for humour and the free imagination and, therefore, a champion for the liberty of children.

As for the 'meaning' that resides in the illustrations themselves, and in the allusions within them, space allows no more than a few samples. The images refer in some instances to earlier Sendak works (as does the *In the Night Kitchen* 'feel' of the whole book). At other times, they are cultural icons, images from the consciousness of our times which reside in our communal culture wholly, and in the individual awareness of each of us individually to a greater or lesser degree, depending on one's life experiences.

Thus in 1993 the little black child – his shape, his colour, his misery – must remind us of newspaper images of starving children in Somalia. The fact that on the book's cover he holds a long halm of grain points to the agricultural disaster that is, today, the Horn of Africa. (We have more to say about the cover later.)

On the very first page, the black child howling, mouth agape, brings to mind the photo we must remember of a Vietnamese youngster standing desolate, bereft and screaming in a road – one of the most horrifying images in the history of our earth.

The iconography of the Mammon-ridden city in which the waifs live is pregnant, too, with meaning – the towers of the metropolis rising in squared splendour amidst the akimbo angles of the children's make-shift dwellings. In case you miss the message, one building bears a sign, the visible portion of which says 'Tower'. The speech balloon covering its hidden portion bears the exclamation, 'Trumped' – referring to the story's bridge game, as well as, of course, to New York's Ozymandian monument to avarice, Trump Tower.

What the city – 'civilisation', if you like – stands for is put into question by an ambiguous projection on a shack, a sort of steeple that looks mighty like an automatic rifle, the cartridge belt of which blends into what may be the Queensborough Bridge, while the towers resemble the smokestacks of the crematoria of the Holocaust. This analogy is reinforced by even viler square, smoke-belching towers in the next 'book', as well as by the quite different background buildings and towers a few pages later in this story in which the rats haul away the kittens and the baby. Here, the main tower makes us think back to the centrefold in Sendak's 1988 book, *Dear Mili.*

Serving as background for the desperate action depicted, the tower has a gaping black entrance and rows of little square windows. On its steeple is a device that appears for all the world (literally) to be a siren. The roof on another of the background buildings is no longer New York-square-glass-and-steel, but medieval-pointed, as in some quaint old German town. Say, Dachau.

In the same picture with the ominous edifices in which the moon – ever empathetic of the action – seems to weep, the rats carry off ten kittens jammed against each other, the mouth of each a screaming O reminiscent of Edvard Munch's rendering of ultimate anguish in his painting 'The Scream'. The wagon itself bears the lying legend, 'St.

Paul's Bakery and Orphanages', all reminders, of course, of other cattle cars, box cars on German and Polish sidings, and filled with their horrible cargoes also going, perhaps they thought, to factories, to 'orphanages', fifty years ago.

And if you are still sceptical, you need only follow those kittens with us into the next section.

'Jack and Guy'

Now, in 'section 2', Jack and Guy are where we left them. They're on all fours, on the moon, in the starry empyrean. Two angels float about, reading newspapers; one baby angel is just on his way up; and a fourth is reading James Marshall's hippo book about 'George and Martha'. The relatively lengthy poem/verse seems even more thinly spread among the pages, for the illustrations are so rich. The linear plot is as follows:

Jack and Guy play in fields of rye, trip over the little black child lying on the ground, and find a kitten. They pick up both. In the foreground we see the tall grasses, in the background, a curious, observant full moon and the square, sharp-cornered factory with black smoke-belching chimney, its sign sinisterly proclaiming 'bakery and orphanage'.

Jack holds the little black child in a comforting manner. Then, with the shocking arbitrariness of the rhyme, he suggests they 'knock him on the head'. The little black child covers his face in terror. Guy, however, counter-suggests that they 'buy him some bread', and the three, the little black child clinging to Jack, along with two white kittens, scurry through the now darker field of rye. Mysteriously, the moon's 'face' has, for the first time, cat-like whisker indentations and a mouth shape echoing that of the kittens' mouths.

On the next page, the boys come suddenly upon a monstrously large white cat – larger than they are – that grins at them toothily. It, too, has whisker dots.

The next spread shows Jack and Guy riding the back of the springing, snarling white monster cat, which, herself, grasps in great sharp claws the two villainous rats. In the background, three rows of kitten faces, all in a line, stare out from tiered pallets or wooden beds. Guy cradles the little black child in his arms.

In the next spread, sitting on a table proclaiming 'Free Bread today!' Jack and Guy feed the little black child bread, and the great white cat lies protectively over a great huddle of kittens that are smiling and yawning and stretching contentedly.

Then buying the little black child *two* loaves, as the rhyme demands, Jack and Guy leap toward the now-cat-whiskered moon, from whose mouth more happy kittens look out. For the words 'and we'll bring him up', the three boys are shown sleeping peacefully, along with the kittens, on the surface of the moon, which, itself, is clearly high in the sky. A periwigged angel – Sendak's Mozart, of course – flies through the air, pointing the way moonward to a small winged baby, a newly minted angel.

The next double spread – the most startling and amazing – shows Jack lifting the closed-eyed, limp figure of the little black baby down from the great golden globe of the moon on which they had all found their comfort. Guy looks on. The kittens scurry. There are no words.

And on the last double spread, a clear echo of the first, all the waifs and kittens we saw at the beginning are shown again, still in their decrepit makeshift homes. However, no longer are these children in postures of stress, anxiety and agitation; the children, and the kittens, too, sleep peacefully, with calm faces. There are no newspapers. The moon is faceless now, simply a moon. In the midst of the children is a sign: 'Sterling Products'. Guy and Jack are in the lower right – that is, the (visual) conclusion of the book – Jack cradling in his arms the little black child, whose face is suffused with a look of deep peace.

So much for the surface text. But again, the images in context tell a larger story than what we see on the surface only. The allusions, the illustrations and the structure of the book itself tell the tale. The book, in fact, is written under two guiding stars. The first is that of the visionary world of William Blake.

William Blake's 'Songs of Innocence' (1789) and 'Songs of Experience' (1794) are sometimes considered literature for children – as are Sendak's books. Perhaps some are. No question though, they – Blake and Sendak – speak *of* and *to* childhood. Sendak hitherto has written, in virtually every book, about the *mind* of the child. William Blake's subject is, in large part, the plight of the children, their suffering as orphans or as chimney sweeps, as victims in a materialistic and hypocritical world of woe. In the end, a number of these children are delivered and are saved by their own resilience and their innocence.

And as in Sendak's 'Jack and Guy' the children fly to the moon, so, too, on the very title page illustration of William Blake's 'Songs of Experience', two children fly into the sky far above terrestrial lamentation and woe.

Sendak's predominantly male waifs, who inhabit the desolate perimeters of the smoke-belching metropolis – Blake's 'dark Satanic Mills'[4] – are surely descendants of Blake's chimney sweeps, small young boys dragooned into a miserable, starved and short-lived existence, their skin turning permanently black, their limbs made crooked, and their lives threatened by cancer of the scrotum.

The startling baldness of Sendak's urchins, then, may be associated not only with the scourge of AIDS – of which Sendak reminds us explicitly in the newspaper texts pictured in this book – but also with William Blake's young 'chimney sweep', who remembers his pal, little Tom Dacre, 'who cried when his head . . . was shaved'[5].

In fact, the hapless infant I have continually referred to as 'the little black child' seems obviously pitiful kin to the poor orphan chimney sweep boy rendered by Blake as

> A little black thing among the snow:
> Crying weep, weep, in notes of woe!
> 'Where are thy father & mother? say?'
> 'They are both gone up to the church to pray.'[6]

Blake's subject, like Sendak's, is the misery of children. It is also the hypocrisy of the [adult] world that goes 'up to the church to pray', even as it subjects the innocent to the horrors of industrialised modernity with its factories and sooty chimneys which, then, in Sendak's paintings, we associate necessarily with the abominable crematoria of the Nazi death camps.

Nor, as we regard white Jack and Guy's rescue of the little black child, is it amiss to recall William Blake's 'Little Black Boy' who, in God's good time, will shed the coil of mortality for a heavenly reconciliation with the 'little English boy'.

Most centrally, however, Sendak's two-part story mirrors the story in Blake's two complementary poems: 'Little Boy Lost' and 'Little Boy Found'. In the first poem, the little black child is lost:

> The night was dark no father was there
> The child was wet with dew.

In the sequel,

> The little boy lost in the lonely fen,
> Led by the wand'ring light,
> Began to cry, but *God ever nigh,*
> *Appeared like his father* in white.
>
> (italics and underlining added)

or, shall we say, like that great and toothful *white* cat who appears truly out of nowhere (*deus/felix ex machina*) being watched in mute amazement by row on row of other victims – pallets of kittens – whose faces and disposition remind us hauntingly of the denizens of Auschwitz who, in well-known photographs, peer pitifully from their bunks.

The great white cat seizes the rats and, carrying Jack, Guy, and the little black child on her back, leaps to the next page, where she shelters forty-four contented kittens, as Jack and Guy feed the little black child, quite in the spirit of William Blake's humble clod who asserted:

> 'Love seeketh not itself to please,
> Nor for itself hath any care,
> But for another gives its ease,
> And builds a Heaven in Hell's despair.'

The white cat transmogrifies, on the next page, into the moon itself, onto which the three children have been spirited (quite literally), and where they and the kittens slumber in peace.[7]

The next page, however, is the one that startles most amazingly, and that points to the second star under which Sendak writes, and by the light of which we must read the tale.

In a traditional story, we could stop with the boys and the kittens saved and sleeping in peace. But in this book, on the next – wordless – double spread, Jack lifts the little black child *down* from the moon. Guy looks on, and the moon itself is now an enormous golden orb against which the little black child's body and extended arm cast a pitiful shadow. Jack lifts from the front, supporting the little black child under the arms, and the little black child faces us, head lolled, eyes closed, body limp, left arm akimbo, casting that deathly image onto the moon!

And of course we recognise immediately what is called a Deposition – Christ, I.N.R.I., being taken down from the cross – as we know the scene from Rembrandt, from Rubens, or, in this case more nearly from the Escorial painting by Rogier van der Weyden or, perhaps, two engravings attributed to Mantegna.

So then, once again, *He* has come to us in the guise of a little child – a 'little black child' in this instance, a little black child who, in the next and last double spread, in the last possible illustratable space of this book, is cradled peacefully in Jack's arms, eyes closed, for all the world (I mean the words literally) a contemporary Pietà.

Sendak's turns out to be an old and oft-told tale.

Jack and Guy have met their test. In the dumps where we are all together, in the world of vermin and smoke-belching chimneys of evil, the urchin boys find the little cowering black babe – hands held out in supplication, 'Help?' – whom they rescue. Unlikely babe; unlikely saints! But, as Jesus said, 'inasmuch as [they] have done it unto the least of these, [they] have done it unto me'.

And the end is peace, not on the moon, not in the aerie sky, but peace here on this earth – such, precisely, as this earth is. Raggedy, rickety, sinful and human.

And then we close the book, and we have that title placed so oddly on the *back* cover. And we puzzle. And we turn the book over, and we see on the front the little brown child rising out of the black maw of the moon, the waifs and urchins looking in astonishment. They hold those straws, those halms of grain. And again with that little round-headed black baby and his grain, we may think first of the famine-stricken babies of Africa today. But the newspapers in which the children are clothed lend themselves, with slight ambiguity, to happier interpretation:

Homeless Shelters
Leaner Times
Meaner Times
Children Triumph
Kid elected president[8]

And the black baby taken down from the moon and resting at the end in sleep-death in Jack's arms comes full circle. He appears, open-eyed, before the amazed lookers-on. We may well think of Andrea Mantegna's 'Descent into Limbo'. That is, technically, the book's beginning. In fact, it was the book's end. But that end – rescue, salvation, resurrection (out of the moon in/on which he slept) – simply marks a beginning. For us

 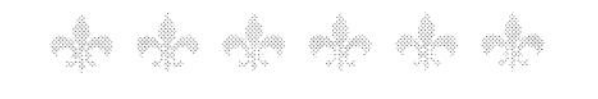

children; for the triumphant book, itself. Because the little Black Baby is come again, announcing, curiously even in the book's design, that 'in my end is my beginning'.[9]

Notes

1 Iona and Peter Opie, *The Oxford Nursery Rhyme Book*, reprinted with corrections (Oxford: The Clarendon Press, 1967), pp. 143, 95. Iona and the late Peter Opie together collected vast numbers of English-language children's rhymes. Their extraordinary collection is now at the Bodleian Library, Oxford. Sendak pays homage to Iona Opie in the last double spread of this book.

2 All such identifications for Sendak's allusions are hazardous. One does one's best.

3 In *Where the Wild Things Are*, as most readers are aware, the margins which decrease as Max enters his all-comprehending dream and the margins which increase as he emerges from his trance bear the major burden of relating the 'true' and 'inner' nature of Max's (objectively) brief voyage 'in and out of weeks'.

4 William Blake, *Blake's Poetry and Designs*, selected and edited by Mary Lynn Johnson and John E. Grant (New York: W. W. Norton, 1979), 'Preface', *Milton*, 1.8, p. 238.

5 Blake, 'The Chimney Sweeper' in 'Songs of Innocence' p. 26, 11. 5–6.

6 Blake, 'The Chimney Sweeper' in 'Songs of Experience' p. 46, 11. 1–4.

7 The fully rational account of the relationship between cat and moon awaits a keener explicator than I.

8 One resists making too much of the fact that the year is 1993, when the sallow and cynical geriatric dynasties in American government have come to an end, and when for so many there is a measure of hope that a new, young administration will lead with compassion and with understanding: 'Kid elected president.' 'Children Triumph.'

9 See T. S. Eliot, 'East Coker', (London: Faber and Faber, 1940). We understand now why, notwithstanding the 'backward' dustjacket, we were admonished to 'open on this side only'. And we have experienced from Sendak once more a book in which design equals meaning.

From *Children's Literature in Education* No. 89, 1993

David Gooderham

David Gooderham read degrees in English and Theology at Leeds and Cambridge and went on to work first in the church and, subsequently, teacher education. He has taught English at the University of Teesside for the last seven years, where he runs courses in Victorian Literature and Children's Literature. He writes mainly in the areas of curriculum studies, Children's Literature and Religious and Moral Education.

STILL CATCHING THEM YOUNG? THE MORAL DIMENSION IN YOUNG CHILDREN'S BOOKS

Morality and children's literature are not easy bedfellows. Maybe it is appropriate to discuss the moral dimension in contemporary adolescent novels, since they deal increasingly with parental divorce, teenage pregnancy, child abuse and problems of this kind. But in the case of books for young children, wasn't the battle between the moral tale and the imaginative freedom of fantasy waged and won long ago, so that now we properly regard them as a locus of play and delight rather than of moralising?

There is, however, a difference between moralising on the one hand and moral structure, development and education on the other. I would argue that, although the moral tale and overt moralising are rightly a thing of the past, in books for children of all ages the moral dimension continues to be of importance and should not be neglected. Goodies and baddies, doing right and doing wrong, being treated well and being treated badly, are fundamental to these texts. And children's experience of reading their first books provides for them as significant an early learning experience in the moral as in any other domain of human knowledge and feeling.

My purpose therefore is to make clear this fundamental dimension, by describing the moral structuring of representative texts and by indicating the kinds of moral engagement they invite from their young readers. I use the term *structure,* since I want to direct attention not so much to the issues that are treated as to how moral assertions are made in the structuring of texts. For this, I shall discuss half a dozen, mainly recent, picture books. I shall venture further, into the problem area of how children engage with such texts, in part because the moral dimension cannot adequately be described merely by the static delineation of ideas in texts, and in part because developmental psychology is now substantially enough advanced to afford some indications of what may be expected of children in the moral domain – and thus of their moral engagement with the books they read. For a critical perspective on this engagement I shall use the work of Lawrence Kohlberg.[1]

A moral dichotomy

Fairy tales have a dual moral structure: that deriving from their archaic past and that constructed by their contemporary adapters. The former, with its clear opposition of good and bad and the final triumph of good, is a universal feature; the latter, a more particular matter for each generation. So strong is the traditional moral logic of the fairy tale, however, that it makes its presence felt in every kind of adaptation.

It can, indeed, keep old-fashioned moralising startlingly alive in a contemporary text. Rita Story's 1990 retelling of *Goldilocks* proceeds unexceptionably until, as the child tiptoes inquisitively into the strange house, the narrator informs readers in no uncertain terms: 'Now Goldilocks was a very naughty girl,' and, as she takes a tentative taste of the porridge, 'Being greedy as well as naughty . . .' Nothing is left to chance at the conclusion of the story: 'Never again did naughty Goldilocks pry into strangers' houses . . . uninvited.'

What a barrage of didacticism! At the end of the narrative, poor Goldilocks remains 'naughty', her childish inquisitiveness becomes 'prying', and the last word reduces realistic prudence to a kind of social fastidiousness!

Lest it be thought that this is just a feature of run-of-the-mill versions, even Tony Ross (1978), creator of striking children's books, is, in his own way, affected by the powerful moral logic of the fairy tale. In his *Jack the Giantkiller*, he feels obliged to append to the retelling a moralistic coda: 'Really Jack stole nothing . . .'! The contorted justification for Jack's thieving is entirely gratuitous. In the convention of the genre, giants are baddies, so there is no need to explain why they should be robbed and slaughtered. Earlier in the narrative, however, Ross has characteristically intruded a vein of ironic burlesque for older, knowing readers of his version: the giant's terrifying attributes include, as the last item, 'bad breath'! In ways like this, the conventional stereotype is modified; this giant is no longer the unquestioned baddie, he has his endearing weaknesses. When the traditional moral structure is modified, however, such is the strength of the moral logic of the fairy tale that checks and balances immediately come into operation; if we now have a humanised giant, we must have him treated humanely – or know the reason why. Hence the moralising in the coda.

With contemporary realist texts, we enter a profoundly different moral world from that of the fairy tale. In Anthony Kerins's *Lost* (1991), another little Goldilocks wanders off along the beach, experiences a dawning anxiety, and is finally recovered by an anxious grandma. The narrative describes what occurs and how the child feels; there appears to be no moral content. This becomes remarkable when the story is set against *Red Riding Hood* or other traditional wandering tales, in which, one way or another, the strays get wolfed up. They meet their fates, culpable or not, as a consequence of the fault of straying. But there is no hint of retribution, not even chastisement or berating, in Kerins's narrative; instead, there is simply mutual anxiety and mutual affection. This is in part a transformation of the moral into the psychological, but it also betokens, nevertheless, a new and quite different moral structure: non-judgmental, altruistic concern.

A second and most unusual realist text is Margaret Wild and Julie Vivas's *Let the Celebration Begin!* (1991) It is an account of the last days in the Belsen concentration camp, which disturbingly challenges our assumption that such a story cannot be told to young children.

The action takes place in the anticipation of release: 'We are planning a party, a very special party, the women and I . . .' In the text, there are some flashbacks to prewar life, but the narrative focuses on toy making, for the children who have never had such things, from tiny scraps of material that can be scrounged together in the camp. The nightmare horrors of sadistic guards, gas chambers and the rest are omitted; the gentle pastel drawings of gawky, shaven women contrive not to frighten; and the tone of the whole blends pathos with hope. This radical adaptation of a story of Belsen represents presumably what is judged appropriate for children. No longer for baddies the retributive torments of hell; wickedness is completely displaced by a celebration of the virtues of humankindness, which can flourish even in such an unpropitious environment.

These books for young children thus present a startling dichotomy: on the one hand, fairy tales which, either directly or in humorous and ironic modes, continue the tradition of moral retribution, and on the other hand, realist texts, from which any such non-humanistic sentiments have been throughly bleached out.

A critical perspective

For older, knowing readers – publishers, reviewers, teachers, book-buying parents, the gatekeepers of young children's reading – these higher morality narratives may be ideologically acceptable. What kind of moral engagement, however, do they offer to young readers? Some of the feelings described – anxiety at getting lost, the comfort of the motherly presence, the pleasure at a party – are within the young child's range of experience. It is questionable, however, whether the narratives offer them significant opportunity for moral engagement.

Lawrence Kohlberg[2] sees the child's early 'preconventional' moral judgments, first, as based on a fear of retributive punishment which can be inflicted by powerful superiors, and then, as an instrumental accommodation to avoid recrimination and to achieve one's ends. (If Peter Rabbit asked himself, 'Ought I to go into Mr. McGregor's garden?' at Kohlberg's first stage, the moral disincentive would be simply that, like his father, he would have an accident there! And at Kohlberg's second stage, that he'd better not show tail or teeth in McGregor's vegetable patch if he didn't want the old man round the burrow with his ferrets.) Following these first two stages, there is a 'conventional' level of morality based on the feeling of solidarity, first with one's own and then with a broader community. (Again, assuming that rabbit moral development is like that of humans: What would his mother think of him? What would happen if everyone started squeezing under everyone else's garden gate?) Only after these further stages do some, later in life, reach a 'principled' level, in which universal altruism figures.

Reading children's books in the light of this developmental perspective, it is clear why fairy tales make so much sense to the young. They embody a rough-and-ready morality, not very congenial to humanistic adults – of any persuasion – but entirely meaningful to young children. Equally, the comparatively slow development of children's moral reasoning means that – congenial though they may be to adults – texts where altruism invites more mature moral response may well be operating at a level of sophistication mysterious to young children. They may get all kinds of things out of such stories, but they are unlikely to be significantly engaged morally.

Three structural imperatives

It seems that, if texts are to touch young children morally, they must, like fairy tales, acknowledge our first retributive and prudential morality: a conservative imperative. Equally, however, if they are to encourage development to more mature moral judgment, they must be appropriately structured to facilitate this development: a progressive imperative. To complicate matters in this prescription, it must also be remembered that the second, adult readership, as providers of children's books, have a strong interest in inducting the young into their own moral world and must in practice also be taken account of. So, to the two imperatives deriving from the logic of psychological development must also be added a third, deriving from the politics and economics of book buying. Texts likely to be acceptable to both children and adults and valuable in helping children's moral growth must, therefore, take account of these imperatives and work at a number of levels.

But who is equal to these things? I shall take two picture books – one appealing to older and one to younger children, one recent and the other tested by many child readers – to exemplify texts which go a good way toward meeting these criteria.

Margaret Mahy's *The Great White Man-Eating Shark* (1989) concerns a sharkish-looking Australian boy who capitalises on his talents by pretending to be a shark and frightening all the locals out of the water so that he can have the bay to himself. Norvin gets his comeuppance when the skill of his imitation attracts the amorous attentions of a female shark. He is not eaten, but for the rest of the summer, he has to watch his neighbours enjoying the water while he stays out.

The narrative is a morally powerful one. It contains a nice poetic justice for a stereotypical baddie and a form of punishment which doubtless touches its readers nearly. There is a danger that this might trap young readers into no more than retributive judgments about Norvin and his fate; it is, however, modified in two important ways. In the first place, stress is laid on relationships with neighbours. They figure importantly, in both pictorial and verbal narrative, as they are first upset and then settle down again in their bay. Norvin has to learn to come to terms with their interests and rights, and in sensing this, the young reader is nudged on from Kohlberg's 'stage one' (retribution, in the shape of the amorous female: 'Marry me at once or I shall lose my temper and bite you') to 'stage two' (coming to terms with his neighbours in Caramel Cove). In the second place, Norvin's success and fall are treated, in Jonathan Allen's pictures, as knock-about comedy and, by the narrator, with wry humour. She comments on the figure in the deckchair on the final page, still drawn to the sea, but well back from it: 'And I think he was very wise not to take any chances.'

The comic and fantastic modes of a text like this take young readers beyond the closed confines of the realist text, to sense, if not yet understand, a larger world of adult value and judgment.

John Burningham's *Mr. Gumpy's Outing* (1970) is a deceptively simple text. Mr. Gumpy takes his boat out on the river and gives children and animals a 'ride' – on condition that they behave themselves. But they don't! On the climactic page, all the conditions are broken (the long cumulative list represents the seriousness of the moment):

> The chickens flapped,
> The sheep bleated,
> The pig mucked about . . .

And the boat capsizes. Interestingly, not only is there no gratuitous intrusion of the narrator at this point, but Mr. Gumpy, who has grounds to complain, doesn't utter a word. He just tells children and animals that they will have to walk home over the fields. He invites them to tea and finally offers, 'Come for a ride another day.'

Unobtrusively, the story comprehends a number of moral levels. There is straightforward retributive punishment: you break the rules, so (Nature sees to it that) the boat capsizes. There is instrumental accommodation: we are all in the same boat, so don't rock it! There is also humanistic altruism, coded in a symbolism open to a Christian reading. For young readers, the story provides significant moral purchase: the capsizing (Kohlberg's 'stage one') and the notion that, if you are going to enjoy your treat in the boat, you must come to terms with the boatman and with the other passengers (Kohlberg's 'stage two'). Both of these stages are comprehended within a larger context. The patterned narrative, the gentle and impressionistic illustrations, and, perhaps most significantly, the use of symbols like journey, fall and reinstatement, wise old man and common meal serve to open up a larger context of aesthetic, moral and spiritual value.

Both Margaret Mahy's and John Burningham's texts thus encompass a number of levels. They contrive not only to acknowledge our first, fundamental morality, but also, through their use of various narrative modes, figures and other devices, to keep open the way to larger worlds and maturer judgments. Texts structured in these ways have the prospect of speaking meaningfully to both children and adults in the moral domain, and, even more important, of helping children in their moral growth.

Notes

1 I use Lawrence Kohlberg's work, since it represents one of the most strongly theorised and empirically tested developments in the Piagetian tradition (Piaget, 1932). There has been debate about Kohlberg's description of higher levels of morality and about consistency in progression, but the 'preconventional' level, which concerns us here, remains comparatively uncontentious among theorists. Kohlberg's work is particularly useful to those who read and talk with children; it not only provides an instrument for analysing moral judgments but is also matched by a practical pedagogical strategy. He advocates discussion of situations and issues with consistent reference to moral judgments a stage higher than those which constitute the majority use – in order to nudge participants into this new way of thinking. The moral discourse of fictional texts can obviously play a significant part in such a process.

2 Kohlberg's theory is of an invariant sequence of levels and stages, through which human beings' views about what is right and their reasons for doing right mature. Each of the three levels, 'preconventional', 'conventional', and 'principled' includes two stages. While minimum ages are identified for the attainment of each stage, these stages are not age-specific, and progression is normally a good deal slower in the moral than in the other cognitive domains.

From *Children's Literature in Education* No. 89, 1993

Geoff Moss

Geoff Moss teaches English in a comprehensive school in Berkshire. He completed an M.A. in Children's Literature at Bulmershe College (now part of the University of Reading) and became interested in the application of literary theory to picture books and to metafictional texts for children. The essence of this work can be found in *Literature for Children: Contemporary Criticism* (1992), edited by Peter Hunt and published by Routledge.

THE FILM OF THE PICTURE BOOK: RAYMOND BRIGGS'S 'THE SNOWMAN' AS PROGRESSIVE AND REGRESSIVE TEXTS

For a reader, the film of the book is often a disappointment. Armed with all the necessary cultural understanding that written and visual forms can have equal status, aesthetically speaking, there is still a tendency to refer to the book as the touchstone, to give it a privileged position from which judgments can be made. Thus, the film is not as good as the book because narrative sequences are altered, events are omitted or added, or, more subjectively, we simply do not visualise the characters in the way in which they are portrayed by the actors in the film. To a certain extent, I appear to argue from a similar standpoint here in looking at the film of Raymond Briggs's book *The Snowman* (1978). However, I admire both and would prefer to propose a wider brief: that the book is progressive, challenging and potentially subversive, while its counterpart might be seen in certain ways as regressive in the way in which it carefully neutralises criticism of the social order and reproduces the conditions of its own production.

The book version of *The Snowman* presents its narrative as a series of drawings which are to 'read' like a cartoon strip from left to right across the page and in sequence down it. There are as many as twelve pictures on some pages, while others fill an entire double spread of pages. There is no written text. Briefly, the story told is that of a young boy who wakes up one morning to find that it has been snowing. He makes a snowman in the garden, and the following night the snowman comes to life, is shown around the house by the boy, takes the boy flying through the air across the English countryside, and then returns to the garden. The next morning the snowman has melted. Essentially, the book presents a fantasy which, thematically at least, might be seen as a story of transcendence, of the innocent child, perhaps in his dreams (for most of the story happens at night and is framed by sections of sleep), entering a world that is magical and other than his own. Considered in this way, the story fits into a tradition of children's literature and popular culture which promotes fantasy as innocent and unrelated to the unconscious. The use of fantasy in works aimed at children is often considered only on the level of its being merely another narrative device available to an author: it is hardly surprising that the narrative closure 'I woke up and it was all a dream' is a device which appears very early in the narrative writing of young children. A number of writers, however, have challenged this view of fantasy writing.

Rosemary Jackson (1981, p. 173) argues that fantasy is not metaphorical but metonymical, that it explores our 'otherness' and challenges the liberal humanist view of character as whole and indivisible. A thematic reading of fantasies which create secondary worlds through religious myth, faerie or science fiction shows them to be compensatory. They make up for the order we find lacking in the 'real' world: 'Their romance base suggests that the universe is a self-regulating mechanism in which goodness, stability, order, will eventually prevail. They serve to stabilise social order by minimising the need for human intervention in this benevolently organised cosmic mechanism.' In contrast, fantasies which draw upon the 'uncanny' (Freud's term), in which drives are *ex*pressed which are normally *re*pressed for the sake of cultural continuity, can, according to Jackson, be deeply subversive and challenging. Because fantasy moves toward dismantling the 'real', moves away from monological forms of discourse toward open, dialogical structures and deals openly with taboos such as sexuality and death, it confronts ideological assumptions. Not the least of these assumptions is the 'value of sublimation as a "civilising" activity.' Thus, the apparently 'innocent' story of *The Snowman* picture book can be seen to confront the disintegration of character in the melting of the snowman so that the boy in the story is faced with the bleakness of the transformed and mutable other self. The transcendence seen in the flight section of the book, with its journey past the exotic architecture of Brighton's Royal Pavilion and pier, is presented in large-format pictures, while the final picture of the melted snowman is small and surrounded by a deep white border. Our attention here is drawn to how the boy reacts, although we can read this only from his posture because we are unable to see his face. The final picture is framed as a closure which, because of the speed shown in the preceding drawings, superficially invites sympathy with the disappointed boy, through the convention of the sad ending. However, this adherence to conventional reading pacifies what Tzvetan Todorov (1975) has termed the 'absolute hesitation' in the reader. He argues that a governing generic feature of fantasy is that readers can neither come to terms with the events in a story nor dismiss them as supernatural. As a result he sees anxiety as an essential part of the structure of fantasy literature. When we see the melting of the snowman as a realistic event and interpret the boy's reaction as disappointment, anxiety is dispelled and the uncomfortable idea of a snowman's coming to life literally melts away.

A radical reading of the ending of *The Snowman* might see the boy's reaction as fascination or as a confirmation of his expectation. The idea that the melting of the snowman merely shows the innocent and misguided view of reality held by the boy who still believes in fantasy seems to me to be inadequate and arises from the view that stories such as this might be civilising. If the boy is disappointed at the end, he will be seen to have learned an important lesson about how to handle 'reality'. If a radical reading is pursued, however, Briggs's tale might be closer to what Jack Zipes (1983) has called 'liberating' fairy tales. Arguing from the viewpoint that conventional fairy tales have been manipulated to encourage social control, he calls for a more subversive form of children's narrative in which:

> The counter cultural intention is made manifest through alienating techniques which no longer rely on seductive, charming illusions of a happy end as a legitimation of the present civilising process, but make use of jarring symbols that demand an end to superimposed illusions. The aim is to make readers perceive the actual limits and possibilities of their deep personal wishes in a social context. (p. 179)

It seems to me that the picture-book version of *The Snowman* works very much in this way to allow its readers, both young and old, to confront disturbing and subversive notions of self, mutability and death. As a picture book, *The Snowman* is a progressive text.

In looking at the book, I have not examined it in great detail. This choice is deliberate because I want to concentrate mainly on the film version to show how these potentially subversive elements within the original are diverted and then appropriated for commercial purposes in the television production.

The film of *The Snowman* first appeared on British television on Boxing Day 1982 and has been shown at Christmas time each year since. It is now available for sale on video. The copyright for the film is held by Snowman Enterprises Ltd., and a large number of artists and technicians are credited with having produced the half-hour television film. Raymond Briggs is credited with a small involvement in the film. It has proved to be very popular, achieving high ratings and gaining awards. In association with the film, Snowman Enterprises also controls the merchandising of the many Snowman products. The song from the film, 'Flying in the Air', was a British top-ten record.

So, what accounts for this phenomenal success? It would be easy to suggest that it is because it is beautiful to look at, charming to listen to, and enchanting as a Christmas entertainment. However, I think that it is also interesting to examine the underlying ideological assumptions and implications embedded within the film to establish a more critical understanding of its popularity.

Max Horkenheimer and Theodor W. Adorno (1972, 1973) have argued that culture reinforces the dehumanisation of capitalism and that cultural production makes people into consumers who relinquish their autonomy to bureaucracy or industry to make their decisions for them. As the aim of production is to create more consumers, mass entertainment effects this by deceiving people into believing that the products they consume actually nourish them. The 'culture industry' is deeply affirmative because reason has become so instrumentalised for the purposes of capitalism that human beings have lost the ability to function creatively or critically. In a number of ways, I feel that the film of *The Snowman* appeals to what its audience already knows in order to reinforce and maintain existing social and economic conditions.

The most noticeable difference between the film and the book is the film's appropriation of Christmas. In 1986, the TV continuity announcer introduced the film as 'the film without which Christmas just wouldn't be Christmas'. This is important for the success of the film, which seeks to become a 'natural' element of the Christmas tradition, represented as it is on Christmas cards, wrapping paper and gifts. One of the central events of the film is the meeting with Father Christmas when the boy receives a gift. On a most obvious level, gift exchange provides a way of maintaining social and personal relationships, while at another level it is an economic activity which leads to large profits for manufacturing and retail organisation. The gift that Father Christmas gives is a scarf, and the scarf is decorated with small snowmen in the film. Thus, the film becomes an advertisement of its own products: the merchandising of the snowman motif becomes naturalised and even mythologised because it is given by Father Christmas himself. Of course, the use of Father Christmas may also be significant because the myth embodied in that figure is that gifts are magical and not the result of mass production. They arise from the benevolence of an old man who personally sanctions the manufacture of millions of individual gifts for the children of the world. It is a myth which disguises every aspect of the economic conditions of production and consumption.

Elsewhere in the film, the viewer is prepared for the merchandise available to the consumer: the figure on the Christmas cake, a miniature snowman, is picked up by the snowman himself to draw our attention to figures of various sizes available for purchase; the crackers that the snowmen pull at their party are blessed with the snowman logo; and at other points, specific Christmas goods (cards, party hats, toys, etc.) are seen and thus closely linked with the snowman theme of consumption. Beyond the film, other market forces have not been slow to recognise the powerful appeal of the snowman image: Toys R Us, a multinational toy chain, used an imitation of the flying sequence for a Christmas television advertisement, and Boots plc echoed the grainy drawing style of the original in its Christmas catalogue.

Many of the products arising from the film are marketed specifically for children, and Christmas tradition, emphasising as it does the family as a cohesive social unit, pays special attention to children. It is worth examining, therefore, the ways in which the film frames the concept of the child.

The 1986 Boxing Day showing of the film begins with film, as opposed to animation, of a man walking across a ploughed field. He pauses and turns towards the camera, which is fairly close to the ground, on a child's-eye level, while an adult voice-over says, 'I remember that winter because it brought the heaviest snows I had ever seen . . . It was a magical day and it was on that day I made the snowman.' Later versions feature David Bowie entering an attic room full of old toys saying, 'This attic's full of memories for me. We spent all our summers by the sea and, in winter, at home by the fire . . . One winter I made a really big snowman.' In both cases, the film then moves into animation, music starts, and the title sequence runs. The world of the film, therefore, is firmly based in the past, and it is, to some extent, controlled by the memory of an adult. The boy in the film is not autonomous, as he is in the book; he is as he is remembered. Nostalgia plays an important part in Christmas festivities, largely because of the focus placed upon the centrality of childhood during this season. Adults frequently refer to their own childhood Christmases as a way of measuring the present. Clearly, this has been a recurrent adult preoccupation since the institution of the 'traditional' Christmas by the Victorian middle classes. However, Cary Bazalgette (1985) points out that:

> Nostalgia is a mutually pleasurable way for adults to exercise power over children. It makes the past seem innocuous and enticing, and it teaches the importance of the unattainable, the things that happened were seen 'before you were born'. (p. 30)

In the film, the domestic world of the family portrayed is a construct reflecting life in a middle-class home of the 1950s. In the kitchen, the taps are not modern, there are no electrical appliances other than a refrigerator, and the floor is tiled in black and white; in the living room, toast is toasted on an open fire, the television is not the focal point of the room, and there are well-stocked bookshelves. In the boy's room, there are no plastic toys, and the general domestic ambience is of austerity broken up by antique furniture, such as the grandfather clock. The picture-book version is not nearly so specific and makes no attempt to throw the story far back into the past. The film uses nostalgia to invite the adult to encourage the child to watch – thus maintaining the hierarchical adult–child structure which the film implies is an essential social pattern.

Another important way in which the film confirms and upholds the adult view of the child is in the way in which it employs a musical soundtrack. Jacqueline Rose (1984, p. 60) claims that there is a very specific theory associated with children's fiction: 'that showing is better than telling: the ideal work lets the characters and events speak for themselves'. She claims that Rousseau's views that language is produced naturally from the objects to which it refers and that childhood is an instinctual and innocent state, have framed an adult view of the child which smooths over economic, sexual and political conflicts with the child. In the film of *The Snowman*, the adult at the beginning has language, whereas the child does not – he has only music – and it seems to me that the music sets up a closeness to Rousseau's 'natural', innocent state more positively than the silences of the picture books. The world is not silent, and therefore the picture book, although eschewing language, actually draws attention to the fact that it is doing so. The film, in using music, disguises the fact that there is no language. The music in the film establishes, through its rhythms, a temporal dimension from which we cannot escape, while the picture book places no such demands on us. Philip Rosen (1980, p.171), quoting Adorno, shows that music disguises real methods of production and prevents any disturbing threats to the unity of character:

> Its social function is that of cement, which holds together elements that otherwise would oppose each other unrelated – the mechanical product and the spectators.

The music provides the social function of communality and a belief in identity. It obscures unapproached issues, such as sexuality or race, in favour of harmony and melody.

In its treatment of landscape, the film is interesting. At first viewing, it is easy not to question the setting and space created in the film, but it is important to realise that these elements are carefully constructed frame by frame. As Lennard J. Davis (1987, p.101) argues, 'These places, that pretend to be open spaces of the real, are actually claustrophobic encampments of the ideological.' In the country, therefore, the snow has obscured all roads, leaving only hedges, the remnants of a more self-sufficient and less state-dominated existence. The cottage is isolated, and there are no telephone wires or electricity pylons, even though the household does need power to run its lighting, television and other appliances. Animals run freely, untrammelled by fencing, and all the trees are native deciduous (except for the Christmas tree in the house, of course!). Country villages are small, consist entirely of detached houses with large gardens, and are focused around a church. At night, when the flight sequence takes place, the country villages are still and unlit; there is no movement to be seen, as if the humans in these villages rest or sleep at night. By contrast, the large town, modelled on Brighton, has its roads clearly visible, and the majority of houses have their internal lights on. Here, too, the architecture is shaped to fit a concept of urban living; close, tall terraced housing with no gardens, arranged in rigid grids of streets. The monotony of this style of living is alleviated only in the images of the Royal Pavilion and the pier. The implication is that this is an escapist or compensatory architecture which is vital for town dwellers. The world we see in the film is a world without factories or even shops; it is a world from which the methods and outlets of production have been carefully removed to imply that consumerism is a magical, hidden business.

When the snowman and the boy fly across the sea (in the picture book, they get no further than the end of the pier), wild animals, such as whales and penguins, are shown as non-aggressive and tolerant of the snowman, so that, in essence, these creatures are actually tamed within the parameters of their wildness. The landscape of the lands across the sea is largely constructed in the same way as before, and on the journey, small communities gathered around churches would appear to be the norm. The film appears to be saying to its viewers: this is how we live here *and* everywhere else – almost as a form of cultural imperialism. Davis argues that early novels used description of place in a similar way:

> The seemingly neutral idea of describing a place and setting action in it carries with it the freight of a middle class interest in controlled property of which the colonial experience is a compelling metaphor. Novels claim space and turn it into a system of meaning – just as countries claim other countries and turn them into systems of meaning. (p.85)

It seems that, in a limited way, the film of *The Snowman* is doing just this and thus is presenting a narrow, regressive view of the world.

There are many instances in the film where ideological assumptions are left unchallenged. The mother is viewed as supplier of the domestic needs of the family: she gives food and washes the dishes. No one in the family is shown to be doing a job of work by selling their labour. Girls look at experiences in astonishment, while boys actually take part, and there are very few snowwomen! Although important observations in themselves, all these examples serve the function of supporting the way in which the film upholds traditional values through appropriating Christmas, disguising its own methods of production, framing a view of the child, and constructing a landscape which is both divisive and imperialistic.

Finally, it is worth examining the closure of the film to demonstrate how it departs from the picture book version in such a way as to turn it from being a progressive into a regressive text. The film shares many qualities with the book until the final moments when the boy, having found that the snowman has melted, turns toward the camera looking upset, takes from his pocket the gift of the scarf, looks at it, and drops to one knee as the view pans out and credits roll across the white snow. As he does so, the piano leitmotif heard at the opening of the film is repeated. The scarf is an important image in two ways: it reminds us of the snowman as product at the very end of the film, and it reinforces the mystery of gift exchange for children at Christmas time. Unlike the ending of the book, the boy's disappointment is made clear, but the soundtrack implies repetition – that the disappointment is temporary, not a death, but part of a cyclical process. The melting of the snowman is an image not of disintegration and chaos, but of regeneration and rebirth, and of course, this pattern is confirmed as the film is repeated each Christmas. Here the Christian undertones become most obvious as the film echoes the mysterious birth, death and resurrection of Christ and thus builds into itself another reason for its popularity at Christmas time. Whereas the book's ending is progressive or challenging in the way in which it subverts conceptions of the unity of personality, the ending of the film is regressive, affirmative and, therefore, seductively appealing.

From *Children's Literature in Education* No. 82, 1991

Remembered from Childhood: Young Readings Revisited

Rosemary Sutcliff

Rosemary Sutcliff wrote more than thirty novels for children, often set in Britain under the Romans or during the Dark Ages. Her awards include the Carnegie Medal for *The Lantern Bearers* (1959). *CLE* invited her to contribute to its series in which an eminent writer revisits a book read with pleasure in childhood. Her choice of *Kim* was not surprising, for her admiration for its author had been reflected in her Bodley Head monograph on Rudyard Kipling in 1960. Rosemary Sutcliff died in 1992.

Kim

I can claim no remembrance of the first time I read *Kim*, or rather, of the first time *Kim* was read to me, for I was one of those fortunate children possessed of a parent – in my case my mother, which was just as well, since my father, being a sailor, was liable to be away from home for two years at a time – who loves reading aloud and does it beautifully. I can only say that by the time I was eight or thereabouts, the book was a long-familiar and much-loved part of my life, as were the *Just So Stories*, *The Jungle Books*, *Puck of Pook's Hill* and *Rewards and Fairies*. I loved them all equally, though in slightly different ways, and I think I still do. Yet it is *Kim* that has a permanent place along with *The Secret Garden*, *The Wind in the Willows*, Professor Gilbert Murray's translation of the *Hippolytus*, and half-a-dozen more, on my bedside windowsill.

Quite why, I do not know. I am in much the same predicament with regard to *Kim* as my first editor with regard to *The Wind in the Willows*, who told me long ago when we were both new to our careers, that he could not judge how good the book was because he loved it so much.

Since that first meeting with *Kim*, whenever it may have been, I have read and reread it many times; not, maybe, regularly once a year, yet I doubt if I have ever gone much longer than three years between readings, and I do not think that I have often gone two. My feeling for the book has of course changed with the passage of time, but it has never grown less. Always the delight has been there, waiting for me. Last week, rereading the book for the first time for a purpose (a purpose, that is, apart from the pleasure of reading it), I was nervous. Would the purpose drive out the delight? Break the spell? I pulled out the battered volume – my grandmother's, when it was new – greeting as usual the elephant with the lotus flower held in the tip of his trunk, whose embossed head decorates the cover, turned somewhat hesitantly to page 1, and began to read.

> He sat, in defiance of Municipal Orders, astride the gun Zam-Zammah on her brick platform opposite the old Ajaib-Gher, the Wonder House as the natives called the Lahore Museum. Who hold Zam-Zammah, that 'fire-breathing dragon', hold the Punjab; for the great green-bronze piece is always first of the conqueror's loot.

And instantly the delight was there, and the old spell weaving itself again.

On the surface, *Kim* is a spy story, and such plot as it has, which is not much, for Rudyard Kipling himself described it as being nakedly 'picaresque and plotless', as are a surprising number of the great stories of the world, concerns a boy's education to be a Secret Agent in the service of the Raj: and that is probably the level at which a child first reads it, with undertones of magic lying sensed but unrecognised beneath. But the plot is little more than a thread on which to string jewels as curious and entrancing as any in the shop of Lurgan Sahib, 'The Healer of Sick Pearls'. This is why the large-scale and vastly expensive film made from the book some twenty or more years ago, as watched for the third time by me on TV recently, is merely the husk, though a colourful and entertaining husk, with all the peculiar essence of Kipling's story drained out of it.

The film is a spy story, its climax the hero's encounter with Russian spies among the High Hills of the Frontier. But the book is so much more, and the encounter is merely an incident on the way, though admittedly one which forms a turning point in the quest of Kim and his Lama. For the story is, among so many other things, a Quest story – of the Lama for his sacred river, and release from the Wheel of Things, of Kim for his true self.

This is a quest that takes them drifting among the drifting vagabond life of India too far down to be coloured by any question of State or politics. Kipling's account of this life is so evocative that reading it, one catches the scent of dust and withered marigolds and the smoke of dung fires where the village elders gather under the peepul tree in the dusk:

> The lama, very straight and erect, the deep folds of his yellow clothing slashed with black in the light of the *parao* fires, precisely as a knotted tree trunk is slashed with the shadows of the long sun, addressed a tinsel and lacquered *ruth* (ox-cart) which burned like a many-coloured jewel in the same uncertain light. The patterns of the gold-worked curtains ran up and down, melting and reforming as the folds shook and quivered in the night wind; and when the talk grew more earnest, the jewelled forefinger snapped out little sparks of light between the embroideries. Behind the cart was a wall of uncertain darkness speckled with little flames and alive with half-caught forms and faces and shadows.

This description of a night scene on the Grand Trunk Road expresses perfectly two of the aspects of *Kim* that linger most strongly in the mind. First, its preoccupation with light. Kipling could never visualise any incident without its setting of light and weather, time of day, and season of the year, but in *Kim* more than any other of his books, one is constantly aware of this play of changing light, windy sunlight brushing across the tawny grass of a hillside, the chill grey of dawn on the waking camp in a railway siding, the smoky flare of torches, white peaks lifting themselves yearning to the moonlight while all the rest is 'as the darkness of interstellar space'.

Secondly, there is its sense of crowding riches – riches so vast that they overflow untidily in all directions and much could not be used at all, though one senses them behind what actually appears, a shifting background 'speckled with little flames and alive with half-caught forms and faces and shadows'.

Kipling himself, in his autobiography, describes the process of smoking over the book with his father:

> Under our united tobacco it grew like the Djin released from the brass bottle, and the more we explored its possibilities, the more opulence of detail did we discover. I do not know what proportion of an iceberg is below the water-line, but *Kim* as it finally appeared was about one tenth of what the first lavish specification called for.

And that is exactly the impression that the reader gets.

I suppose it must have been about the time that I started to write, and my awareness of the working of the craft in others was therefore beginning to waken, that I first realised the kinship that undoubtedly exists between *Kim* and *The Jungle Books*. Kimball O'Hara, whose father was a Colour-Sergeant in an Irish regiment and his mother a nursemaid in the Colonel's family, and who, after the death of his parents, was brought up – insofar as he was brought up by anyone except himself – by a half-caste woman who smoked opium 'and pretended to keep a second-hand furniture shop by the square where the cheap cabs wait', is in the same position as Mowgli, a boy belonging by birth and heritage to one world, thrown into and accepted by another, and faced in the end with the same choice to be made. Mowgli has to choose between the Jungle and the Village, Kim between the world of action for which he has been trained, and the timeless Eastern world he knows in his bones and in his heart's core. And though we are not actually told so, we know that like Mowgli he will go back to the Village, leaving the Jungle behind him, and that he too will break something within himself in doing so. But because of the very nature of the world for which he has been trained, he will remain always just a little a citizen of two worlds, with all the strains and stresses and heartbreaks that such a position entails. For to be even just a little a citizen of two worlds must of necessity mean to be not completely a citizen of either.

Like Mowgli, too, Kim has his sponsors in his adoptive world, and in his case, in the world of the Secret Service, the Great Game, also. First and foremost there is the lama himself, the most completely good character that Kipling ever created; the only perfectly good character, I think, that I have ever met between the covers of a book, who contrives also to be unreservedly attractive – generally speaking, human beings, actual or fictional, need a fault or two before it is possible to love them. Then there is the masterful old dowager of Saharunpore, the owner of the jewelled finger aforementioned, who emerges vividly and irrepressibly and outrageously among the rest, though she remains (more or less) behind her embroidered curtains and is never actually described at all. Mahbub Ali, the lean and ferocious horse dealer with the dyed red beard, is the only one of Kim's sponsors to stand for him in both worlds, and is believed to be based on a friend of Kipling's early days, a Pathan of 'indescribable filth but magnificent mien and features', who brought him the news of Central Asia beyond the Khyber Pass. Lurgan Sahib, 'The Healer of Sick Pearls' and another player of the Great Game, was also based on a real character, the keeper of a curiosity shop in Simla, Alexander Jacob by name, a man of Turkish ancestry, and possessed of uncanny powers. And for the fifth and last, there is the soft-bellied Bengali babu (clerk) with the heart of a lion – for surely no courage can match that of the man who is always afraid.

Ironically, he is the clever, half-Westernised Hindu whose kind later spread to form a 'middle class' which India had never had before, and from which much of the backing for Self Rule was to come.

But this, having little feeling for politics, Rudyard Kipling could not foresee. Nor could he foresee that by that time the word 'Empire' would begin to take on shameful undertones. Empire building and holding, all the things that much of his work seems to stand for, would be widely considered a disreputable occupation. Further, he could not foresee that because he stood for these things, the charge of jingoism would be flung at him by people who had not noticed that the accent of his work is on service, rather than mere mastery. His *A Ballad of East and West* (1889) would be quoted in support of the charge: 'Oh, East is East, and West is West, and never the twain shall meet', by people who had taken the lines out of context, without reading far enough to see that the verse ends:

> But there is neither East nor West, Border, nor Breed,
> nor Birth,
> When two strong men stand face to face, though they
> come from the ends of the earth!

I can sympathise, as Kipling could, with the Native's hunger to have his land and his culture to himself again (I have made that clear enough in some of my own books). But born and bred as I have been in the tradition of the so-called Fighting Services, I feel very close to Kipling in most of his values. I do not think that an Empire is necessarily a good thing, but I do not feel that it is necessarily something to be ashamed of either. I can appreciate also, from the same Service background, his opinion of people behind desks or in pulpits at home, who have no clear idea of what things are actually *like* at the scene of action, but who know exactly how everything should be done nevertheless. I can appreciate his feeling for the difference between the outsider, sometimes to be considered as 'fair game' by the initiated, and the individualist and rebel, to be encouraged within reason (Kim belongs very much to the second of these two categories).

So, in the later part of his life, in the years after his death, and by some people even today, Kipling was and is looked on as the jingoistic upholder of an oppressive Raj. And yet the Bengali writer Nirad C. Chaudhuri could claim that *Kim* was not only 'the finest story about India in English', but also that the book was the outcome of Kipling's

vision of a larger India than meets the most penetrating outward eye, 'A vision whose profundity we Indians would be hard put to it to match, even in an Indian language, not to speak of English. . . . We Indians should never cease to be grateful to Kipling for having shown the many faces of our country in all their beauty, power and truth.'

Kipling loved India, and not with a love that stemmed from the outside looking in, but very much from within, from the long hot fever-smelling nights when as Assistant Editor of the *Civil and Military Gazette* published at Lahore, and still in his late teens, he would explore the ancient Muslim city crouched under its ghost-ridden fortress from which Ranjit Singh, the Lion of the Punjab, had ruled his short-lived Sikh kingdom. On such nights, no one could sleep much, and most of the life of Lahore went on in the streets and on the rooftops. These nighttime prowlings were to bear fruit and flower later:

> He [Kim] knew the wonderful walled city of Lahore from the Delhi Gate to the Outer Fort Ditch; was hand-in-glove with men who lead lives stranger than anything Haroun al Raschid dreamed of; and he lived in a life wild as that of the Arabian Nights, but missionaries and secretaries of charitable societies could not see the beauty of it. His nickname through the wards was 'Little Friend of all the World'; and very often, being lithe and inconspicuous, he executed commissions by night on the crowded housetops for sleek and shiny young men of fashion. It was intrigue, of course – he knew that much, as he had known all evil since he could speak – but what he loved was the game for its own sake, the stealthy prowl through the dark gullies and lanes, the crawl up a water pipe, the sights and sounds of the women's world on the flat roofs, and the headlong flight from house-top to house-top under cover of the hot dark.

And Kipling's contact with 'White Man's India' was not Vice-Regal Lodge or the Simla parties for which he had a splendid contempt, but the company at the Lahore Club, where tired representatives of Army, Education, Canals, Forestry, Engineering, Irrigation, Railways, Medicine and Law met and talked in great detail each their own particular brand of 'shop'.

The only 'shop' which he does not seem to have drunk in with joyful avidity was that of the Church. He had above all no use for the Missionary, however valiant and well-meaning, who did not understand native culture or traditions or allow for the possibility of other truths than his own. He had a deep religion of his own, but it was not particularly a Christian religion. And he stated his own belief in his splendid *Song to Mithras* (1917):

> Many roads Thou hast fashioned
> All of them lead to the Light.

And in *Kim*, when he wishes to make a saint, he makes him a Buddhist, not a Christian.

The lama possesses charity in its broadest sense of love with understanding and acceptance; the two Army Chaplains, one Anglican, one Roman Catholic, good, well-meaning men both of them, are entirely lacking in that quality. But even the lama only gains his vision of his Sacred River after, for love of Kim his *chela*, he has denied his own philosophy of unattachment to earthly things and the severing of all human bonds.

Kim is a strange, beautiful book, written on many levels, and beneath the Secret Service adventure story, and below the spread of constantly changing scenes, curious incident and laughter, and the delights of smell and sound and colour, the raggle-taggle riches and the half-glimpsed glories, at the deepest level of all, it is a story that has to do with the Soul of Man; a story whose real theme is love.

From *Children's Literature in Education* No. 47, 1982

Philippa Pearce

Philippa Pearce grew up in the mill-house in Great Shelford, near Cambridge, which provides the setting for her classic novel, *Tom's Midnight Garden*, winner of the Carnegie Medal in 1958. After taking a degree at Cambridge, she worked as a writer and producer for B.B.C. Radio, and as an editor for Oxford University Press and André Deutsch. She has written several widely admired novels as well as six collections of short stories and the texts of a number of picture books. Her stories have been televised and broadcast on radio – *Tom's Midnight Garden* on several occasions.

The article which follows was another in *CLE's* series in which distinguished authors return to a book remembered with pleasure from childhood. Philippa Pearce's choice was Henry Gilbert's *Robin Hood and his Merry Men* (1912), illustrated by Walter Crane.

Robin Hood and his Merry Men: a Rereading

I had a Robin Hood period in childhood. Like most childhoods, mine is patchily remembered, misty. Through a mist – one of those delightful early summer morning mists, unfrightening, full of promise – I perceive the green figures of Robin Hood and his men slipping, sliding, wavering. Over how long a time? I don't know. Perhaps one summer? Surely several?

Certainly the season was summer, or spring; not winter. I remember standing with string tied round the middle of my cotton dress, on a corner of our lawn against the archway cut through one of the yews. I also remember strolling slowly across the meadow opposite our house – in full view of its windows – very probably in a similar dress similarly belted. I wasn't doing anything particular that anyone could observe: not speaking, not gesticulating. But, on both occasions, *I was Robin Hood.*

Note that I did not need to act Robin Hood in some dramatic situation, such as I knew well from his story. Simply, I *was* Robin Hood. At some time I would make a bow – a token bow that easily broke if bent;

and I made hazel twig arrows capped with elder – that craft I had from my brothers. I longed for a quiver (I loved the very word) for my arrows, but I had not the ingenuity to make one, and it never occurred to me to ask my mother, who probably would have helped me. The bow and arrows were a valued addition to being Robin Hood; but not essential. Only (I think) the string was important: tied round my doubtful waist it changed me utterly. I was wearing a leathern belt 'neath which could be tucked a dagger for carving roast venison or an arrow against some proud prelate: *I was Robin Hood.* I became part of the literary style of Henry Gilbert. Behind all the green mistiness of that time stands factual, certain, a book: *Robin Hood and his Merry Men* by Henry Gilbert, illustrated in full colour by Walter Crane. The book belonged to one of my elder brothers, the one next to me in age. A book-plate stated that he had won this prize for his Work in Spelling and Writing in the year when I was five.

I do not know how much of the book came to me at first through its owner. Perhaps my brother read it aloud to me at least in parts; perhaps he just explained the pictures. (In the end, of course, I must have read the book for myself.) The book was always very closely associated with him. He had his own drama of Robin Hood; I don't know exactly the nature of his play, but I observed a good deal of it. 'Very cautiously Robin made his way between the trees, taking care not to step on a twig as he walked rapidly over the grass, his quick eye meanwhile bent in every direction.' Then my brother's quick eye would detect what (I suppose) he himself had previously laid there. 'On the bare ground were a few broken twigs which to the ordinary eye would have seemed to have been blown there by the wind but with hands on knees Robin bent and scanned them keenly. "One bent at the head and eight straight twigs," he said under his breath; "a knight on horseback that will mean, with eight knaves afoot. They are halted on the western road, not far from here. . ." '

This brother actually owned a cow's horn, almost completely scoured out; and he made what seemed to me a huge bow of real yew seasoned over months in our mother's airing-cupboard. So he had his own, opulently equipped play of Robin Hood. I don't think we ever played the play together. For one thing , I would have been allowed to be only Little John – always, I think; no turn and turn about. Or I might even have been condemned to Maid Marian.

At the age of five, then, Robin Hood entered and took over my

imagination. (*The Scarlet Pimpernel* had the same effect upon me to a lesser degree, some time later.) This was a totally different experience from my response to stories such as (my favourite) *Miss Jemima* by Walter de la Mare. That story, by the power of its writing, drew the reader into itself, rather than invading the reader's daily life.

Yet our *Robin Hood* (my brother's; but *ours* too, by right of love) was not ineffectively written; and the pictures – oh! the marvellous, marvellous pictures! The book as a physical thing – the weight of it in my hands, the dog-earedness of certain pages, the literal detachment of some of the illustrations: all that is with me still. Children should *own* books they like or love for this reason alone, if for no other.

So, rereading Gilbert's *Robin Hood* I cannot be coolly critical. I could not properly evaluate it, for instance, against any other Robin Hood collection. Even the old ballads – the source of it all – seem imposters of authenticity compared with our *Robin Hood.*

In retrospect, I believe I see certain things that were not visible to me all those years ago. Obviously, the foremost appeal of Robin Hood has always been the spaciousness, the freedom – the escape to freedom – for which Robin stands. He is against bad authority; but all human authority is potentially bad. So he is simply against authority – although he himself is a good, green authority. Justifiably, a law unto himself, in a green kingdom.

He has power, from several sources. His woodcraft and bowmanship are almost superhuman – those peeled hazel wands split by his unerring shaft *snoring* its way over umpteen hundreds of yards! He also has his merry men. Now there are various ways of looking at Robin and his men. They can be considered as a team, if you like – a sports team of some kind of which Robin is captain. The interpretation fits. Or Robin Hood can be a gallant army officer deploying his forces and leading them into action. Again, that fits. But the interpretation I adopted was in Arabian Nights style. Robin Hood conjured. He set his horn to his lips and blew 'a curious blast'. Then archers in green (or brown, according to season) 'seemed to rise from the ground and to issue from the trunks of the trees'. So the cow horn in my brother's room was as fascinating to me as would have been an oriental lamp such as Aladdin rubbed.

There was power in the Robin Hood stories; also mystery. Henry Gilbert not only invented new Robin Hood adventures, but also interwove them with the legend of the Little People who live inside the grassy hillocks. There is nothing flimsy-fairy about these Little People. They are devoted to Robin Hood, of course; but they are also sworn to dreadful private vengeances. I shuddered at the weird, croaking cry of: 'Colman Grey! Colman Grey!' (That my father ate Colman's mustard with his cold boiled bacon regularly only made the cry more actual and therefore yet more mysterious.)

Mystery and power express themselves again and again in disguisings. Robin disguises himself as a potter, as a minstrel, as a 'ragged wastrel' and so on. His enemies also sometimes disguise themselves: the most horrifying and inexplicable disguise is Guy of Gisborne's: a horse's hide, complete with head. (There was a Crane picture for that.) Finally, King Richard himself is in disguise as an abbot; and then, in a supreme moment, he flings aside his abbatial black to reveal 'the rich silk surtout blazoned with the leopards of Anjou and the fleur-de-lys of France'. (Again, a dazzling picture.)

I see now that Henry Gilbert strove to give some kind of historical setting and relevance to his Robin Hood stories. (He says in his preface that 'I have added incidents and events which have been invented so as to give a truthful picture of the times in which he lived'.) But *then* I never bothered about history at all; I did not even bother about common sense. I never wondered that the outlaws always looked so healthy, well-groomed and *clean* in the Crane pictures. Their diet never seemed doubtful to me: there are very many references to roast venison and a great variety of other game; and one mention of 'stewed kale or cabbage'.

On the other hand I noticed – and treasured the thought – that all this had happened here, in England. I knew that there was a Nottingham, and there had been – or even was, vestigially – a Sherwood Forest. And if there wasn't a Sheriff of Nottingham, then that was only because Robin Hood, in final exasperation, had killed him off. Times shifted and met in my mind. If I ever reached Kirklees, I thought, surely I could find Robin's grave, still tended.

What I could not understand in Robin Hood's life history, as presented by Henry Gilbert, I passed over and forgot. The rightness of his loyalty to a King nicknamed Lionheart was obvious. His devotion to the Blessed Virgin Mary, on the other hand, was outside my grasp, since I had a non-conformist upbringing. I understood and accepted his anticlericalism. All his enemies, in fact, were my enemies: 'rich snuffling priests, proud prelates, evil lords, and hardhearted merchants'. To rob that lot, for the poor, was dead right.

Nowadays, as a professional myself, I see weaknesses in Gilbert's

writing; even, alas! absurdities. But his tendency is to overwrite, in a way clearly enjoyable to himself and not without joy to his readers. He can do his own justice to a great occasion, such as the destruction, almost at the end of the book, of the Evil Hold at Wrangby. Already some of the villains (not villeins; I had had that sorted out for me by my brother) were killed, and the two worst of all had been lynched in an 'act of wild justice': Sir Isembart de Belame, Lord of Wrangby (and 'grandson of the fiend of Tickhill') and Sir Baldwin the Killer. Meanwhile, the Evil Hold is fired:

> Leaping tongues of fire darted through the ropy reek and coiling wreaths, and soon, gathering power, the fire burst up through the floors of the great hall and the chambers above, and roared like a furious torrent to the dark sky. Great noises issued as the thick beams split, and as balk and timber, rafter and buttress fell, the flames and sparks leaped higher until the light shone far and wide over the country. Shepherds minding their sheep far away on the distant fells looked and looked, and would not believe their eyes; then crossed themselves and muttered a prayer of thankfulness that somehow the Evil Hold of Wrangby was at length ruining in fire.

To top this description came the Crane illustration of the scene the next morning. In the background (I describe from memory) the Evil Hold still smoulders and the gibbetted bodies swing. In the foreground, centrally, Robin Hood sits astride his horse:

> Doffing his steel cap, Robin bent his head and in silence gave up a prayer to the Virgin, thanking her for the help she had so amply granted him .... From over the plain came a crowd of peasants – some running, some walking slowly, half disbelieving their own eyes. Some among them came up to Robin, and old men and women, their faces and hands worn and lined with toil, seized his hands and kissed them, or touched his feet or the hem of his coat of mail with their lips.

Robin Hood sits up there, like the central figure in a Doom painting, bareheaded, his hands outstretched on either side, palms outermost, towards the people to whom he has brought salvation. His downward-looking face – fair hair, short beard – is gentle, saintlike, divine. This was a Christ-figure.

Of course, I did not articulate the idea then; but now I seem to see it clearly. I can also identify more closely the power that is in Gilbert's Robin Hood – anyone's Robin Hood. It is *virtue,* in its richest sense:

virtue as supernatural efficacy, that is also power for good – that is good.

I see myself as a child, with that piece of string tied round my middle, responding eagerly to all that I imagined Robin Hood was, from the presentations of Henry Gilbert and Walter Crane. That impulsive, unsophisticated response seems to me to have been a generous, creative one; and I can still respect it.

In a letter Philippa Pearce adds:

Since I wrote this piece my daughter, reading Wordsworth's *Prelude*, pointed out to me the relevance of Book V, *Books*, to what I had written. Wordsworth describes the child whose education is totally supervised: he/she (no, Wordsworth doesn't even envisage a 'she') is 'noosed'. This kind of overdirected academic (and moral) education is 'a pest', and he is devoutly glad he escaped from it. Instead, he read a random miscellany of tales. And the book as 'a physical thing' (I quote myself) is what Wordsworth owned and loved:

> A precious treasure had I long possessed,
> A little, yellow, canvas-covered book,
> A slender abstract of the Arabian tales...

And then he actually refers to the Robin Hood stories:

> Oh, give us once again the wishing-cap
> Of Fortunatus, and the invisible coat
> Of Jack the Giant-killer, Robin Hood,
> And Sabra in the forest with St. George!
> The child, whose love is here, at least doth reap
> One precious gain – that he forgets himself.
>
> *The Prelude*, Book Fifth:
> *lines 341-6 (1850 edition)*

From *Children's Literature in Education* No. 58, 1985

Patricia Beer

Patricia Beer was born in Devon and educated at Exmouth Grammar School, and at the Universities of Exeter and Oxford. She has taught English at universities in Italy and England, and is now a full-time writer. She has published eight volumes of poetry (most recently, *Friend of Heraclitus*, 1993) alongside critical works, a novel and an autobiography. She also contributes regularly to the *London Review of Books*. When *CLE* invited her to write about a novel she recalled with pleasure from her early days as a reader, she chose Robert Louis Stevenson's *Kidnapped*.

KIDNAPPED

In the thirties in Britain, Robert Louis Stevenson's *Kidnapped* was a great favourite with adolescent girls, such as myself and Sandy, antiheroine of Muriel Spark's *The Prime of Miss Jean Brodie* (1961).

> 'Sandy, you must take this message o'er the heather to the Macphersons,' said Alan Breck. 'My life depends on it and the Cause no less.'
>
> 'I shall never fail you. Alan Breck,' said Sandy. 'Never'... Alan Breck clapped her shoulder and said, 'Sandy, you are a brave lass and want nothing in courage that any King's man might possess.'

It was Alan, of course, that Sandy and I and all the others fancied. David the hero was too close to us in age and inexperience.

There is no doubt that fancying is what it was. After the tomboyish passage just quoted, the day-dreaming turns from the heather to the drawing-room:

> Alan Breck would arrive in full Highland dress. Supposing that passion struck upon them in the course of the evening and they were swept away into sexual intercourse? She saw the picture of it happening in her mind, and Sandy could not stand for this spoiling. She argued with herself, surely people have time to think, they have time to think while they are taking their clothes off, and if they stop to think, how can they be swept away?

These speculations were unnecessary as Alan's clothes were not designed to take off; and Sandy and I and the rest of us soon turned to other fictional heroes whose were.

I imagine all this no longer applies. So many things have changed in the last forty years that I cannot suppose youthful reaction to *Kidnapped* to be an exception. And I am sure that the advance of feminism will have affected the response of girls to Alan Breck, who is a male chauvinist pig both in his behaviour and in his advice.

Stevenson thought he was writing *Kidnapped* for boys, and he liked the idea. In the dedication of the sequel *Catriona* to his friend Charles Baxter, to whom *Kidnapped* had been dedicated seven years before, he trusts that there may be left in Edinburgh 'some long-legged, hot-headed youth' who would be ready to pursue David's adventures from where he was left outside the Bristol Linen Company's bank at the end of the first book. He knew boys were not his only audience, but in a letter to Sidney Colvin, written in 1894, he was not prepared to envisage his readership as including more than two further categories: journalists and fellow novelists. Henry James, incidentally, considered that Stevenson was all too aware of his boyish audience and that Uncle Ebenezer, whom, strangely, James found unconvincing, was created with an eye to serialisation in *Young Folks.* Young folks were of course boys.

Jenni Calder, in her repetitious biography of Robert Louis Stevenson, *RLS: a Life Study* (1980), makes considerable mention of his sympathy with women and his concern at their social exploitation. This may well have been his theoretical attitude; certainly a comment from *Virginibus Puerisque* (Stevenson, 1881) has a very modern ring:

> Man is a creature who lives not upon bread alone, but principally by catchwords; and the little rift between the sexes is astonishingly widened by simply teaching one set of catchwords to the girls and one to the boys.

But little of this sympathy for women makes its way into Stevenson's fiction as a whole; into *Kidnapped* virtually none. When news of the murder of Campbell of Glenure is brought to Aucharn, the wife of James of the Glens, who sits by the fire and weeps, as well she may knowing that her husband will be the chief suspect, is presented as a figure if not of fun, of embarrassment. Her expressions of gratitude – emotional but not more so than the occasion calls for – to David and Alan for their help, make David 'stand abashed' and Alan 'look mighty silly', and they depart into the night as soon as they decently can, perhaps sooner. The maidservant at the inn who helps them to cross the Forth on the last stage of their flight is treated no better. She is hoodwinked and emotionally blackmailed into rowing them over the firth to safety. It is true that their lives are at risk, but as a result of their exploitation of her so would hers have become.

In *Catriona* (1893) women play a much larger part but this makes matters even worse. Catriona herself is really rather sweet, but no more than a nice child dressed up as a heroine; she tells David how at the age of twelve she rode with the clan in the '45 rebellion, and it is this touching image of her that predominates even in her womanhood. Barbara Grant, wealthy young patroness of both David and Catriona, though no doubt meant to be spirited and original, comes across as a misogynist's dream, poking her nose into other people's private affairs and manipulating them like a deranged social worker.

Whatever sexual fantasies readers bring to bear on *Kidnapped*, they must do all the work themselves (a young feminist, for example, might daydream about reforming Alan Breck from his horrible attitudes); there is nothing in the book to help them. What then are its themes and which of them can we expect to appeal to young people nowadays?

The title would point to a highly acceptable subject if kidnapping meant to Stevenson what it does today. But as he is for the most part using the word in the original sense of carrying off people by force for service on the American plantations, he cannot offer the elements which make contemporary kidnapping into world news and fill the media to choking point. There is no anxious relative trying to raise ransom money; there is an anxious relative certainly – Uncle Ebenezer – but his sole concern is that the kidnapping should succeed. As the affair is known to so few people, there is little suspense except what the victim, David, himself experiences, and he is not waiting for rescue by interested parties, only for some lucky accident. No newsworthy amounts of money are involved, only the businesslike sums paid out by Uncle Ebenezer and, if things had reached this point, the owner of the plantation.

Another subject equally popular today and a godsend to the media, that is, legal trial, might well have been central to *Kidnapped*, but in the event virtually got away. James Pope Hennessy's biography of Stevenson (1974), a lively work, indicates the point at which Stevenson first became involved in the story he presents. It seems that in 1885 his wife, Fanny, perennially ambitious to be an author too, was studying a selection of Old Bailey trials with a view to writing a play. The bookseller who supplied the necessary records included in the parcel, through either inefficiency or good salesmanship, an account of the trial of James Stewart in Appin. Stevenson, already professionally interested in the murder of Colin Campbell, apparently received a conclusive impetus from reading this report. If this is so, it is fascinating to reflect how and why the trial itself slips out of *Kidnapped* altogether, except in powerful adumbration ('Alan, it'll be a jury of Campbells'), and takes place in *Catriona* only offstage, its purpose being to provide David with an agonising moral dilemma.

Agonising moral dilemmas can be interesting, of course, to a thoughtful young reader, provided the concepts involved are accessible, and Stevenson's fascination with the question of what one should or should not do in given circumstances could well be imparted and even provide a motive for reading his books. *Kidnapped* certainly is full of situations where moral decisions have to be taken, and the relevant concepts are perfectly accessible to the young. The theme of loyalty is the most important in the sense that it occurs most frequently. It is introduced early on, in a light enough way. When David leaves home, or, in Stevenson's more vivid words, when he takes the key for the last time out of the door of his father's house, he is accompanied as far as the ford by the Minister of his village, Essendean. David realises that the good man is distressed by his departure:

> My conscience smote me hard and fast, because I, for my part, was overjoyed to get away out of that quiet countryside, and go to a great, busy house, among rich and respected gentlefolk of my own name and blood. 'Davie, Davie,' I thought, 'was ever seen such black ingratitude? Can you forget old favours and old friends at the mere whistle of a name? Fie, fie; think shame!'

His priggish but essentially decent dialogue with his conscience could form a subtitle to the whole of *Great Expectations.*

The theme darkens. It becomes more complicated and deals with issues that are physically more lethal; as in chapter 19, when Alan and David arrive at the house of James of the Glens after the Appin murder. In this excellent scene we have three interlocking conflicts of loyalty, with lives at stake. James wavers between hospitality to a stranger and duty to his own family: having provided David with clothes, food and weapons for the flight, he announces that he will have to 'paper' him, that is, send out a description and offer a reward for his capture. In these circumstances Alan, in his turn, has to decide between the claims of friendship, which would make him persuade James to do no such thing, and the claims of kinship, which would allow James to go ahead. As a result of all this, David has either to permit James to paper him, out of affection and gratitude to Alan, or to remain true to his own common sense and feeling for justice by insisting that the one who should be papered is the real murderer. But then, he is a Cameron . . ., and so on.

It is all part of the dilemma – and of the realism – that the viewpoint of none of them can be pure. As the Whig Lowlander sees it, the Jacobite Highlander's notions of what is right contain an element of sheer lunacy, while the Highlander considers the Lowlander inflexible and insensitive. But though each is profoundly influenced by his own code, each is acting according to his own character as well.

The characterisation in *Kidnapped* would provide a jolt – welcome or unwelcome according to the buoyancy of the recipient – to any inexperienced reader accustomed only to goodies and baddies. Take James of the Glens, for example. The stereotype of the Jacobite chieftain in danger of death – Ewen Cameron in D. K. Broster's *The Flight of the Heron* or Archie Cameron in her *The Gleam in the North* – is a miracle of fortitude, goodness and honesty. Under stress James can be both cowardly and mean, just like all the rest of us, and when it comes to self-deception, he exceeds most of us: he solemnly swears that he will never divulge David's name to a living soul, when in fact he does not know it himself. For a writer so concerned with morality, the extent to which Stevenson refrains from censure is astonishing. There is probably no actual evil in either Alan or David – he would have to condemn *that* – but their faults, and Alan's especially, are those that do in fact damage the personality. Perhaps the weaknesses he condones in his characters are his own; certainly he is known to have been as vain as Alan Breck Stewart, always glancing at himself in the mirror.

Whether or not Stevenson's presentation of moral dilemmas was in any way modified by the fact that their setting was historical is hard to say; probably not. Surely the moral conflicts listed above would have been of much the same kind, though perhaps with less acute implications, in any age. For some decades now it has been the fashion to say that Stevenson has no historical sense. I am far from sure what that means, but it always involves a comparison with Sir Walter Scott, to Scott's advantage, of course. The invidious coupling of their two names was current in some form or another in Stevenson's lifetime, as we would know if only from his splendidly spiteful remarks on Sir Walter Scott in his article in the *Idler*, 'My First Book':

> With the map before him he [the novelist] will scarce allow the sun to set in the east, as it does in *The Antiquary*. With the almanac at hand, he will scarce allow two horsemen, journeying on the most urgent affair, to employ six days, from three of the Monday morning till late in the Saturday night, upon a journey of, say, ninety or a hundred miles, and before the week is out, and still on the same nags, to cover fifty in one day, as may be read at length in the inimitable novel of *Rob Roy*.

I would argue that in *Kidnapped* Stevenson does display historical imagination. An author who sets his story six years *after* an event which has engrossed, indeed obsessed, so many writers and readers of fiction must have at least historical curiosity. Whatever romance the Jacobite rising of '45 may have held at the time – probably very little – there can have been even less in 1751, with the clans helpless and humiliated, families bereaved and still in danger, so much poverty and so many people still on the run. But to Stevenson it was obviously a more significant moment: when the captains and the kings had departed, when the sins, or at least the actions, of the fathers were being visited on the children, and when initial widespread violence had dwindled to sporadic murder.

Stevenson's view of history is likely to be more to the taste of young readers today than to those of a generation ago. For over a decade now the media, following the appropriate theorists, have been getting us all accustomed to the idea of Everyman (as in B.B.C. Radio's *The Long March of Everyman*) with his crude jokes, his repetitive songs, and his inarticulacy: his only recorded remarks at the great battles are on the lines of 'Here comes the calvary (sic)' as he plods along behind leaders who are rendered as less important than himself. *Kidnapped* might not seem to belong to this genre: Alan and David are educated men with claims to gentility, of which they are both acutely conscious, and one would not dare to describe either as Everyman, certainly not Alan and especially not to his face; but all the same the novel leaves us with a broad sense of followers rather than of leaders, of those who suffer rather than those who act. Two of the characters who might marginally be considered as leaders are – one from each side – Cluny Macpherson and Colin Campbell. We are shown them only in glimpses or by hearsay, but their portraits, such as they are, stand eloquently against the historical and social background which helped to form them.

An interest in history must involve an interest in geography. Stevenson wrote *Kidnapped* in Bournemouth, of all places, and soon after finishing the book he left Britain never to return. Both his plan to emigrate, in pursuit of health, and his well-founded suspicion that he would never come back, never see Scotland again, must have been with him during the months of composition and may well account for much of the poignancy of his descriptions of place. There was another factor too: as a student he had contemplated training to be an engineer, the profession of his father, who was Commissioner of Northern Lights, and with this aim in mind he accompanied him on his tours of Scottish lighthouses. The tours convinced him, to his father's disappointment, that he was not cut out to be an engineer, but they also convinced him of the miraculous ability of the scenery to evoke the past. So a mixture of guilt and nostalgia for youthful journeys may have further sharpened the haunting atmosphere he creates.

In the course of one tour he spent three weeks on the Isle of Earraid, and it is there that David is cast away when the *Covenant* sinks. The paragraph which describes the boy's arrival on the island is masterly. Stevenson achieves a strong sense of location with almost no descriptive details, and a strong sense of loss and terror with the most restrained language. The passage is not purple nor does it hold us up. It is part of the narrative:

> With my stepping ashore I began the most unhappy part of my adventures. It was half past twelve in the morning, and though the wind was broken by the land, it was a cold night. I dared not sit down (for I thought I should have frozen), but took off my shoes and walked to and fro upon the sand, barefoot, and beating my breast, with infinite weariness. There was no sound of man or cattle; not a cock crew, though it was about the hour of their first waking; only the surf broke outside in the distance, which put me in mind of my perils and those of my friend. To walk by the sea at that hour of the morning, and in a place so desert-like and lonesome, struck me with a kind of fear.

Quoting this paragraph renews the incomprehension that I always feel when Stevenson's style is attacked, as it frequently has been and is to this day. Some of the criticisms can be quite easily dismissed. When Virginia Woolf, for example, speaks of his 'dapper little adjectives', one has only to reflect that her own adjectives on this occasion are both dapper and little. But when John Bayley, in his considered and well-argued article in *The Listener* (November 9, 1980), trounces Stevenson's stylistic principles and practice, I admit I am shaken. But still I cannot see it.

Stevenson himself apparently had no doubts about his own style. It would be strange if he had had. Brought up in an age when fine writing was widely considered to be a craft that could be mastered by dedication and hard work, he did work hard at it and made sacrifices in its pursuit. His only area of anxiety was concerned with dialogue. In 1875, at the beginning of his career, he wrote to his cousin Bob Stevenson: 'I have been working like Hell at stories and have, up to the present, failed. I have never hitherto given attention to the buggers speaking – my dialogue is as weak as soda water'. In fact, he need not have worried; in general, the buggers speak quite convincingly. They certainly do in *Kidnapped*, for here he has the inestimable advantage of using a dialect which is native and natural to him, but which is at the same time exotic enough to non-Scottish ears to convey something of history, distant lands and adventure, without a blow struck. I leave the controversy about Stevenson's style to others, but as my brief is to discuss the suitability of a certain book for children's reading, I would simply say that a child who gets no worse style than that of *Kidnapped* put before him today will be quite miraculously lucky.

In *Aspects of the Novel*, E. M. Forster (1927) provided posterity with the now famous dictum 'Oh dear yes, the novel tells a story', and it is perhaps at this comfortable point that a discussion of the merits of *Kidnapped* could rest, for Stevenson's ability to tell a story cannot be seriously disputed, and he never told a better one than in this particular book. His aim, as we have seen, was not to lure old men from the chimney-corner but to keep children from play, not in any churlish spirit, but to give them food for creative imagining, something to be enjoyed at the close of play, or indeed of work. He says this explicitly in the dedication of *Kidnapped* to Charles Baxter:

> This is no furniture for the scholar's library, but a book for the winter evening school-room when the tasks are over and the hour for bed draws near; and honest Alan, who was a grim old fire-eater in his day, has in this new avatar no more desperate purpose than to steal some young gentleman's attention from his Ovid, carrying him awhile into the Highlands and the last century, and pack him to bed with some engaging images to mingle with his dreams.

Like nearly every other classic, *Kidnapped* is a thoroughly professional work written for money by a full-time author, yet it is also a communication that is meant as a gift, a kind of legacy. From Bournemouth, on his way to the South Seas, Stevenson sends out, to his readers and to his friend in particular, the hope that by means of his story he may bequeath to them 'those places that have now become for your companion a part of the scenery of dreams'. The bequest is valuable.

From *Children's Literature in Education* No. 48, 1983

THE ACT OF READING

Margaret Mackey

Margaret Mackey grew up in Newfoundland, but has spent much of her adult life in England. In recent years, she returned to Canada to live in Edmonton, Alberta, where she has completed a doctoral study of ten adolescent readers and their encounters with a young adult novel. She has written several articles for journals. The most recent of a number of outstanding contributions for *CLE* was included in the 25th Anniversary Issue of Spring, 1995.

MANY SPACES: SOME LIMITATIONS OF SINGLE READINGS

Once upon a time, the prose in a novel seemed transparent, a window onto an imaginary world. Nowadays, with self-conscious manipulation of narrative forms, we are more likely to think of that prose as a construct, something shaped by an author.

However, there may still be an illusion lingering. We are more aware of the text, but we often still think of the reading process as transparent, the necessary route to the constructed world of the novelist or poet.

In fact, the word *reading* hides a multitude of sins – sins of omission, of conflation, of lack of clarity. We use the word in many imprecise ways; all too often, we do not wonder if we clearly understand somebody else's usage – or even disentangle our own.

If I propose to speak or write in public about a book, I will certainly read it more than once. By the time I compose my opinion about the book, however, I have thoroughly mixed up these discrete readings within my own mind. Sometimes I retain a memory of being confused or disturbed by a misunderstanding during a previous reading; all too often, the misapprehensions blur and fade away as my understanding deepens. I can easily forget that I once was baffled or mistaken about a reading of a book.

However, if I am teaching a novel and I take the reasonable precaution of preparing beforehand, I run a serious risk of bamboozling my pupils about what goes on during reading – indeed, I have probably fooled myself. For even a capable reader may often perform a single reading which is partial and inadequate. Students perceiving their teacher's insight into a text may assume that good readers can produce this kind of understanding on one single but thorough read. Their perception of their own reading ability may be correspondingly diminished. This would be a great pity even if it reflected the true situation; since the 'critical read' is usually a construct, composed of more than one reading, this misunderstanding is all the greater problem.

I consider myself a reasonably competent reader. With due attention and effort and interest, I can usually compose some kind of intelligent appreciation of a text. However, in the course of trying to come to terms with the complexity of the mental processes involved in reading, I set myself the exercise of recording my immediate responses to one particular reading of a book. The results surprised me and led me to think very hard about what we do in classrooms when we 'teach' a novel.

Dangerous Spaces

The book I chose to read was *Dangerous Spaces* (1991) by Margaret Mahy. To tell the complicated plot in brief, it is the story of two cousins, Anthea and Flora. Anthea's parents have accidentally drowned, and Anthea has moved in with Flora's family in the old house built by their common grandfather, Lionel. There is some suggestion that the old man still haunts the house and prevents his son, Flora's father, from finishing the alterations he has started. Anthea is miserable about the loss of her parents and upset by the noise and disorder in Flora's family; Flora is jealous of Anthea's romantic orphaned state, fairy-tale beauty and dainty possessions.

One day, Anthea discovers an old stereoscope, a viewer which merges two matching pictures into one three-dimensional effect. This stereoscope, along with its set of cards that contains the duplicate pictures, had belonged to her grandfather, Lionel, and his younger brother, Henry, who died as a boy. Looking at the pictures through the viewfinder, Anthea recognises a scene from a nightmare she had the previous night. The pictures which belong to the stereoscope actually form a preview of Anthea's adventures in subsequent dreams, night after night. Eventually, Flora moves into the dreams as well. Anthea is being tempted by her dead great-uncle Henry to stay in Viridian, an imaginary land he created and wrote about before his death. Flora, meanwhile, confronts the ghost of her dead grandfather who wants his house to remain as he left it.

In Viridian, the two brothers are renamed Leo and Griff. Eventually, after many adventures, Anthea and Flora challenge these two ghostly boys and persuade them that they belong together in death, and that the living belong to their own times. Anthea also begins to come to terms with her overwhelming grief about her parents. She and Flora are now ready to settle down together in the house, which Flora's father is finally beginning to fix.

A reading history

I read this book a total of three times and flicked through it many times more. I took notes on the second reading. Now, in retrospect and in as much detail as I can reconstruct, I want to resurrect aspects of those three readings, to see how they informed each other and contributed to my present understanding of the book. For the sake of clarity, I will label each reading and be as precise as possible about what I now recall from each.

I bought this book when it was newly published. It is unusual for me to buy a children's hardback, but I did so without hesitating when I read a review by Peter Hollindale (1991) which compared this book to earlier Mahy triumphs:

> It is characteristic of Mahy that from this hotch-potch of narrative clichés she has fashioned something rich and strange, a story of dangerous alienation which is original and compelling. . . . Such borderlands between reality and fantasy are true Mahy territory, familiar from *The Changeover* and *The Haunting*, and *Dangerous Spaces* is another such story in which psychological realism and supernatural phenomena echo each other.

The Changeover (1984), *The Haunting* (1982), and also *The Tricksters* (1986) had previously impressed me to such an extent that I immediately put down the review and telephoned the bookstore about acquiring a copy of *Dangerous Spaces.* I owned the book before nightfall. It was certainly worth the price of a hardback to me to see if Margaret Mahy could match her earlier efforts.

Reading A

I read the book in less than a day and kept no record of any kind while reading. This was the reading I shall refer to as Reading A. Six months later, I found I had forgotten almost everything about the book. What remained in my mind was a very small collection of fragmented images and a feeling of disappointment. Although *Dangerous Spaces* is not a bad story, it did not seem to me to be as astonishing as other Mahy books. I was not alone in this reaction. I loaned my new book to three colleagues, who all expressed a similar sense of letdown.

Six months after Reading A, I read *Dangerous Spaces* again. Before I began the second reading, I tried to summon up my recollections of Reading A. I had forgotten most of the plot and the vast majority of the images. Only two fragments remained in my head with any vividness: the picture of the stereoscope and a vague image of galloping horses. The idea of the horses was linked in my mind with a kind of irritation which I could not place. It was the stereoscope which I remembered most clearly from Reading A, though I could not articulate what I found pleasing about it.

(Other readers might be surprised at this lack of recall. I had, after all, been enthusiastic about reading this book; how could I obliterate all useful memory of it so quickly? Louise Rosenblatt's (1978) analysis of reading, however, describes just such a reaction. She distinguishes between 'aesthetic' and 'efferent' reading, and, indeed, defines 'efferent' in terms of its Latin meaning of 'to carry away'. In efferent reading, the reader's concern is with what he or she will take from the reading; in aesthetic reading, the reader's attention 'is centered directly on what he is living through during his relationship with that particular text'. My experience with *Dangerous Spaces* was aesthetic in these terms, and my later irritation with note taking probably also reflected my considerable bias towards reading for the experience of the moment within the text. Recall is not a priority in this kind of reading, so my nebulous and fragmented memories are perhaps not so surprising after all. The contrast between reading in this way and the kind of reading that goes on in many classrooms is considerable and deserves attention; even keeping a reading journal may alter the experience of this kind of aesthetic reading.)

Reading B

So I set about recording my second reading (Reading B) of *Dangerous Spaces*. My notes were written on yellow Post-it slips, stuck to the sides of the pages; they mainly consisted of single words and phrases drawn from that page. I am a fast reader, and I wanted to find a recording method which would slow me down as little as possible. Even so, I found that Reading B felt very forced and laborious.

When I look back over these notes, I find they bring back at least some of the sensations I had while reading the book. Since I took my wording from the phrases on the page and made no effort to rewrite or sort out my own responses, I find I now have some access to the accumulation of inarticulate emotional reactions which piled up as I read. I can now clarify and analyse the feelings I felt then, but what the notes themselves record is an emotional ebb and flow – not just of responses to the events of the plot but of reactions to the way the book was written as well. I felt, for example, irritation at some aspects of the organisation of the story. What I would like to make clear is that this response was an affective one, not a cognitive one. Any analysis of what made me feel the way I recorded at the time was very much an afterthought. My early response, even to a second reading, was a collection of emotional layers.

I suspect that in many literature classes we do not make enough allowance for the exceedingly inchoate nature of our initial responses to texts. It may indeed be that many students think that as *teachers* read, they respond with fully formed critical analysis at once. We do students more than one disservice if we allow them to continue under this misapprehension. First, we can undermine their confidence in their own reading strategies. Second, we may be encouraging them to think that a lack of engagement represents a more mature reading response.

There are other problems with a single reading, and my record of Reading B brings some of them to light. I am an experienced reader, and I was taking unusual care and paying particular attention to *Dangerous Spaces* simply because of the artificial requirement to note responses as I went along. Despite (or perhaps because of) this fact, I made illuminating mistakes.

Like most practised readers, I have a working schema in my head of how a story is likely to be shaped. I expect the seeds of later developments to be planted early in the text. I would have said I know how to be alert to those seeds as they disappear into the ground, as it were. But this is what I did on page 6.

The family is at breakfast.

> 'The bread's cut. Use the toaster in the kitchen!' Molly said. 'That one there fused yesterday. Old Lionel again! How did a nice boy like you ever

come to have a father who goes around fusing toasters when he should be busy pushing up roses?'

'Oh, well, you've got to expect that sort of thing, living in a haunted house,' said Lionel cheerfully.

It was a family joke that the house was haunted by the ghost of his father, old Lionel, who had grown up in this house when it was only two rooms and an outside lavatory. He had loved it dearly. Now his descendant, young Lionel, dived into the kitchen, making the bead curtain chatter crossly to itself behind him.

Anthea saw Flora look uncomfortably around the room at the mention of ghosts, and she looked, too – just in case. There were no ghosts. All that haunted the room was the usual disorder.

The living room and the dining room had once been separate, but young Lionel had knocked out a wall to turn them into one space, and had stripped off the old lining so that the plumbing could be improved, the pipes relagged and new electrical wiring installed. Because he had never finished the work he had started (there had been a pile of smooth tongue-grooved boarding covered over with green plastic at one end of the living room ever since Anthea had come there six months ago), living in Flora's house was like living inside a sort of skeleton, skin gone, and bones, nerves, and blood vessels revealed. Even the bedrooms weren't private in the way Anthea had been used to, for there was a hole in the wall between her room and Flora's. The first thing she saw every morning was Flora's freckled face peering through the hole at her, peering but not smiling.

Any experienced reader might be expected to pick up the mention of the ghost. A ghost – particularly a specific, named ghost – does not usually appear in the early pages of a book without some repercussions later on in the story. Yet, in my notes, I passed over any hint of old Lionel, and wrote:

Living in Flora's house – like living inside a skeleton.
Hole in wall between bedrooms.
Bead curtain.

As far as I can now reconstruct my reading from those notes, it seems to me that I was thoroughly impressed by the metaphor of the house like a body with no skin. I recall taking notice of it as a vivid example of the kind of writing Margaret Mahy does best. What may have happened at this point is that the ghost, still being processed through my short-term memory into my working memory, got knocked aside by this startling image. I cannot be certain; it is also possible that the fact that the ghost was dismissed as a joke also played a part in its disappearance from my mind.

In any case, whatever the cause, by the time I wrote my little note, I had already forgotten about the ghost. What were the consequences? They lingered throughout the second reading of the entire book. I had construed the story shape as focused on Anthea's loss and great grief. The metaphor of the skinless house seemed to tie in well with that focus; Anthea must feel similarly vulnerable. In fact, the story goes on to make this comparison many times, and it may be some forgotten remnant of Reading A which affected my processing here. Whatever the roots of my oversight, I found that every time the ghost reappeared in the story – and he comes to be very important indeed in the plot – I was annoyed. The ghost always felt like an intruder on the story to me, an impediment to closure, an interference with the design I anticipated. This particular emotional response was the consequence of my own inadequate reading in the very early stages, yet it remained a real and intrusive aspect of my reaction to the novel.

My lack of sufficient attention to this detail of the story affected my response to the whole book. The work of Reading B also threw light on a problem left over from Reading A.

After Anthea finds the stereoscope, she and Flora look at all the pictures. Flora has seen them all before and has had time to pick out her favourite. She tells Anthea to look at it (pp. 26–27):

> Storm clouds rolled behind low hills in the distance. In the foreground, wild horses galloped, shoulder to shoulder, across an eerie plain, one black horse just a little ahead of the rest.
>
> 'Terrific,' Anthea said. 'Think of riding a wild horse.'
>
> Flora had often thought of it. From the time she had first been allowed to use the stereoscope, this picture had seemed to hold all the beauty and wildness of the world. She had often imagined herself to be part of that wildness, riding on that leading black horse, its mane blowing out behind it, while her own hair blew back in a dark cloud. Only when she had stopped looking through the mask, did Flora remember, with confusion and surprise, that she had short mouse-coloured hair which, even in a storm would only bob around her ears. Anthea's hair, though, would certainly stream around her, pale against the storm clouds, as she went galloping . . . galloping . . .
>
> 'I suppose we'd only fall off,' Flora said, sounding very practical, 'and the other horses would tread all over us.' And she put the picture of the wild

> horses in a pile that she had privately labelled Nature. 'What's the next one?'
>
> 'We've come back to the beginning,' Anthea said.

It seems to me now, looking at this passage from the perspective of many readings, that Margaret Mahy has here laid out her counter as plainly as we could possibly desire. This card is the last one in the pile. It is Flora's favourite. We are clearly expected to pay attention to it. It takes her into a world where she can imagine herself free and glamorous, but when she comes back to reality she realises yet again that Anthea is far more suited to be the romantic heroine on the horse.

In my notes, I commented on Flora's wish for long hair and glamour. I wrote the single word 'horses', so I did take account of the scene. During Reading B, I recognised this scene as related to the image of wild horses that I remembered from Reading A. But sometimes, despite our best efforts, we repeat mistakes from one reading to another.

At the climax of the book, Flora is trying to use the stereoscope to get into the imaginary land of Viridian, where she knows Anthea is in danger. Instead she winds up confronting her dead grandfather, old Lionel, who is still fretting about keeping his house exactly as he built it (pp. 130–131):

> 'What's the use of worrying about the shape of the rooms when the people of the house are giving up and getting ready to go,' Flora cried. 'Houses wear out! They have to be changed.'
>
> 'Families change!' repeated the faint voice beside her. 'Wood and tin keep their shape longer than flesh and bone.'
>
> Flora sent most of the cards flying off her bed with a sweep of her arm.
>
> '*I'm* your true house,' she cried fiercely, holding her arms wide so that he could take a good look at her. 'Well, part of it. So's Anthea. Why go haunting wood and nails while the blood gets lost in nothing?'
>
> 'The blood!' He sighed and fell silent.
>
> Without looking up, she knew he had gone, for suddenly there was Taffeta [the cat] in bed beside her, pressing close to her and kneading with her front paws. She purred, but it was from anxiety, not contentedness.
>
> 'If at first you don't succeed . . .' said Flora stubbornly, sliding a picture into the stereoscope, and sticking out her tongue at the vanished ghost. Adjusting the card holder in its grooves she suddenly found the exact place where the picture became three-dimensional, but this time it was more than simply three-dimensional. This must have been the one scene that had been waiting for her, for it rushed toward her, a gaping mouth which swallowed her up in darkness and storm and the beating of horses' hoofs.

As I reached this point in Reading B, I was aware that we were entering the scene recalled from Reading A. I knew that Flora was about to move into a stereoscope picture with wild horses. But again, I could not clearly recall the initial description of this picture. It was only later, when I checked specifically in the early chapters, that I really took in the details of the description of this card which foreshadows the inevitable closing scene. It became clear that I was annoyed by this scene (which is probably what made me remember it from Reading A) because I had not properly stored the early account of Flora's favourite card. Mahy makes it as clear as possible in Chapter 3 that the picture of the horses will be important. But this card is then not mentioned for many chapters, and by the time I got to the scene where Flora picks it up again, I had forgotten about it.

Marcel Just and Patricia Carpenter (1985) describe how such forgetting can occur:

> Integration can also lead to forgetting in working memory. As each new chunk is formed, there is a possibility that it will displace some previous information from working memory. Particularly vulnerable are items that are only marginally activated, usually because they were processed much earlier and have not recently participated in a production. For instance, the representation of a clause will decay if it was processed early in a text and was not related to subsequent information.

In some kinds of novels, particularly detective novels, writers may be trying to slide in bits of information so discreetly that they are not processed. It does not seem likely that Mahy's intention in this book was that a reader would twice forget the details of the description of the key picture. However, for the purposes of this account, the allocation of responsibility for my lapse is not the issue. What I would like to point out is that if I were composing a critical assessment of the book, I would almost certainly suppress the inadequacies of my own readings, not out of embarrassment but simply to accord with the conventions of a literary essay. All too often, when we write about a book, we are really writing an account of how we think we *ought* to have read it.

However, in the real readings, instead of calling up a precise recollection of the stage setting from the early part of the book, I turned, as a substitute, to my wider experience of reading Margaret Mahy. The scene continues with a description that could be written only by Mahy (pp. 131–132):

> Flora found herself on a huge grassy plain, with a sharp wind striking into her face, ruffling her hair. It was evening. The sinking sun flooded the whole plain in an unearthly light – all the stranger because the sun was shining narrowly between the horizon and the rim of a rolling line of black clouds. Flora had never seen such a storm. The clouds were rounded, and for all their blackness were illuminated by the western light creeping in under them, so that their curves were both luminous and lurid. Flora had never seen threat and wonder so dissolved into each other. Looking down at her hands, she saw her skin had the sinister glow of the storm, its freckles embedded in it like specks of gold. Her blue pyjamas glowed. She, ordinary Flora, was transformed into a girl of precious metals and jewels, frightening and thrilling herself.

In my notes at this stage, I commented on the family resemblance to *The Tricksters.* It was in the hopes of just such scenes that I had started the book in Reading A, looking forward to this vivid and extravagant Mahy voice. Yet my response was tempered by disappointment. In dealing with the complex of merging plots which occupies this stage of the book, I was doubly handicapped: I was irritated by the ghost of old Lionel, and I was processing the importance of the stereoscope scene of the wild horses with less than complete recall of the initial description of the card. I knew in a schematic kind of way that I was very close to the resolution of the story, but emotionally I was unsatisfied. In an important way, at this stage of the book I was reading as if I were involved – but I knew I was bluffing.

Do practised readers articulate, either to themselves or to less proficient readers, just how they may fall back on intertextual experience to fill gaps in their processing of a text? The ability to compensate tacitly for insufficient data is an important one and deserves more attention than it often receives.

I am not the only reader to be less than satisfied by the book as a whole. After I completed Reading B, I turned to other readers to compare responses. I had read the book; now it was time to talk about it. My colleagues who had read it six months earlier had all felt some sense of disappointment and found themselves with little coherent recollection of the story as a whole. Because I am a relatively 'professional' reader, I also checked reviews. Here, too, I found confirmation of my own feelings. While some reviewers agreed with Peter Hollindale about the exceptional quality of the book, others came closer to my own views. Audrey Laski (1991) said:

> For admirers of Margaret Mahy's brilliant combinations of magic and everyday life, this ghost story may be something of a disappointment. It has two excellent central ideas: that a child who has been unable to accept the death of her parents in an accident may be dangerously drawn towards the idea of death, and so vulnerable to the demands of a lonely ghost; and that an old stereoscope can be the way into the ghost's dream country, constructed out of its pictures. It also has the charm of this author's scenes from family life, noisy and absurd and difficult for Anthea, who has been an only child until adopted by her relations. But it does not work as well as it should.

Ilene Cooper (1991) commented:

> The fantasy elements of this New Zealand-set story sit a bit uneasily next to the physical world of Anthea's grief and Flora's anger at the changes in her household. Also, the lure of the dream world is not as strong as it should be.

Another reviewer, for the *Bulletin of the Center for Children's Books* (1991), was also unhappy:

> Mahy has always realised her ventures into fantasy with a consistency of detail that made them credible. This time, the detail is present without the consistency. Statues loom, battles erupt, crayon arrows point the way through a nebulous limbo that is more confusing than ominous. The concepts are fascinating; their development needs sharpening.

In looking at the book critically, after all these readings, it was useful to me to consider other perspectives, to weigh other readers' reservations against my own, to consider the more enthusiastic reaction of Peter Hollindale and some other reviewers. At the time of Reading B, however, I was engaged in a more nebulous response, and one which was more emotional than intellectual. Such inarticulate responses are often fleeting; the discipline required to record reactions as I read was irksome, and I certainly would not want to do it very often. The compensation is that, as I look over my notes, I can recall quite vividly a range of unexpressed and quite temporary feelings. If I had not set out to express a more developed response to this text in this essay, that set of feelings would be one of the major ingredients in my total reading of the book. The very act of articulation altered how I think about this particular reading experience.

How often does our response to a book involve nothing more than an accumulation of different emotions, fleeting and unconsidered? I suspect the answer to that question, depending on the reader, may actually be: *most of the time.* Recreational reading does not necessarily call for anything further. Even a considered reading may well work from the starting point of this first, transitory emotional response.

Classroom reading is artificial for a number of reasons. Frank Hatt (1976) suggests that real reading involves the chance to choose a title which may meet your own personal needs. In a classroom, where this choice may be made in advance by the teacher, he says, what follows is a *simulation* of real reading. I believe that in our classrooms we run the risk of other kinds of simulations of real reading as well. The kind of engaged first or even second reading that gets swept away, that simply wants to know the outcome, that amounts to an accumulation of fleeting affective responses, may often disappear in the rigours of classroom routines, where we may all read together at an artificial speed, where we may not be able to give out the books for reading at home, where we may stop at the end of the chapter to write answers or discuss developments.

Simulations often have substantial educational value. But it is hard to believe that the virtue of a simulation is the same if nobody knows it actually is a simulation. Some children read *only* on classroom terms. As teachers, the least we can do is be aware ourselves of the limitations of that kind of reading experience.

Reading C

Reading B is not the end of the story of my relationship with *Dangerous Spaces.* After I had attached the last yellow Post-it note to a page, I laid the book aside for a while. Some time later, however, I found myself in a bookstore. I had not stopped thinking about *Dangerous Spaces,* and it occurred to me to check the meanings of the characters' names. I knew from reading other Margaret Mahy books that the names might be charged with extra layers of meaning.

I had thought that far, yet I was not really prepared for what I found in a book of *Names for Your Baby. Flora* means 'flower', as I knew. What I had not expected was that *Anthea* means 'flowerlike'.

In a way, Reading C began before I even got home and looked at the book again. If Flora and Anthea are two versions of the same name, that fact must surely alter the importance of the stereoscope and its duplicate pictures as a crucial image in the story. As corroboration, the Viridian names of the two brothers are Leo and Griff: 'lion' and 'lionlike' (a griffin is part bird, part lion).

I began to read again, but this time concentrating on pattern and shaping. In Reading C, I made a much more literary reading, looking for evidence of craftsmanship, focusing on the organisation of the book and not on the emotional impact of the story. And at the level of craft, the novel, in my view, is more effective.

Margaret Mahy pays considerable attention to the image of the stereoscope. All the way through the book, she uses the word *space* in a charged way, but the word is used most evocatively in referring to the stereoscope pictures, where, of course, the space is illusory. Here is Anthea's first look through the stereoscope (p. 17):

> At first she saw two pictures (one with each eye, perhaps), but then her sight shifted in some way, and she understood that the two pictures were trying to melt together into a single picture which would have a mysterious depth to it. The flat card would suddenly blossom with hidden space.

Margaret Mahy emphasises the idea that such a space is portable. For example, at the end of Chapter 2, Anthea looks at a photograph of her great-uncle Henry holding the stereoscope (p. 19):

> He smiled a little – triumphantly – she thought, like someone who has a space all his own, held safely between his own two hands. But it seemed to her this was a space he was offering to share.

The repetition, the marked position at the end of the chapter, the echo of the title (and the contrast of the word *safely* with the title as well) – all these ingredients point to the importance of the idea of this space. In Chapter 3, it is repeated when Flora looks at the stereoscope (pp. 23–24):

> Flora found herself fascinated, almost against her will, by the moment when the two flat pictures fused into one deep one. The scenes filled out with a space that did not really exist – space that could be folded up into a box that looked like a book; space that could become as flat as a bookmark and as easily hidden.

All this I had taken in on my second reading, yet it was only later and in retrospect, that one significant element of the text took shape in my mind. I was ready to make a link between the stereoscope and a book, a connection made explicitly in that last quote, but I had not registered the direct relationship between the stereoscope and *this* book. As I stood in the bookshop with the name dictionary in my hand, realising that

Flora and Anthea are two versions of the same name, I could feel my assessment of the story shifting almost precisely in the way that Margaret Mahy describes: two flat pictures fusing into one deep one. I came home and looked at the book again, sure that there was something I had missed. And there was. For much of the book, the organisation is very explicitly paired: a chapter about Anthea followed by a chapter about Flora. It is the equivalent of the two pictures before they blend into one, before the three-dimensional merge takes place.

Chapters 4, 5, 6 and 7, for example, alternate the heroines. The gradual blending of the two stories is accomplished deftly. The divide between Chapter 6 and Chapter 7 is crossed by a repetition of one two-word phrase. The two sets of words come very close together but are clearly divided by the chapter boundary and by the separation of the stories of the two girls. Chapter 6 ends (p. 50):

> Her [Anthea's] heart jolted as it would never have done for a spider. Lying at her feet was a fat black crayon.

Chapter 7 begins (p. 51):

> It was as if Flora's heart jolted.

It is easy to read this as the two stories coming closer together, and that is certainly how I took it: that the jolts to the heart happened at the same moment, and that Flora's story was becoming entangled with Anthea's. Naturally, I had been expecting this to happen, but the repetition of two simple words strengthened the sensation of the story's moving inexorably onward.

Not all chapters are paired in this way, but Chapters 10 and 11 again alternate Anthea and Flora. By Chapter 11, Flora has moved into Anthea's dream, searching for her when she finds her bed empty. Chapters 14 and 15 are also paired, and it is at this stage in the adventure that Flora finally gets to ride her wild horse.

By Chapter 16, as the adventure comes to an end, the stereoscope world of Viridian has collapsed and turned back into pairs of cardboard pictures (p. 136):

> The sea and its island often seemed not like space, but like a painted wall, risen up only inches before her face and stealing air from her. There was almost no space left for her in Viridian, almost no space at all.

The theme of duplication returns, almost as if the stereoscope were losing its power of merging the two pictures. As Anthea and Griff reach the beach, they see two dragonish islands floating breast to breast. The statue that stands at the beginning of the road has a double at the end, but this one is smiling, not weeping. 'Its tears were used up. Its grief was gone'(p. 140).

The major metaphor of the book is also duplicated. The image of the house, stripped to its wires for renovation, appears regularly through the book. The parallel image is of Anthea feeling she can see into her own body (p. 30):

> At some time during the night Anthea found she was staring at a hand . . . staring right *into* it, past the skin, past the wonderful embroidery of its blood vessels and nerves, to the very bones themselves, spread out against a pattern of red and white. All of this seemed to be nothing to do with the hand itself.
>
> 'When did I wake up?' she thought, not frightened but astonished, still staring into the hand which reminded her of something. A house somewhere. Yes! Stripped of their smooth outer surfaces, hands, like houses, were all pipes and electrical wiring and joists.

In the scene of confrontation between Flora and Lionel, we can see these metaphors merging. '*I'm* your true house,' Flora says to the old man. 'Why go haunting wood and nails while the blood gets lost in nothing?' (p. 131).

At the end of the book, however, while the Viridian pictures have collapsed back into duplication, the house–body image remains fused. Flora's father finally begins to work on the house. The unlined walls are covered up. Anthea recalls the stripped effect and, by allusion, its relation to her own emotional healing (p. 145):

> To her surprise she was almost sorry to see a corner of the skeleton house vanishing under a new skin. She would never forget that, under painted surfaces, houses had their own secret spaces filled with wiring and pipes and insulation, or that everything was secretly connected even if people did not want to look closely at the connections.

Conclusions

There are two ways of looking at the discoveries that I made in my different readings of this book. One is to reach the conclusion that

Margaret Mahy addressed the shaping and patterning of this book in a very striking and successful way but perhaps was not so successful in organising the emotional weight of the story. Perhaps the stylistic pyrotechnics were too successful; in a way, *Dangerous Spaces* reminds me of a vivid mosaic where the separateness of the individual tiles is always just too noticeable, so that viewers are never swept away by the picture as a whole.

That, however, is to look at the text. The whole point of this exercise has been to look also at the reading. In my account of Readings A, B, and C, I have tried to highlight some of the ways that any one reading may fail to do justice to a text. My Reading A was almost entirely transitory; I was astonished during Reading B by how very little I remembered. Reading B itself was limited in different ways: although I was trying to pay attention very carefully, I was still capable of being distracted at crucial points of storing information in my working memory.

It would be a mistake, however, to look at Reading C as the stage where everything clicked into place. Reading C was never a complete reading, for a number of reasons. I read carefully through the first five chapters, marvelling at what I had missed before; but after that, I skimmed and skipped, looking for evidence of patterns, not for one moment caught up in the emotional impact of the story. Reading C provided much of the data for an analysis of some of the effects of *Dangerous Spaces*, but it was, in a different way, equally restricted.

In any case, when I now talk of my 'reading' of this book, I am referring to a layered and intermingled version. Only the notes which contain the skeleton of Reading B give me any access to the way in which the layers built up. We have naturalised the word 'reading' to render this kind of intermingling just about invisible, and by so doing, we run the risk of seriously misleading apprentice readers – or even ourselves.

Even as I have tried to disentangle these different readings, I have not laid any claim to a definitive or 'true' interpretation of the book. The one element of the story which struck me decisively throughout all these readings was the image of the stereoscope. When I analysed it, I found the relationship between the stereoscopic image and our fictive imaginations in reading to be immensely powerful. I can argue the case that the stereoscopic metaphor influences the structure of the book as a whole. But I cannot legislate this interpretation for other people.

Three colleagues read this book; not one mentioned the stereoscope when I asked them for their recollections of the story, six months later. I found ten reviews; fully half do not even mention the stereoscope as an ingredient in the plot.

Just as not everyone is struck by the image that seems to me to be the most vital in the book, not everyone has the same kinds of reading strategies and problems. My own difficulties nearly all come from reading too fast, from a pell-mell approach that would baffle and horrify many other readers. I am not describing a universal reading process any more than I am providing a definitive analysis of the story – and that needs to be remembered as well. For a highly conventional activity, reading is incurably various.

Implications

I have talked to adolescent readers about what they think makes a good reader. Many suggest the importance of the ability to see below the surface of the text, to get a deeper meaning; and many teachers also regard this capacity as a sign of good reading.

But this ability does not necessarily manifest itself on a single reading of a text, and it is unfair to students to let them believe that it does. Knowing that good readers make mistakes, overlook important points, forget others, work out compensatory strategies so that they can read *as if* they had noticed in the first place – knowing that any single reading is probably much more fallible than even the reader really internalises or acknowledges – surely this is a useful insight for learning readers. The corollary of this point is the importance of rereading, of continuing to think about a text, of exploring questions it raises. This activity is also vitally important for readers at every level. Students in classrooms organised as reading workshops may be doing too many single readings and not enough rereading and reflecting, so that their views of reading may be limited in different ways.

Not all books, not all authors, are worth the investment of multiple readings, and that is worth knowing, too. In the case of *Dangerous Spaces*, although I came to have a considerable respect for the virtuosity of its composition, I never did stop feeling that, one way or another, this book is flawed. The craft is greater than the content. Margaret Mahy raises important fictional issues and shapes parts of her story superbly well, but in the end, in my opinion, she does not create such a balance that craft and story support each other. To use her own metaphor, the two pictures of the stereoscope never quite blend into the three-dimensional effect; I always felt that each eye was looking separately.

That is an aesthetic judgement, with which others may not agree. Whatever our conclusions about *Dangerous Spaces*, however, I think we benefit by clarifying our thoughts about the limitations of any single reading, about the composite nature of any articulated reaction to a book.

From *Children's Literature in Education* No. 90, 1993

Jon C. Stott

Jon C. Stott is a Professor of English at the University of Alberta. Among his publications on children's literature are *Mary Norton* (a bio-critical study for Twayne-Macmillan) and *Representing Native Peoples in Children's Literature* (Oryx). His current project is entitled *Words of Wonder: Literature for Canadian Children* for Harcourt, Brace. Since 1975, he has worked regularly in Edmonton Schools developing children's literature programmes. He travels widely across Canada giving professional development seminars for teachers and school librarians and also serves as a member of *CLE*'s North American Editorial Board.

'Will the Real Dragon Please Stand Up?' Convention and parody in children's stories

The most important basic element of literature is not originality or creativity, but conventionality. That is because literature makes use of language, one of the most conventional tools of those most conventional creatures, human beings. Human beings communicate linguistically by means of widely accepted word structures, and the most structured use of words occurs in literature. Until we have mastered the conventions of our native tongue – its vocabulary and, more important, its grammar – we cannot converse. Until we have mastered the conventions of a culture's literature – its symbolic vocabulary and its narrative grammar – we cannot read that literature with true perception. It is necessary for us to internalise conventions, make them our own, before we are free to engage in the interaction between author and reader which constitutes the act of reading. If we do not understand the conventions the author is using to tell the story, he or she is speaking in a tongue foreign to us even though he or she may be using words and grammatical structures that we hear in our everyday speech. But if we do understand the author's conventions, we are engaging in an act which will continue long after the initial physical act of reading; we will truly be engaged in a creative and original enterprise.

I start with these commonplaces because they have great importance for all of us who read literature and who teach literature to children. Because the types of words and the grammatical patterns of the stories we read are those of the newspaper and the radio, we often tend to think that reading a newspaper, an encyclopedia, or a textbook involves the same processes used in reading a short story, a novel, or a play. But that is only partly so. Within the same vocabulary and sentence structure is contained a startlingly new and different language, a special code that requires training and practice to acquire and use correctly, well, and fully.

Let me give you an example. Last year, a teacher working in a remote Alaskan Inuit community told me of a special event which took place every Friday in her school. One of the elders came to her classroom to tell one of the old stories. He spoke in simple but good English and the children loved his stories, reacting strongly to them. 'At first,' the teacher said, 'I was lost. I just couldn't understand the point of them. They didn't seem to have any meaning to me. But by the end of the year, I was looking forward to the old man's Friday visits as much as my students were, and I was reacting as strongly to his stories as they were. I loved them!' Hers was an extreme case, for she was in a distant land, in an alien culture. But the stories were in English. Essentially, she had had to learn the literary language, the vocabulary and narrative structures, which were contained within the 'normal' English in which the stories were told. *Learn* – that's the key word; she had to learn the conventions of a literary language. And we all have to if we want to read stories. That's how we are able to understand them.

If we are omnivorous readers, devouring everything, good and bad, in print, hiding a flashlight under our pillows, turning, as they used to say, into bookworms, we learn this language unawares, in the same way we learn our native tongue. But if we aren't omnivorous readers – and in this day of television, video games, computers and community-organised sports leagues, most children aren't – we come to good stories, those which make skilful (shall we say original and creative?) use of the conventions, like foreigners learning a new language, and we must be systematically (that does not mean dully) taught the vocabulary and grammar. Unfortunately, for many of us, this instruction began in high school or even college, and often as not, we were, to shift the metaphor, thrown in at the deep end and told to sink or swim. Most of us, and I certainly was one, sank at first. Luckily I came back to the surface; but I struggled for many years before I was able to swim without too much trouble.

What I will take up now is really a practical demonstration of the theoretical material I've just summarised. What are some of the conventions of literature? How do they work? What do they mean? And more important, how can we introduce these to elementary school children in such a way that they can become more perceptive and appreciative readers of literature? How can we guide them without making them bored and without turning them off? To answer these questions, I'd like to consider one of the most fabulous creatures ever found in literature, a creature who is far from extinct, who is, in fact, proliferating in stories at a rate that puts rabbits to shame: the dragon.

No one has ever seen a dragon; yet everyone has a general idea of what dragons look like and what they do. Dragons do exist, but only in one place: in stories. The earliest dragon stories are shrouded in the mists of antiquity, which is just a way of saying that no one can give an accurate date for the creation of the first one. Certainly they were being told thousands of years before the birth of Christ. Stories about dragons came from two general areas: the Orient and Europe. Our focus will be on European dragons, particularly those most popular in legends and tales told from the Middle Ages onward.

If no one has ever seen a dragon, where did the details that fill the hundreds of dragon stories come from? The answer is simple: from other dragon stories. Just as children learn to speak by listening to and imitating the language they hear and by relating words to appropriate aspects of the world around them, so storytellers imitated the stories they knew and related the various conventions to their inner, imaginative lives. In fact, by the time of the Middle Ages (and probably much earlier), it wasn't necessary to borrow from a specific story. A biology of dragons existed in people's minds, and even in learned tomes. People knew what dragons looked like, their characters, habits and habitats, even if they had never seen a dragon. In other words, a set of literary conventions had established itself; there existed a general vocabulary and grammar of dragon lore. Just as we do not readily possess every word and grammatical combination of words, but a general structural pattern which we apply to specific linguistic situations, so, too, storytellers possessed a literary grammar and vocabulary to be used for specific dragon stories.

Everyone knows the general physical characteristics of the European dragon: generally winged, it was huge, had a virtually impenetrable body covering, long sharp claws and teeth, a lethal barbed tail, and flaming breath. It was a terrible sight to behold, even when sleeping, as Tolkien's hobbit, Bilbo Baggins, discovers. Physically appalling, dragons were psychologically frightening as well, for they were extremely clever and had terrible tempers. Angered, they would wreak havoc on entire villages, breathing flames over everything. Their greatest love was treasure, not their own, but stolen or usurped treasure. However, working, it would seem, on the old adage that possession is nine-tenths of the law, they jealously guarded their ill-gotten wealth. Should the tiniest part of it be stolen, they literally flew into terrible rages and set about seeking revenge.

Dragons, of course, had to eat, and their favourite delicacies were virgins. Fearful villagers, to save themselves from the resident dragon's anger, would sacrifice one of the town's virgins to the dragon at regular intervals. For the ordinary virgin, there was little to do but to submit to the inevitable. But when the supply of ordinary virgins was exhausted and a royal princess was scheduled to be the next victim, it was a different story. Then a knight in shining armour, generally riding a white (that is, pure) steed, would perform a daring rescue, not only ridding the locale of a great menace, but also earning the right to the princess's hand. These then, were the conventions of dragon lore, the vocabulary and grammar out of which individual stories were crafted.

Why, it should be asked, were these stories so incredibly popular? Early scholars suggested that the stories arose out of attempts to find answers for mysterious natural phenomena. Far-off, rumbling, flaming volcanoes were perhaps strange giant creatures; lightning flashing and thunder rumbling over distant mountains came from these beasts. When people attempted to describe the creatures, they took elements from animals they knew (bat wings, bear claws, lizard bodies), magnified them, and created a terrifying, monstrous amalgam.

Modern scholars generally reject such interpretations and search for answers in the nature of the human mind. Stories, it is argued, are linguistic structures that give shape and, therefore, meaning to our imaginative and psychological concerns. The dragon, with its appearance, size and personality, represents those forces which we find most fearful and threatening. The dragon is the power of evil – physical, moral, psychological and spiritual – which threatens to overwhelm us all. In the dragon story, small, frail and vulnerable human beings face virtually insurmountable odds with little more than their goodness, courage and intellect; and they emerge victorious. The slaying of the dragon is thus a victory for the human soul. Not surprisingly, the medieval dragon was often associated with the Devil, and its opponents were good Christians. Edmund Spenser, an ardent supporter of the Protestant Queen Elizabeth I, went one step further. In *The Faerie Queene* (1590), he identified the dragon with the Catholic Church, bent on destroying England.

Over the last hundred years, a different type of dragon story has emerged: the parody. Parody, a very sophisticated form of literature extending back at least to the days of ancient Greece, is solidly based on established literary conventions. The parodist takes the grammar and vocabulary of a well-known story type or individual story and completely inverts them. The result is usually a humorous satire. For centuries, one of the favourite kinds of parody has been the mock-heroic. The patterns of such well-known epics as the *Iliad*, the *Odyssey*, the *Aeneid*, and *Paradise Lost* and of romances of questing knights have been used to tell the stories, for example, of an oversexed barnyard rooster tricked by a sly fox, or of a society quarrel caused by the snipping of a lock of a belle's hair. Over the last century, the theories of evolution and the terrors of world wars have seriously undermined the belief in heroic human endeavour. Small wonder that dragon stories have been used for ridicule. What if the knights are wimps, the damsels pump iron, and the dragons are cream puffs? If the writer could demonstrate the ridiculousness of the conventions of dragon stories, she or he could also cast doubt on the social values they embodied.

Kenneth Grahame's 'The Reluctant Dragon' (1898), Ogden Nash's 'The Tale of Custard the Dragon' (1961), and Robert Munsch's *The Paper Bag Princess* (1980) are three of the best-known dragon parodies. But perhaps one of the best is, unfortunately, one of the least-known: Edith Nesbit's *The Last of the Dragons* (1900). When a princess is informed that, at age sixteen, she will have to be tied up and rescued from a dragon by a prince, she objects: 'All the princes I know are such very silly little boys. . . . Couldn't we tie up one of the silly little princes for the dragon to look at – and then I could go and kill the dragon and rescue the prince? I fence much better than any of the princes we know.' When the great day arrives, she and the prince conspire to face the dragon together. However, when they enter his lair, they discover that he doesn't want to fight. He tells the couple that all such fights are fixed, that he wouldn't want to eat a princess anyway – 'I wouldn't touch the horrid thing' – and that he wants to be left alone. However, when the princess calls him 'dear', he begins to cry and informs them, 'I *am* tame. . . . That's what nobody but you has ever found out. He attends their wedding, becomes their gentle and devoted servant, and is named Fido.

One immediately sees the parodistic elements; this isn't what we expect from a dragon story. The princess, not the prince, is the skilful and brave person; the dragon is tame and isn't slain. However, underneath the parody, the story is every bit as serious as the typical dragon story. In mocking the literary conventions, *The Last of the Dragons* criticises social conventions which blind us to true and better realities. The prince and princess are fettered by their socially imposed roles. She is expected to be delicately and uselessly feminine; bravery and physical abilities are not encouraged. However, underneath the royal exterior, we find, as well as bravery, true concern for others and tenderness. The prince, an incompetent as far as typical princes go, genuinely loves the princess and is willing to face what he thinks will be certain death for her sake. But the greatest victim of preconceived conventional notions is the last of the dragons. Whether or not others of his species have lived up to their biological and psychological characteristics, he has not. And because people expect princes to fulfil their assigned duties, he is in danger of dying without his true nature ever being known. Only because he meets a royal couple as unconventional as he is does he get to lead a fulfilling life.

The Last of the Dragons is a rich and satisfying story. And the reader who is fully aware of the literary conventions that the story contains and the way in which Nesbit uses them is in a position to get a great deal more out of the story than the reader who is not aware of them.

Our general overview of literary structuralism, dragon lore and parody has all been a preamble to the important business at hand: the teaching of these elements to a good Grade 4 (nine-year old) or an early Grade 5 class. When we have finished, the children should be able to understand the concepts and should be able to apply them to *The Last of the Dragons*, to other stories they encounter, and to their own creative writing.

Although children may think they know a lot about dragons, they can learn a great deal more by looking at a series of slides taken from dragon pictures in *Dragons*, by Peter Hogarth and Val Clery (1979). Each slide can be used to illustrate some of the points we have noted above.

After looking at them, the children are given a sheet entitled 'European Dragon-Lore', on which they list as many characteristics as they can remember. A general discussion follows in which children are able to hear each other's answers and add to their own lists. We now have the conventions – the literary grammar and vocabulary – to apply to the parody we read, *The Last of the Dragons.* As we go through the story, students are asked to raise their hands when they recognise a departure from the conventions.

When we have finished reading the story, we briefly discuss it generally and then consider the deviations from the conventions, noting that nearly everything seems to be upside down or reversed when compared to what we know about usual European dragons. At this point, the term 'parody' is introduced: a story which turns things upside down, or that looks at serious story conventions humorously. *The Last of the Dragons* is a parody because it reverses typical elements of a dragon story and makes fun of them. Students are surprised when they are told that, although 'parody' is a new term to them, they already know quite a few parodies. To illustrate my point this year, I wrote the words 'Weird Al Yankovich' on the board and asked the children why I'd done that. After a moment or two, the students recognised that he is the composer of 'Eat It', and that 'Eat It' is a parody of Michael Jackson's smash hit, 'Beat It'. 'And that's not the only parody you know,' I tell them, asking if anyone can remember the TV series 'The Greatest American Hero' and who it parodied. Those who read *Mad Magazine* – and large numbers of the children do – quickly realise that *Mad* often parodies popular TV shows and movies. Finally I have a couple of *Time* magazine 'Persons of the Year' covers, which I show along with a *Time* 'Person of the Year' card with a polaroid snapshot of myself and a *Mad* cover in which the person of the year is Pac Man.

Appreciation of parody requires that the reader do more than see general parallels: precise parallels and reversals exist. To emphasise that point, the children are asked to review their dragon-lore sheets. They are then given a sheet with the heading 'Parody' and are asked to list all of the differences between the lore they noted and the story *The Last of the Dragons.* Parody, they learn, is not a careless or casual art.

They also learn that, in addition to having fun with the conventions of story types, parody can be used to convey a serious message. As we have seen above, *The Last of the Dragons* criticises a society which assumes that conventional notions of people and dragons represent the truth and which doesn't take the trouble to discover the true natures of individuals. After asking the students how the king, the people, and even the prince and princess expected the dragon to act, we can consider why they had these expectations and how these initially prevented them from seeing the dragon as he really was. We can also ask why the princess was expected to be the victim and the prince, the rescuer. Here we want the students to see that social roles are imposed in spite of a person's abilities or qualities. Finally, we discuss how the prince, the princess and the dragon achieve fulfilment because they refuse to be restricted by convention and to see others as they really are.

Our lessons on dragon lore and parody, and, implicitly, on literary structuralism, do not end here. After discussing *The Last of the Dragons,* we read Ogden Nash's poem 'The Tale of Custard the Dragon'. The title itself suggests that the poem may be a parody, as the name and the species are in conflict. Our object in studying this poem is to decide to what extent the poem is conventional and to what extent parodistic. Children are asked to justify their point of view with specific references to the text, and most assert, correctly, that the poem is a mixture of convention and parody.

In one school in which I work, the teacher has created an individualised learning centre on dragons to help reinforce the conventions and the concept of parody. The students can listen to tapes describing famous dragons and can read dragon stories. Writing activities include entering words into a dragon dictionary kept at the centre (the words are those heard on the tapes which describe the dragons), filling out dragon lore and parody sheets for the stories read at the centre, and writing dragon stories. For this last activity, we have a lined sheet which supplies the title, 'The Day I Met a Dragon'; the instructions, 'In this story, you are to tell what you saw, what you did, and how you felt'; and this opening, 'It was a cold and windy day. There were clouds covering the sky, and the wind made sad sounds. I was walking through a valley filled with large, grey boulders. I turned a corner of the path, and there it was.' For the centre, the teacher has also gathered several books discussing dragons and several extra dragon storybooks. She uses these as the basis for report writing, a major activity in her language arts curriculum.

Our final activities involve further reinforcement of the concepts of story structure and parody. In Grade 5 classes, the major novel we study is Jean Craighead George's *Julie of the Wolves* (1972). Along with it, we have looked at Paul Goble's *The Friendly Wolf* (1974) and have talked about the movie *Never Cry Wolf* (1963) and European folktales relating to wolves. With our experience with dragon lore and parodies as background, we are able to reconsider these wolf stories. We first introduce the ideas that stories can be classified and that groups of stories have definite characteristics: spy stories, desert island stories, dragon stories and wolf stories. We list as many European wolf folktales as we can, and then we list their characteristics. Then we discuss the actual qualities of wolves, the qualities that native Americans have always known about and that modern researchers are only just discovering. *Julie, Never Cry Wolf* and *The Friendly Wolf* are used to help us compile our lists. Using *The Last of the Dragons* as our model, the class discusses how it might write a parody of wolf stories and what they might include in such a parody. Each member of the class then writes a parody. The results have, of course, been of varying quality, but generally they have been surprisingly good – perceptive and humorous.

Now that we've looked at some aspects of literary theory and analysis and their relationship to teaching literature to children, the questions remain, 'So what? Why bother? All this is interesting, but how is it important educationally? We're only dealing with stories, after all.' True, we are only dealing with stories. But if, as I believe, stories represent humanity's highest use of its special skills of linguistic communication, what we are doing is very important for several reasons.

First, in studying the conventions of dragon lore and their uses in specific stories, we are helping children to comprehend more fully the implications of the actual words they read or hear. We are helping them to get more out of specific works.

Second, in examining the nature of parody, we are helping children to understand the conventional nature of literary language. We are showing them that structural patterns inform all literature, and that when we have discovered the pattern of a specific story and related it to the general structure from which it derives, we can better understand the unity of the story. Not that we just look for the skeleton of the story and ignore the flesh; but the skeleton gives shape to the flesh. The literary pattern gives a framework which provides coherence for the details.

Finally, and most important, through our approach to literature study, we are strengthening the basic human intellectual impulse, what the poet Wallace Stevens called the 'blessed rage for order'; that is, the need to discover and create meaningful structures out of the unshaped chaos of experience. Knowledge is not merely an accumulation of unrelated facts. Indeed, a grab bag of facts is of use only to someone who wants to appear on 'Hollywood Squares' or to play 'Trivial Pursuit'. Only when the human mind organises these facts into patterns – discovers, the scientist would say, laws – is knowledge achieved. Literary study is a way of introducing the children to the structural basis of all knowledge. By learning the conventions – the vocabulary (facts) and the grammar (structure) – of dragon lore, they are doing what they must do in all areas of study.

Long before there were microscopes, telescopes or computers, people turned to the storytellers, both religious and secular, for knowledge. These linguistic structure-makers used words to explain the meaning of the spiritual, physical and social worlds in which people find themselves.

Nowadays, we don't often listen to our storytellers, our structure makers, as closely, as carefully, as we could. There are those people who would suggest that this is one of the reasons we find so few meaningful structures to give validity to our lives. And so, for those of us who teach language arts, what we do when we bring stories and children together is of vital importance. Through the stories we share, we are bringing young readers into the presence of some very good structuralists.

Through the way we present stories, the questions we ask and the activities we initiate, we are helping young readers to understand better the significance of the structures created by great storytellers, and most important, we are helping them to acquire the ability to create their own structures, to give or find meaningful patterns for their lives, and to give their lives richness and dignity. The poet Robert Frost, who saw metaphors as basic poetic structures, once wrote that the only lost soul was the person who got lost in his material without a gathering metaphor (that is, structure) to give it shape and order. We do not want the children we know to be like Frost's lost souls. Through helping children to become better readers of literature, we can help them to find, not only themselves, but also the wonder and glory, the structures, of the worlds they relate to.

From *Children's Literature in Education* No. 79, 1990

Margaret Meek

Margaret Meek's influence in the fields of literacy and literature is immense; any conference on these subjects is energised by references to her thought. She has worked with students and teachers in many countries, from university summer schools in Canada to township schools in the new South Africa. She was for many years the Reviews Editor of *The School Librarian* and received the Eleanor Farjeon Award 'for distinguished services to children's books' in 1971. Her numerous publications include *The Cool Web* (1977) (as joint editor), *On Being Literate* (1991) and the influential *How Texts Teach What Readers Learn* (1988). The piece which follows was her response to the editors' invitation to contribute to the 25th Anniversary Issue of Spring, 1995.

THE CRITICAL CHALLENGE OF THE WORLD IN BOOKS FOR CHILDREN

Forgive, please, these first skin-shrinking platitudes. I need them for what follows.

The notion of children's literature is based on the implicit premise that children can be expected to learn to read the books that their elders write or make for them.

Other aspects of common knowledge related to the educational process that counts as learning to read are barnacled upon this one. The kinds of reading associated with literature and 'the literary' depend on the learner's confident assumption of the role of a reader, a growing fluency and independence and an extending range of encounters with different kinds of written language, especially in books. Texts for early reading are mostly narratives and poems. Efficient learning lies in the discovery that, on a page, the words stay as they are for each rereading. Development advances as readers come to know how written language is patterned and that they can reproduce it to make their own meanings in writing. Successful readers engage in what D. W. Harding once described as 'a bond with the author', whereby they learn to become both the teller and the told. Importantly, children read the texts of their times. Those who discover reading as enjoyment and a kind of deep play grow, often quickly, in both competence and experience.

Stories are central to these processes. The reasons are well understood and often repeated, perhaps because of the delicate ambivalence that associates stories with fiction, and thus with the 'made up' and the untrue. The history of children's learning to read in our culture has never quite lost its Protestant overtones: the reader's right to unmediated interpretation of a text, especially the Bible, and the rationalisation that reading is learning and therefore bound to do us good. Narrative is still as Barbara Hardy (1968) described it: 'a primary act of mind'. Carol Fox's (1993) overwhelming evidence of the effects on children's language development of hearing literary stories read aloud confirms, more than adequately, Ursula Le Guin's (1992) assertions that 'narrative is a central function of language. Not, in origin, an artifact of culture, an art, but a fundamental operation of the normal mind functioning in society. To learn to speak is to learn to tell a story.' Stories teach children the verb tenses of the past and the future when they are intensely preoccupied with the present. Before they have memory as reflexion, or understand prediction as more than repetition, they discover the 'what if' of imagination, its *but, could, might, would* and *should*; the past as forgiveness and the future as promise, in the literature of their culture. In a story like *Hansel and Gretel* listeners and readers live with possibilities as part of the everyday.

All of this is in the consciousness of readers of *Children's Literature in Education.* Twenty-five years of careful attention to books and writers offered as *readings* of texts new and old have contributed to a poetics of this literature: a description of its nature, the theorising of its making, with imagination as a core construct. What Ted Hughes prefigured in his essay in the first issue has taken strong root, like a vine clipped every year, firmly set for good yield and gathering. Critical analysis, especially the kind that foregrounds readers' responses, has ensured that children's literature, however defined, is recognised in these pages as being at the heart of the English language arts curriculum, and therefore of children's education.

We know well that authors, artists and publishers profit from this kind of attention. It encourages explorations and innovations in the making of books for the young. Those who, like me, are interested in children's interactions with books and texts, are persuaded that modern storytellers and poets actually beget both new readers and new kinds of reading. The young are a challenge, an opportunity to extend, almost to reinvent, what reading and books can be like. New visual and language 'expressions' engage readers in new ways of listening, saying and seeing. By inviting a reader to pore over a page, modern picture books show readers how to explore different ways of making meaning. As their eyes inspect and interrogate the details, of clothes and rooms in addition to actions and sequences (see the picture on the wall on the first page of *Where the Wild Things Are*), children are not simply extending the ways in which they watch television. Artists and picture storytellers know that, so they purposely offer different kinds of reading secrets. *Where's Wally Now?* is a bookish experience which needs a new kind of description. What are the current readers of the Weetabix packets looking at when they seek out the red and blue figure in the plethora of cave man details? Is this puzzle a new or an old set of reading practices? What is the current equivalent of Edward Ardizzone's conviction that the best way to show a child's feelings in a picture is to draw it from the back? As new readers have few fixed notions of narrative and pictorial conventions and no prejudices about what books and stories *should* be like, they enter into page turning with hopes of surprises to come.

We are bound to acknowledge, however, that the kinds of world-making that we associate with narrative fiction are no longer confined to oral story telling or to books. As adventurers and as readers of the texts of their times, children are familiar with a range of media presentations of stories, including different versions of the same stories which may occur simultaneously. Think of how many different ways there are to read *The Snowman*: the original, the video, on cups, plates, T-shirts, Christmas wrapping paper, wallpaper, pillows, greetings cards and in the Ladybird hand-me-down. Also, there may be forms of readerly behaviour we know less about than we should. Children who control, and know that they are controlling, moving video images so that they can wind fast forward familiar sequences and choose to 'frame' their favourite incidents may be exhibiting 'readerly' behaviour in ways we have yet to describe. Margaret Mackey (1994) tells how a Canadian child from a family that is far from wealthy 'lives in a world of multiple versions of fiction' as the result of her multi-media experiences. 'Inexorably,' she says, 'children's ideas about fiction and how you behave with it are being affected by the kinds of fiction they meet. Cross-media hybrids are everywhere.' Thus our critical models and activities have to be enlarged to deal with the varieties of these forms and the nature of these encounters. Can we confidently say that children are reading Beatrix

Potter's account of Mrs Tittlemouse as they uncover the print on their porringers? If not, what kind of reading *is* that?

I have taken you over familiar territory so that we may together encounter the waste land: all the other books that are written, or perhaps more correctly, made, to teach children about the world *directly*, so that they will think about it as actual, real and learnable. However, the world is presented in books generally called 'non-fiction', the assumption is that it is, indisputably, there. More than half of children's school-based reading relates to 'subjects' and curricular programmes of study. Books designed for this kind of reading and understanding are rarely counted as literature. Reference books of all kinds, from encyclopedias and dictionaries to brochures and leaflets, together with the varying notations of maps, mathematics and music relate different kinds of reading to acts of learning. Where books offer information, their use is seen as transactional. Their texts enable us, in James Britton's (1992) phrase, 'to get the world's work done'. The general assumption is that books of information for adults are to be consulted rather than absorbed, although there is ample evidence that people look up time-tables and collect travel brochures in order to make imaginary journeys as they also consult catalogues and magazines to dream of cars, houses, holidays and clothes they will never buy. But children in school are to find in books designed for their instruction, ways of confirming, ordering and extending what they may have already discovered piecemeal, by bumping about in the world. They are to remember, to add to a 'store' of information on a subject, whatever has been designated for this purpose. Part of the learning is to acquire a certain competence in writing in the manner deemed to be conventionally appropriate for the topic.

As children become more accomplished and confident they discover that stories 'make worlds'. The book language of stories is the formal magic of the teller's or artist's invention, the ways they devise for tapping into the imagination of the reader or listener. Quite early readers recognise different authors from the characteristics of their presentations; they rarely confuse Shirley Hughes with Anthony Browne. Also, stories are metaphors for ways of thinking and feeling before these can be deliberately explored. All this is counted as learning to read. In contrast, reading to learn means encountering text books and topic books designed (usually as a team enterprise) on the premise that whatever is to be known can be put into writing, diagrams, maps or pictures, and *studied* by the learner. Non-fiction texts are to take readers through steps and stages of reasoned thinking, from descriptions and categories to concepts as abstractions, across a whole range of hierarchically arranged knowledge systems. The language of this kind of writing is said to be 'scientific'; that is 'regulated by the requirements of consistence and non-contradiction'.

These are Jerome Bruner's (1986) words, part of his intriguing argument that there are 'two modes of cognitive functioning, two modes of thought, each providing different ways of *ordering* experience, of constructing reality' (my italics). He suggests that the novelist and the scientist both deal in 'possible worlds', but the imagination works differently in each. In this assertion he has the history of science and the conventions of formal education on his side. In ordinary school terms, non-fiction is about the world observed and recorded in words whose formal arrangement is sanctioned by those who have contributed to 'the vast knowledge of how science and logical reasoning proceed'. So children are expected to learn the registers and the logics of a subject as they assimilate its content. Long before they are likely to realise the nature of the scientific imagination, they are to engage with 'facts', a word that confounds rather than helps our understanding of how children learn. Narrative recedes in book learning as topic discourses, different kinds of statements and propositions are emphasised as ways of knowing. This knowing is assumed, especially by psychologists, to follow a linear progression that extends throughout the years of schooling despite evidence that language is learned recursively. There is still what Barbara Hardy called 'a widespread and, I suggest, dubious but understandable assumption on the part of wishful believers in life-enhancement that human beings begin by telling themselves fairy tales and end by telling truths'. We return to this point later. Meanwhile we should look at information books to see how they are to be read, for the simple reason that, with certain notable exceptions, (the works of David Macaulay, for example), they are rarely given consistent critical attention.

Modern topic and information books are new in the history of publishing, although the rationale for their existence is as old as that propounded by Comenius (1672) for *Orbis Pictus*: what we cannot experience of the world directly we can see in pictures in a book. Born out of the 1967 Plowden Report emphasis on children as autonomous learners, books for discovering the world contain thousands of different segments of it to be studied in response to curricular demand or teachers' choice of subject matter. Christine Pappas (1989) analysed a hundred or so of these books and found, under the surface differences of presentational forms, a kind of recipe for their production. They all had obligatory elements, such as 'the presentation of the topic' (Birds); 'descriptions of attributes' (Feathers); and 'characteristic events' (Nest Building). Optional elements are 'category comparisons' (Singing Birds and Others), and a 'final summary'. Despite the infinite variety of topics, the repetitive structure of these books is unmistakeable. The double page spread is another common feature. Once the format emerged, its usefulness was confirmed and conventionalised.

As information goes out of date, like groceries, the validity of many information books is only temporary. Often the packaging is renewed to give the impression that the contents have been revised. Attempts to structure the sentences of the prose text to suit the assumed reading skill of the learners usually lead to short, abrupt sentences with insufficient redundancy for the reader to understand the import of what is written. Yet, from the words and pictures, the maps and diagrams, children are to 'retrieve' information about the world which they are to regard as *true.* This naive realism which assumes a world 'out there' we come to know by naming it, is a long way from the scientists' imaginative world-making. I have found no book of this picture-and-text design which explains to its primary school readers how we have come to know what they are expected to learn, or why these particular parts of a topic have been chosen to represent the whole.

Critics of children's literature are apt to exclude information texts (and magazines, to which they bear some resemblance) from their accounts of what children read. Yet for many young readers, these picture and caption books are their preferred texts. We know too little about how children actually read books with titles like *Roman Britain*; *Stars and Planets*; *Light.* There is evidence that when five year olds are invited to 'read' aloud two different kinds of texts, the intonational patterns of their attempts are different and distinguishable. When older children, mostly boys, pore over topic books of subjects which interest them, they are usually in pairs or larger groups. They talk as much as, if not more than, they read. They dart about the pages, stabbing their fingers at words and pictures. They do not always follow the book sequence from beginning to end. This behaviour is sometimes thought to be reprehensible; in other classrooms it is encouraged. Formal teaching about the books themselves always includes directions about how to use the index and the contents page as part of an induction into 'study skills'. I am usually reluctant to be unduly critical of any of these procedures because I know that where they happen, teachers are taking care. Many schools are so meagrely resourced that 'topic work' with books rarely happens.

Instead, the worksheet takes over, or exercises in the 'course' book. Both are designed to engage the learner. In fact, the information content of these devices is even more prepacked, predigested and simply to be copied or ticked in response to multiple choice questions. My colleagues and I discovered that the answers to questions on SRA cards could be divined by the pupils without their having read the passage which contained the information required. Sadly, a fair amount of this 'busy work' still goes on in the later years of junior school and the first years of secondary education. In their heart of hearts, teachers know that this is neither a serious literate practice nor an efficient learning one.

How the joint sessions of children reading together, or other kinds of encounter with the contents of a book, turn information into understanding is not yet well documented, but discussion is certainly an important and relevant part of the operation. Readers who give passionate and continuing attention to books on topics which enthral them convince me that they are engaged in the same quality of imaginative interaction as we attribute to readers of stories. My evidence comes from a seven-year-old snake expert whose devotion to what his teacher calls 'facts' is an important element in his reading competence. We shall draw on his experience again, later. His reading may be in a different kind of world-making from that of his friends who prefer animals in Farthing Wood, but world-making it assuredly is. If you find this difficult to believe, read W. H. Auden's account of the imaginary lead mine he carried in his head for six years of his childhood. You will discover how he chose and read books about geology and mining machinery in order to select the most effective technology to make it work. You will also be impressed by Donald Fry's (1985) account of Clayton, a young reader hesitant about reading stories but devoted to books and articles about farming. He typifies for me the 'young expert' for whom children's non-fiction books are of too little use and no match for a wealth of first-hand experience.

Then you will understand why I believe that it is world-making and not rationality that distinguishes information texts from narrative texts. We need to know much more about how texts teach children *about learning*, especially when the relation of texts and books to the world they purport to describe for study is so constantly changing. To what extent is it possible to describe a book in Vygotsky's terms, as a 'zone of proximal development' where the expert lends his or her mind out to the readers? How could this be characterised as something other than a 'level of difficulty'? Critics of children's books are bound to be interested in the moves children make in relation to the texts they are offered. It isn't enough to say readers are 'bright' or 'interested' as if that described children's intellectual development. We need critics who are prepared to judge the nature and quality of the engagement required by the information offered.

When we talk about 'scanning', for example, as something to be deliberately learned for the purposes of information retrieval and 'study skills', do we really mean that this is something different from what children and adults do when they look at the designs and graphics of advertisements? At present there seem to be more passionate convictions than evidence. My hunch is that, behind every dispassionate scientist there is a committed young explorer, male or female, of what is *to be* known, a reader who asks why things are *said to be* thus.

The general acknowledgement is that this kind of explorative reading of 'expository texts' is the result of 'giftedness', or the product of long schooling in academic disciplines and extended study. We make all sorts of assumptions about reading because we who have survived the years of devotion to specialised subject matters are those who determine what counts as learning. But surely our experience confirms that information texts are, of all kinds, the most unstable. Where once the rainforests were to be wondered at as exotic aspects of the Amazonian jungle, now they are objects to be 'saved'. It is indeed regrettable to watch a forest die, but the causes and effects are political, socio-economic and moral as well as ecological. I haven't discovered from the books on this topic when it is important to make this clear as part of the learning. What the young are to learn about natural phenomena is shot through with other implications. So part of the lesson is that there are no neutral texts in any topic domain. Very few books make this clear. But I do know that many, many children are ready to find in books of information not simply the ordered presentation of what they are expected to memorise. Instead, they want encouragement *to think*, as an imaginative as well as an intellectual endeavour. Our failure to see that books can and should support intellectual activity as *desire*, and not as a series of set-piece interventions with text taught as 'skills' to dig out 'facts', whatever these are, has resulted in poor teaching of how books of information can add to children's understanding. Publishers and teachers are not indifferent to children's learning. On the contrary, they are earnestly on the side of the learners. But because they are not sufficiently reflexive about how reading *becomes* learning, or how piecemeal acquisitions of information ('pre-disciplinary' is Peter Medway's term) develop into the publicly acknowledged forms of knowing, they are hazy, in my view, about the role books play in these processes.

Margery Fisher understood this well. In 1972 there came *Matters of Fact*, a lighthouse in the wasteland of information books. As the titles she discusses are nearly all out of print or superseded, her book has remained as an unread classic. But we can still be impressed by the case she made for what children learn about reading as they read to learn.

> A child uses information books to assemble what he knows, what he feels, what he sees, as well as to connect new facts. His reaction to something as ordinary as a loaf may be, at one time or another, one of wonder, excitement, interest, aesthetic pleasure, physical satisfaction, curiosity. He needs books which can combine warm individuality and clear exposition, a mingling of words that colour the subject and words that clarify it, a recognition of past as well as present. He seldom finds such books.

In a later article in *Children's Literature in Education* (*CLE* 22, 1976) she goes over this ground again: 'We all want better information books for the young . . . . This means better writing, a more enterprising use of material, a greater respect for the reader's intelligence (together with a sensible eye to the degree of stamina and perspective that can be assumed at any particular age).'

One move to make school information books more like their serious adult counterparts has been the introduction in the papers of the English National Curriculum of the notion of 'non-chronological' texts. That is, children are to move away, or on, from narrative, on the grounds that information cannot be presented as a story. At once there are problems. Think of history. Events, even events that occur and are recorded as a chronological sequence, do not relate themselves. Their sequence becomes significant when the historian gives them a structure. Then they become evidence and have meaning. To become a historian is to discover how, from different sources, different stories of the past can be told with authority. Lately in England and Wales we have had furious discussions about which sequences from history our children are to learn. But no one has suggested seriously that history, the great story, should not be narrated. History includes discoveries, inventions, laws, moral judgements, ideas and whatever else creates our social consciousness. The discourse rhetoric of these individual topics becomes conventionally familiar, the proper habit, as children advance in understanding the contents of each special subject. Like other mannered conventions, different kinds of writing are learned in use.

What is it, then, that provokes a curious fundamentalism in those who are keen to promote reading to learn and yet want to outlaw narrative, even in early books about the common things of life, like fire, air, earth and water because the treatment of these must always be 'scientific'? How, if not by imagination, can a six-year-old envisage what is meant by the statement 'More than half of the planet is water'. Bobbie Neate, in her book *Finding Out About Finding Out* (1992), is convinced that children do not learn 'facts' from stories. Again, the word is confusing. But this simply cannot be the case. How many readers of Arthur Ransome have come to understand a great deal about boats and boating? If I were to cancel all I'd learned about Russia, the Sargasso Sea, Purcell, chermoula, the great fire of London, the great fourteenth-century plague and a thousand other topics that are reasonably part of my mental furniture, gleaned, sorted and understood from autobiographies, biographies, novels and poems, what would my world be like? Agreed, as Margery Fisher points out, *King Solomon's Mines* is not the safest guide to African history, but then we also know about the different purposes for tellings and reliable and unreliable narrators. The importance of culture and human relations, including legal systems, their consequences and the significance of different points of view, are first awakened in the reading of stories. Are these not central to learning to think and to think about thinking?

Part of the trouble lies in inept descriptions of fact and fiction and the distinctions assumed to exist between narrative and non-narrative discourses. When my daughter was reading Laura Ingalls Wilder's *Little House in the Big Woods* (1932) to my grandson, the snake expert, they greatly enjoyed the description of how the people in the story made things. At the end of the chapter which describes the collection of maple tree sap and the making of 'sugar snow' she said: 'You remember that Mamou told us that she saw the people in Canada making maple syrup when she was there. She sent us some in a jar.' Then my grandson: 'How could she see these maple trees? They're only in this story, and it isn't true.' There followed an even longer discussion about how writers write what they know; people know things in life *and* in books.

Grandparents shouldn't intervene, but Sam and I have book talk. I discovered he'd been told at school that you can't believe stories because they aren't 'the facts'. A fact, he said, is the difference between the coral snake and the milk snake. Only in *The Jungle Book* did a snake have a name and that was because he was 'a character, like a person'. However, it soon became clear that it wasn't the books or the texts that made Sam separate fact from fiction. (Thanks to John R. Searle (1969), we know that the words do not by themselves reveal the truth or falsehood of an utterance or statement.) Instead, his teacher had insisted that you don't *believe* stories: something much more far-reaching for beginning readers. The information Sam needed wasn't about fiction and non-fiction, but, at this stage, about who was telling the story. In this interim period, information is authenticated by the teller. He learned by consulting the story book again, that Laura, the author, is the grown-up who was Laura, the little girl who tells the story in the book. The narrator and the author were the same, and the book had been written so that people could know what life in North America had been like long ago. Once it became clear, that things which happened 'a long time ago' could still be what his teachers called 'facts', Sam, who had never enjoyed story writing because you had to 'make it up', also discovered that what had happened to him could also be told as a story; how he saw the milk snake in the zoo, for example. Then, when he was telling what happened, he could explain to his reader why he knew it was not a coral snake.

Narrative is not a genre, a single kind to be set against another, expository text, from which anecdotes and stories are banned. Narratives are storehouses of multiple mixed ways of telling things. That's what children's storytelling shows. Adults expect transactional writing to be tidier. But, think of biography, that rich, important, current trade in curiosity about what certain people and their families, friends and acquaintances were like, how they lived, thought, sinned, spoke and acted, all plaited to show and interpret the sheer complexity and differences of being human. The writer claims to tell the truth as she or he sees it, but, as Harold Rosen says, we never get the whole story. The very little evidence we have of children's topic reading shows how their imaginations are captured and sustained not by the generality of things, but by unique examples, single instances, the anomalous case. Margaret Mallett (1992) reports that when they are shown photographs of squirrels, children concentrate on the one that has mange. Then they demand to know about *cause*, the story of how it came about.

Biographical writing for children has slipped into low gear. It's difficult to persuade publishers that a text about Mozart doesn't need underlining with freaky drawings. It needs an expert on the topic, writing out of full understanding and sympathy, looking for the next generation of readers and listeners. Most designers of books about space, cars, pyramids and computers, format the contents as eternally present. The details engage the imaginations of the young, no doubt, but not always in ways that encourage further enquiry, and sometimes only fleetingly. Quite often readers want to know something more off piste than the direct run of things: how an aeroplane 'got its name', for example. They are also curious about how adults know things, and if, when they are adults, they will know other things. As J. A. Appleyard suggests (1990), topic learning has, for children under twelve, the excitement of a *quest* tale if the teacher's imagination is engaged with the way they *can* learn. It isn't always the way of the book.

Modern publishing and the technologies which have been developed for book making to be as impressive as, but different from, television, bring whole worlds into children's hands to be looked at as well as read about. In the arena of book learning, those who work with Dorling Kindersley have triumphed in the presentation of information as something clearly and exactly to be seen. The seeing eye is the advanced lens of the camera. The pages of the books from this house are composed of immaculate photographs on high quality white paper. Learners are 'eyewitnesses'. The claim is that the readers can now see things in books and understand them 'as they are', by means of a system called 'lexigraphics'. That is, the images 'slow down' the looking, while the print, in neat segments of differing lengths and density, 'speeds up' the reading.

These books subject all possible topics and subtopics to this treatment; they are universally available, instantly recognisable. They are to appeal to adults as well as to the young. Clearly, children enjoy looking at those which deal with topics they already know about or are curious about. The very uniformity seems to act as a way of recognising a familiar way of going about finding out. Comenius would instantly recognise the technique. In bookshops and libraries children choose Dorling Kindersley books by their logos. The central reading scene is usually around the books about dinosaurs. When I was checking some details of the universal appeal of this topic I haunted libraries and bookshops. I asked some readers how we knew about these creatures, and if they were not just monsters that someone had imagined. The rush to explain to me about 'evidence' was impressive. Clearly the evolution, feeding habits, size and the ultimate disappearance of the creatures had all been studied. The distinction was firmly established between them and anything 'made up'. Asked if the books had photographs of real dinosaurs, these young experts laughed me to scorn and explained the part played in the enterprise by the Natural History Museum. How did they remember all the details of the time scale? There was a chart in their classroom. (Was that, I wonder, what Vygotsky called 'a perceptual bond'?) Was it difficult to imagine a million years? Yes, but you didn't need to count; just imagine a world without people. Younger children could find similar examples in different Dorling Kindersley books; older ones were given to speculation about why the dinosaurs disappeared, a topic they found in the books as part of the text.

What seems to happen is a series of discussions, in twos or threes, where those who are looking at the photographs decide where they will focus their attention. Then they seem to offer bits of what they see to each other and make a 'heap' of common knowing which they then interpret to each other or set out to explore further. This is a cheerful scene, for the general view has been for some time that information books have been less than inspirational. Does not such a remarkable turnaround in children's books deserve some particular notice? There has been admiration but little real critical exploration of these productions to match this total endeavour to present the world in pictures so as to promote book learning. What are its general successes in the matter of children's *learning*, beyond looking?

The mummy in the museum, the pinions of birds' wings, the veriest details of Egyptian jewellery, every intricacy of what the design teams and compilers have brought together to constitute a topic is seeable in Dorling Kindersley's Eyewitness books. But, the photographs don't take themselves; someone is behind the lens. Photographs don't explain things. As Frank Smith points out, photographs are not the medium 'in which creative artists, those who go beyond the literal, traditionally work'. (I hear the mutter, 'Cartier Bresson' and protests from all teachers of photography in art schools. That's the point; we need to discuss it.) The captions have to do half of the work and in some cases they are generous in their naming, giving children the kinds of words that enchant them, many of which are stored for special ways of showing off. But, if children see in a photograph on a white page what they are told is there, is that the same as being an eyewitness? Are lexigraphics the answer to our problems about children's reading to learn if the high powered use of advanced technology still needs narrative and expository texts? Will the transfer of these visuals on to CD-ROM with voiceovers take information-getting away from books even when we know that books may be better for thinking than screens? When children are caught up in the seeing, do they believe that this is what makes a difference to what they know, or is there more for them to do in order to think differently? Are not these questions some things that critics of children's literature, whose work gives them insights into imaginative reading, might think and write about?

I am not asking for answers, just speculating about what kinds of inquiry would help us to know how children actually read *The Ultimate Dinosaur Book* and what they think about dinosaurs thereafter. Sometimes, when I am looking closely at the collected works of the Dorling Kindersley force, I am reminded of the series of cigarette cards which were the source of illustrated topics in my childhood: sailing ships, castles, wild flowers and the rest. My zest was in the gathering; the notes on the back remained unread. I had other reading for castle scenes. The claim for Eyewitness books is that the design of the pages lets the readers integrate what they see with what they already know. Has anyone checked this out in readers whose knowledge is so varied, so difficult to characterise in terms of ages and stages, despite repeated attempts of psychologists to do so?

In the matter of books for learning, including learning to read, we are at an important turning point, so we should be critically aware of what is happening. Current technologies make much more information available in many different formats, with the result that we cannot be sure exactly how children select and interpret what we believe they are bound to learn. We know that reading a screen is not the same as reading a book, but most of the evidence comes from my generation of the bookish. What is it like for those who have never been without television? Most children I know are more comfortable with a whole range of technologies than I shall ever be. If, then, we want the young to discover the advantages of print literacies that are constituted in books, an effortful accomplishment in every century since books became common, we cannot assume that books will always be the same.

Modern technologies encourage children to see non-print text as *changeable.* (I wish I knew more about their views of various versions of Shakespeare, cartoons, films, modern dress variants, different productions.) Convinced as I am that reading is construction and not decoding, and knowing that modern texts for adults are deliberately made unstable, I am concerned that children should discover in book learning not a fixed pattern of the world's events, but an imaginative engagement with different versions of the world and its inhabitants. That is, they will discover what is important information by direct engagement with its use in world-making. This will probably mean they will discover different ways of reading to learn; indeed I hope it does. But they need better books than those offering a kind of learning package, some authorised version of the world which shrinkwraps their thinking and stultifies their imagination.

So I hope that young children, before they are school-bamboozled by insistencies about fact and fiction, narrative and non-chronological writing and the rest will encounter the series of books called *Read and Wonder* produced by Walker Books. In principle, they are books of information for those who are still learning to read independently. But simply to say that is to downgrade the intellectual and imaginative subtlety of their conception and production. They are far away from any notion of 'beginner books' or 'starters'. The communicative act is embedded in the totality of the books as 'literary' presentations, like metafictive picture books, except that, this time, the reader learns about certain continuing aspects of the world by interpreting different kinds of signs within a single cohesive text.

As I write, there are twelve titles in the series; the only common feature is their size. Like the best picture books, each is a collaboration of artist and writer to produce a topic-learning event supported by advanced publishing techniques of colour reproduction. The representations of eels in *Think of an Eel* (1993) are not photographs, but more eel-like as the result of the movement of Mike Bostock's paintings. There are two texts in different print styles. The calligraphic text says things like, 'Baby eels are born in early spring'. The other text is a poem which makes an eel world of both feeling and information:

There's a warm, weedy sea
to the south of Bermuda.
It's called the Sargasso.
No wind ever blows there
no sailing ships sail there.
For thousands of years there
a secret lay hidden:
this salt, soupy sea
is where eels are born.
Deep down where it's blackest,
eel egg becomes eel.
He looks like a willow leaf,
clear as a crystal.
His fierce jutting mouth
has teeth like a sawblade.
He eats like a horse and
swims up through the water.

The main thrust of the detail is to take the reader with the eels on a journey by saying on the cover: '*Imagine* (my italics) you could find your way to a place you'd never been before'. It's a quest which doesn't exclude poetry or narrative as ways of understanding and knowing. In *Think of a Beaver* (1993) the words echo the prosody of *The Song of Hiawatha. My Cat Jack* (1994) is a first book for children watching cats play. The movements, and the words to go with them, are based on the old game of alphabet-adjectives. (I learned it as 'The minister's cat is an *awful, bad, clumsy . . . yellow, zany* cat.' You were out if you repeated anything that had already been said.) In *Caterpillar, Caterpillar* (1993) a little girl learns from her grandfather how to watch the metamorphosis of a tiny egg on a nettle leaf into a butterfly. He restrains her impatience and teaches her to look. The delicate interaction of words and drawings is a network of feelings: anticipation, impatience, relief, disappointment, joy, as the mystery unravels itself. It is also worth spending time on *The Wheeling and Whirling Around Book* (1994) if we want to redescribe scanning. Here's the first sentence in the information text. (The page is full of fairground activity.) 'When something spins, two opposite things are happening at once: flying-apartness and holding-togetherness.' Around the drawing of two children holding hands and circling are the words: 'Try this. What would happen if you let go?' In *A Piece of String is a Wonderful Thing* (1993) there is enough intricate detail of how many things are held together or made into something else by this apparently ordinary device. The question then arises: how did our ancestors 'think it up'? Then how did 'to string' become 'to tune, tense, key up, thread, hang, fasten, arrange in a line, provide with a string, extend, stretch, tease. . . .'? The collected examples show how abstraction is a function of language. Another concrete virtue of this topic is its suggestion that there are still things to be known about 'how things work'.

Each book in the series deserves close reading to unpick the ways in which the words, pictures, signs and detailed information make a patterned whole. Each text is a metaphor for a way of knowing that emerges from looking and wondering, in the sense of asking with curiosity, surprise and awe. Each page is part of a *score.* A linear account of these books undoes the vision and underplays the way the information is woven into the composite text. They need the kind of reading that David Lewis gives to John Burningham's, *Where's Julius?* in his 1992 article 'Looking for Julius: two Children and a Picture Book'. The difference is, *Read and Wonder* is reading to learn as well as learning to read. It is also imaginative world-making in ways that are not, at this stage of learning, separable. We have to consider the possibility that descriptions of the world 'as it is' are much more problematic, complex and important than many a 'non-fiction' book makes them seem.

It would be even more difficult to do justice to these books by writing about them in this way if I hadn't learned from Jerome J. McGann that 'the linguistic and linear reading model may not by any means comprehend the structure within which the reading model is to be executed'. I had a hunch about this before, from Gerard Manley Hopkins who wrote about the 'to-fro trambeams' of the eyes in ways of looking. McGann's word for this kind of reading is *radial.* His example is the poems of William Blake which, in the original versions, have pictures which remind us of 'the crucial importance *spatial relations* (my italics) play in the structure of texts'. In terms of children's book learning there is no doubt about this. McGann's most interesting example is, of course, something that readers take for granted. Think of the number of times when you have been reading something and you have put the book down and gone to consult another one before taking the first one up again. You needed to fill a gap in one text with the information in another but you are still, while so doing, engaged in reading the first text. The gaps in the Dorling Kindersley texts are the white paper around the photographs; the radial reading lies in the relations the reader makes between what is to be seen, what is looked at, and what is said about each icon and the relation of all of these things to other articles, objects and details on the same page. The lexigraphics handbook suggests that the relation is that of the part to the whole, yet the scale and the size of the objects have sometimes to be inferred before they can be understood.

We are only beginning to understand that we can take nothing for granted in information texts, whether on paper or on screens. We shall not get to the bottom of what we still need to know about how children interpret all kinds of writing about the world (note, I no longer say 'as it is'), unless we also look carefully at the books children are to learn from, and at as many other ways as possible of conveying what they are to know. Until now, we have sometimes assumed that information books might do children's thinking for them. Instead, even the simplest text to be read for information 'retrieval' (whatever that is) implies a complex network of interactions and intertextuality in terms of sources, selection, emphases, and claims to verity, actuality and speculative endeavour. Children and adults experience different versions of events simply by going about the world from day to day and thinking about what happens. There are two distinct age-differences in that activity. Children expect to learn so they are inclined to look ahead, to tolerate change, for they are changing all the time. They are more inclined to speculate than to be certain when they are still finding things out. They apply to computers for information in ways they believe they can control. In books for children, experts, those who want children to share their enjoyment as freely as their knowledge, show how they make worlds out of their experience. We see them bringing together observation, speculation, amazement to make learning into something that is both rational and imaginative at once; the 'what if' of the story and the 'what if' of the hypothesis. (I have in mind *Spiders* by Michael Chinery, 1993.) These are not necessarily different modes of thinking. Rather, they are bilateral awarenesses and different emphases and orderings, according to the writers' and readers' purposes and contexts, including reworking the past and anticipating the future. Here is Frank Smith:

> Our imaginary realities are furnished with the same basic structures and relationships as those found in the world around us, not because our imaginations are limited to what we have experienced, but because experience is constrained by what we can imagine.

If this is so, and I am still thinking about it, how can we make books for the young 'about' the world they inhabit emphasise imaginative thinking as something they can powerfully do with their experience of both books and the world? What kind of a critical enterprise would that be?

From *Children's Literature in Education* No. 96, 1995

Reasons for Confidence: The Future of the Book

Aidan Chambers

Aidan Chambers taught English and Drama in secondary schools for eleven years before becoming a full-time author of fiction for young people and a writer and lecturer on literary education. His best-known novels are *The Present Takers* and *Dance on my Grave*; his most recent, *The Toll Bridge*. His latest books on teaching are *The Reading Environment* and *Tell Me: Children, Reading and Talk*, both published by the Thimble Press, which he and his wife Nancy founded in 1969 in order to publish the magazine *Signal: Approaches to children's books*.

This article was originally given in 1992 as one of a series of lectures which commemorate the work of Sidney Robbins, the founding editor of *CLE*, who died in 1971.

THE DIFFERENCE OF LITERATURE: WRITING NOW FOR THE FUTURE OF YOUNG READERS

In the late 1960s, when Sidney Robbins was planning the first of the Exeter conferences in celebration of children's literature, children's books in Britain were in a season of high bloom. Take 1967, a convenient quarter-century ago, as a sample. That year the following books were published in the UK for the first time:

Smith by Leon Garfield; *The Mouse and His Child* by Russell Hoban; *The Piemakers* by Helen Cresswell; *Charlie and the Chocolate Factory* by Roald Dahl; *The Dream-Time* by Henry Treece; *Flambards* by K. M. Peyton; *To the Wild Sky* by Ivan Southall; *The Dolphin Crossing* by Jill Paton Walsh; and *Charley, Charlotte and the Golden Canary* by Charles Keeping.

And that's not all. Two others must be added to the list. One of them, *Where the Wild Things Are* by Maurice Sendak, had taken five years to cross the Atlantic and reached here at all only because of the determination of an editor, Judy Taylor at the Bodley Head, who refused to be swayed by the general opinion, among librarians, teachers and other publishers who had seen a copy of the American edition, that the wild things would frighten the life out of little children and not sell. Now we recognise it as the work that most clearly demonstrates the poetics of the picture book as a literary form. With it, the picture book came of age. The other book, *The Owl Service* by Alan Garner, was very quickly, though not uncontroversially, recognised as a novel that redefined the possibilities in writing of adolescence.

When these two books appeared, I was working part time as a teacher-librarian in a secondary school for eleven- to sixteen-year-olds, and part time as an author trying to write a novel that took twelve years to finish. Its title was *Dance on My Grave*, I didn't know then that it was the beginning of a six-book sequence. The fourth, *The Toll Bridge*, has just been published. If it takes me as long to write the last two as it has to write the fourth, I'll be ten years older before I've finished, this century will be over, and we'll be two years into the next millennium. Will my books still be in print then? Will *Wild Things* and *The Owl Service*? Indeed, will literature in book print survive for long into the twenty-first century? There are those who say it won't, and who don't care if it doesn't. There are those who think its days are over already, that it is outmoded and survives only because a group of élitists keep it going. And there are always the millennialists, who thrill themselves with an apocalyptic view of the world and for whom the year 2000 will set off a revolution that will sweep away the book culture of the last thousand years.

Of course, there is bound to be something of a fuss as the century turns. We'll be prone to thoughts of making a fresh start and will want to prune away shards of our old ways that we feel hinder us or are too closely identified with what used to be: the baggage we'd rather not carry with us into the new life. By the time I've written the last of the six books in the *Dance* sequence, what will be the state of children's books as a whole – if, that is, there is still anything wholesome left to talk about? What will be the state of 'the book'?

The rest of this lecture will occupy itself with itinerant thoughts on some of those questions. And it will be an episodic narrative because I am a fiction writer and that is the kind of mind I have.

To start with I'd like to say a little more about *Where the Wild Things Are* and *The Owl Service*. If toasting glasses were in our hands, I'd ask you to raise them in celebration of those two eximious works of art. In the days that followed their publication, I gave them to the teenagers I was teaching, each in the same way: I read them aloud. Both had the same effect on my pupils as they'd had on me. I can best describe it as 'greedy astonishment'. We were astonished by their unfamiliarity, their unexpectedness, by the strength of the emotions and ideas they provoked in us – in other words, by the intensity of the pleasure they gave us. There was more to them than we were used to getting from books of this kind, and we were greedy for more. The ways this greed showed itself were in an impulse to read the books again at once, and in a demand for more like them, a demand which of course couldn't be easily satisfied. I remember pupils who had never dreamt of spending money on a book going off and buying copies, not just because they couldn't wait for their turn to borrow the school's but because they wanted copies of their own. (Please note: we're talking hardback books at hardback prices, not mass-market paperbacks at ice-cream prices.) Only a little while before, some of these same pupils had told me there were no fiction books in the library they wanted to read.

On me, the experience had two particular effects. It taught me that the dogma spewed upon us nowadays by such disinterested philosophers as Mr. Rupert Murdoch, that people know what they want and should be given it, is one of the fashionable half-truths of the late twentieth century. The half that is true is that people often do know what they want, but only if they already know about it. If something doesn't exist, or if we don't know that it is there because we aren't shown it or given access to it, how can we know we want it? It is the work of artists to bring into being what doesn't exist yet; and it is the work of teachers and librarians to show children what there is and give them access to it. In particular it is their work to introduce to them what is least familiar.

One of the lessons I have learned as a result of my twentieth-century life is to be wary of anyone who talks about 'the people' and to distrust completely anyone who claims to be acting for 'the people'. 'The people' do not exist, any more than 'the child' beloved of writers on education exists. What does exist are people, individuals living together in various and multifarious relationships, among whom are some living in a state we call childhood, a condition of human life that is far from singular and that is not at all the stable, quantifiable and describable entity some of us think it is.

The second thing *The Wild Things* and *The Owl Service* taught me was that we frequently underestimate ourselves (as writers and as educators) and, even more, the young people for whom we are responsible. We are all capable of far more than those who want to manipulate us tell us we are. Those pupils I mentioned showed me they could far exceed anything they were thought capable of doing because a great piece of writing engaged their minds and emotions and enabled them to extend their reach. *The Owl Service*, especially, did the same for me as a writer: it revealed to me possibilities I hadn't thought were graspable within the confines (and I thought of them as confines then; I don't now) of fiction for teenagers. It was an experience that taught me, as Margaret Meek puts it, *How Texts Teach What Readers Learn* (1988).

When I look back at my own history I realise that it is the people who have encouraged me, helped me and enabled me to reach beyond what I thought I could grasp whom I honour and remember with gratitude and affection, and who still live in me. Some were right there beside me: my parents, some teachers, my wife, a few friends. Many others were met and still live for me in their writing. These are the people whose company I keep and whom I would not live without. I'll hazard a guess it is the same for you.

If literature for children is to continue through the next millennium, it will depend on writers who make a difference and on adults who make that difference available to children. Talk of the millennium and the company I keep reminds me of the great modernist Italian author Italo Calvino. His book *If on a Winter's Night a Traveller* (1981) is *the* great novel about reading. He was to give the Charles Eliot Norton Lectures at Harvard in 1985 but died on the eve of his departure for the United States. He had written five of the six lectures, having spent nine months, his wife records, working on them obsessively. He called them *Six Memos for the Next Millennium* (1992). It seems appropriate that the death of this exemplary modern author left us, his readers, the job of thinking out the ending for ourselves, an indeterminacy Italo Calvino would have relished. Perhaps he was so obsessive about them because he sensed he was dying; certainly his signing of 'the values, qualities, or peculiarities of literature' he wanted, as he put it, 'to situate within the perspective of the new millennium' make a wonderful last testament. I expect you remember how, at the beginning, he writes, (p. 1), 'My confidence in the future of literature consists in the knowledge that there are things that only literature can give us, by means specific to it.' I note he doesn't speak of confidence based on belief, but of confidence based on *knowledge*. What is it we can *know* about the speciality of literature? If each of us were to write down in the next half hour a list of 'those things that only literature can give us', I wonder what we'd find at the end? I've been playing that game myself lately and have to say I've found it much harder than I expected. A few of my answers are here.

But now I want to make a digression, the point of which will, I hope, become clear very soon.

As a teenager during the 1950s I was devoted to the theatre. Around 1953, television swept across the land, and in its wake theatres closed everywhere. Old, established repertory companies were disbanded and historic theatres were pulled down. People were saying that the theatre was dead, a demise begun by cinema and radio and finished by television. I remember sixth-form debates on such motions as 'The theatre is dead, long live the theatre'. And it's true, the majority of plays at that time were tired, bland, empty-headed affairs. The producers with power were a few monopolistic moguls who disliked anything that smacked of intellectual, emotional or technical challenge. There were many who said the theatre was so bad, so clapped out, so out of date, that it deserved to die.

But what happened? Some writers, a few independent producers and directors, younger actors, designers, one or two critics, and an academic or two asked whether the death of the theatre was inevitable. They loved it and believed it possessed unique qualities that were essential to human life. They set about analysing what was special to theatre, what it could do that cinema and radio and television couldn't do at all, or couldn't do as well. And they based their work on that understanding. The result was that for the past thirty years in Britain, we've had the most flourishing theatre we've known since Shakespeare's day. There are signs of a falling-off again, but that's another matter.

Some of the people involved are now established figures: leaders among them were Peter Brook, Peter Hall, Joan Littlewood, the late George Devine and his English Stage Company, Samuel Beckett, and Harold Pinter. What they identified was that theatre is primarily about the dynamic physical presence of the human body interpreting a text orchestrated by the sense-making music of the human voice: words in speech embodied in flesh and blood right there in the room with you. So they argued for small theatres in which everybody in the audience is close to the actors; they attended carefully to the subtlety and density of the text and to how it is spoken; they got rid of cluttered fake scenery and other fripperies and emphasised instead the use of light and colour and the arrangement of shape in the *temenos* of that ancient circle Peter Brook called 'the empty space' and we call the stage; and so they created an emotionally and intellectually powerful, tactile theatre. It is a history now well known. I sat in the beautiful little Swan Theatre at Stratford-on-

Avon the other night marvelling at an exquisitely measured, precisely articulated production by Peter Hall of *All's Well That Ends Well* and thinking that there, at arm's-length from me, was the maturely sophisticated expression of the analysis Hall had begun for himself thirty-seven years earlier in his famous production of Samuel Beckett's *Waiting For Godot*, the play that to my mind is the iconic text for all this; and as I watched, I knew – knew in my guts as well as in my mind – that here was something of a nature and value I could possess and make my own no other way.

My contention is that, as we move into the next millennium and what some call 'the post-industrial era of technology', we book-loving people will have to perform the same act of rediscovery for literature-in-print as those people did for theatre. And the best way this will be done is not so much by studying the question in theory as by thoughtful practice: by writers and readers working it out together through their experience of writing and reading books that exploit the difference of literature, just as theatre people worked it out in the production of texts. The more I try to perform that act myself, the more sure I become that the results could be the same for book-literature as it was in theatre: a great new flourishing just at the time when it looks as if the form is dying.

In *Six Memos*, Italo Calvino explores some of his own practically worked-out understandings, and sums it up this way (p. 45):

> In an age when other fantastically speedy, widespread media are triumphing, and running the risk of flattening all communication onto a single, homogeneous surface, the function of literature is communication between things that are different, not blunting but even sharpening the differences between them, following the true bent of written language.

If your own experience of exploring what those differences are is similar to my own, you'll have discovered that we have to investigate some deep-rooted assumptions.

As, for example, our assumptions about what a book *is*.

A couple of years ago I was teaching the opening session of a one-year course in children's literature with a group of first-year undergraduates. Our subject that afternoon was the picture book. We'd spent half an hour browsing round a collection of about a hundred titles. I wanted the students to think about the poetics of the picture book. So to start the seminar off I wrote on the board these words:

Picture book
Picture-book
Picturebook

and asked if these different combinations mattered. The students looked at me warily, being well versed in teacherly traps, and finally muttered that yes, it probably did matter. But they couldn't tell me why. I then made a move I had not planned. I suggested that as the picture book, whatever difference the spelling made, was above all a book, we might as well begin there. 'Define a book for me,' I said, expecting an instant answer. Nothing.

Does this surprise you, as it did me? Or do you already know what we found out from each other, that in all of their and of my own schooling, no one had ever either defined a book for us or asked us to define it – in their case fifteen years of formal education, in mine fifty-two, in which the primary mode of communication after speech was book print, and yet no one had thought it necessary that we should think about the form itself. Not surprisingly, in fact. While a form of communication is dominant, we tend to take it for granted, or to assume that we all know all about it. Only when it is under threat or has been overtaken in predominance by another form do we begin to wonder whether we need it at all and why. The book, and especially the literary book, is in exactly that position nowadays.

Well, we set about trying to define the word 'book' and had a difficult time. The dictionary was a help but seemed to miss some essentials. Here's what we finally arrived at as the basic minimum:

> A book is a sequence of pages on which appear meaning-communicating marks, all of which are bound together in an authorised order.

Of course, we'll need subdivisions which deal with modifiers: *picture* book, *note* book, *sketch* book, *account* book. But for anything to be counted as a book, it will have to conform to the primary sense. A book is always a sequence of pages, which are always bound together, and the pages are always in an authorised order. The key word here is *authorised.* The authority of the book is that it is authored.

Whatever we have learned about the reader being in charge, about the reader being able to do whatever he or she wants with a book, it is also true that a book is created by a writer arranging marks on pages in a sequence that she or he wanted the reader to acknowledge and attend to. Wayne Booth has reminded us that both authors and readers have particular responsibilities to texts. To both of them, the central matter is – or should be – the written text; that is what books are for and that is why authors write them and readers read them. In no activity more than in reading a book is responsibility left so completely in the hands of the individual person without imposition or policing by institutional authority; and now here is the ideal of responsibility made more practical and graphic – it has, after all, to do with the graphemic itself – than during the reading of a book. It is essential to the nature of the Book. It is one of the reasons why totalitarians of every stripe – political, religious, educational or bureaucratic – are so much bothered by books that they try to ban or even burn them.

Not that we should give uncritical allegiance to any individual book's authority. We learn to discriminate; we pick and choose, giving our attention to those which persuade us by their authenticity. We often talk with children about a book's subject matter, or the characters in the story, perhaps too little about the language itself. But something we talk about hardly at all is that, as W. H. Auden put it, 'the underlying reason for writing is to bridge the gulf between one person and another', or, as Harold Brodkey expressed it, 'Reading is an intimate act, perhaps more intimate than any other human act. I say that because of the prolonged (or intense) exposure of one mind to another.' What gives us the deepest continuing pleasure is the company we keep with the mind, the personality, the being we call the author.

John Berger, another author whose company I like to keep, explains what makes for authenticity in an essay on the credibility of words in his book *Keeping a Rendezvous* (1992):

> Authenticity in literature does not come from the writer's personal honesty. There have been great writers who were mythomaniacs. Writers in general break their word at least as often as most other sedentary people. Moreover, many writers – not all – are excessively egocentric, blind to everything that turns its back on them. The disappointment of readers on meeting an admired writer probably begins with this confusion about the source of authenticity. It has little to do with either honesty or wisdom; still less with a devotion to beauty or aesthetics . . . . Authenticity comes from a single faithfulness: that to the ambiguity of experience. Its energy is to be found in how one event leads to another. Its mystery is not in the words but on the page.

'Its mystery is not in the words but on the page.' John Berger is leading us to the heart of the matter. In no other form of verbal communication, in no other art than the art we call literature, is the communicator as much in command of the medium as when composing a book; in no other is the recipient as much in control of the medium as a reader is when reading a book; in no other is the mind of the recipient in such direct touch with the mind of the communicator; in no other is there as much left for the recipient to do in the making of the experience as there is for the reader; in no other is it as possible to achieve such density, such subtlety, such inexhaustible ambiguity, such multiplicity of meanings as it is in a book. And the mystery of this, Berger says, is not in the words – a bookload of print-like words can be beamed at you from the screen of a word processor – the mystery is not in the words *but on the page.*

What is the mystery of the page? Young children, when they are learning to read, demonstrate one aspect of it that literary adults often forget. They chew books and hug them and paw at the pages. One of the reasons the page is so important is that it is tactile. The book, an object made of pages, is designed for holding in the hand; the binding is designed so that the pages can be turned. The physicality of book reading, its appeal to our fingers, is hardly at all attended to by researchers into reading. In earlier times, when the book was dominant, this didn't matter. Now that there is a variety of electronic print that does not involve pages, the book's touchability does matter, makes it special and different, and needs to be thought about. Not just because it affects the reader but because it affects the writer. Writing for a page is different from writing for electronic display. The boundaries are different; the grouping and bordering of lines of words are different. The way the turnover of the page can be used is obliterated by electronic display. And, as we'll remind ourselves in a moment, the stable nature of the page is lost in electronic display.

The experience of reading a story or a poem on book pages is also noticeably different from reading it on an electronic screen. For me, electronic print not only reduces my pleasure considerably but also diminishes the quality of my attention: I am less patient with it, take less in, and am less aware of the play of meaning.

Why? Perhaps because there is a considerable visceral, emotional, and intellectual link in human activity between the hand and the eye. After the Iron Man in Ted Hughes's famous story has fallen from the top of the cliff and smashed himself to bits, it is only when the hand finds the eye and then the eye directs the hand that the Iron Man can rebuild himself. The ways in which hand and eye work together, what each does, determine the nature of the experience, the pleasure we enjoy, and, where reading is concerned, not just the meaning we make of the words but the meaning we make of the whole event: of selecting what to read, of visiting the words through the medium of the book or an electronic machine, of considering what we've read and revisiting the words in order to reconsider them.

The book possesses other qualities that make it profoundly different from every other medium. These have been rehearsed fairly often and don't need more than listing here; the user-friendliness of the book and of book-print, and the way pages of book-print – their size and shape, the design of typography, the length of lines, the use of spacing, the texture and even the colour of the paper – have been refined over two thousand years to a format and appearance that exactly fit the human hand, so that the object is a pleasure to hold, and suit the human eye and what it can take in as it moves over print.

Anyone who has spent any length of time working on a word-processor while also using books, as I am doing right this minute, will know how different it is looking at the words on a screen and looking at words on a book page. The book exists only for print and for reading; that is its purpose in life. Every form of electronic print is simply part of something else, a machine that has other uses, and is designed primarily not for reading or writing words, but for manipulating electronic pulses. If it is reading written language that matters to us, then what we want is the book, because the book is the home where written language lives and where readers live with written language.

But we aren't finished yet. Another essential quality of book literature, another aspect of its being, is length.

Though a book can contain many smaller units, like a collection of poems or short stories, or ancedotes, or even one-line jokes, it implies, by bringing them together, relatedness: a reason for those units being gathered in one volume, and therefore the suggestion that they should be attended to as a whole. In other words, book-print is the site of coherent, concentrated attention.

I was talking about this recently with my friend Alan Tucker, a bookseller and poet. In a letter afterwards he wrote:

> What people (children) read for is the literature, the words. When the text

> is secondary to the illustrator it is already appealing to the senses more than the mind. There is no shortage of nice things for the senses in children's (or adults') lives here and now.
>
> *Only* the book can discuss the million critical issues of our society (a world society). The press is (1) too ephemeral, short term; (2) too frightened of being boring; (3) too brief, aiming always at spurious simplification. The same is true of the other media. Only books are long and detailed *and uninterrupted* enough to grapple with anything serious.
>
> And they can only do this, and civilisation survive as a culture rather than a fun fair or theme park, if people are physically capable of concentrating their minds. As ever, most things come naturally to children. The one great asset schools can give children is *intellectual stamina*, stick-at-it-ness, which comes from reading literature, by the process we all agree on – pleasure in reading.

Because these words are being read aloud to you, you can't see those to which Alan gives typographic emphasis, so I'll repeat them. '*Only* the book can discuss the million critical issues of our society,' 'only books are *uninterrupted* enough to grapple with anything serious,' and 'the one great asset schools can give children is *intellectual stamina*,' which comes from reading literature with pleasure. Hear! Hear! I say to that.

There are two points I want to pick up from Alan. The first has to do with detailed length.

In pre-electronic times, sustained length was considered a virtue. Think of Samuel Pepys, for example, complaining in his diary if the Sunday sermon lasted less than three hours. Think of the long periodic sentence so brilliantly composed by writers like Dr. Johnson, George Eliot, and Dickens. Think of the three-decker novel. Since the arrival and development of electronic media, brevity has increasingly been counted a virtue and sustained length is disliked – so much so that now politicians are trained to speak in ten-second sound bites, the average length of a shot in an advertisement on television is less than two seconds, and anyone in an interview who speaks for more than a minute is interrupted or cut off. By that standard, this lecture is already long past endurance; even as I write it, I do not expect the majority of you in the audience to be listening. That is why, in many institutions of tertiary education, where sustained concentration would, you might suppose, be part of learning, the formal lecture is now on the decline. I don't necessarily regret this; I merely point it out as a fact of contemporary life.

However, because this is so, it does not follow that sustained attention – intellectual stamina – is no longer a good thing or is unnecessary. On the contrary, because so many aspects of contemporary life work against it, it has become all the more important that we acquire it. This doesn't mean, though, that we must read three-decker novels written in long periodic sentences as the equivalent of a mental workout. There are ways of writing literature which mesh with contemporary rhythms of thought and yet still exploit length. Italo Calvino, who himself brilliantly explored some of these narrative forms, puts it this way in *Six Memos* (pp. 51 and 120):

> In the even more congested times that await us, literature must aim at the maximum concentration of poetry and thought.
>
> ... But I would say that today the rule of 'Keep It Short' is confirmed by long novels, the structure of which is accumulative, modular, and combinatory.

The irony is that the more concentrated the meanings we pack into what we write, and the more modular and combinatory we make the structure, the more we need to read it in book form because of the greater need there is to reread it, and to move back and forth and pick and choose and mix and match in the way a book makes easy. We need what the book encourages: time to dwell on the page, and the most efficient control of the writing within the authorised sequence. If that's true, then the book is far from finished and is entering an era when it is more necessary than ever.

The other point I wanted to pick up from Alan Tucker has to do with literature being fun. This is one of those issues about which you must be careful what you say or you'll be branded a kill-joy moral didacticist, a promoter of boring lesson-teaching solemnity, but I'll risk it. As long ago as 1978, Penelope Lively wrote in the *Horn Book* that 'We do actually believe now that children's books need to be fun and nothing else'. This is now a fashionable opinion. I have difficulty understanding the sense of it. Surely, fun is not a thing in itself, something that can be delivered to you like a bag of candy, but is the name we give to the feeling we get when engaged in an activity that gives us amusement and pleasure. We can get fun from thinking hard as much as from lying in the sun and, as we put it, 'doing nothing'. People who, like me, are lucky enough to be doing what they want to do get fun out of their work. Fun is not an absolute determined by only certain kinds of behaviour.

Besides, linguists, researchers into ideology, and feminist and literary critics have all shown us how it is impossible for a story to be 'fun and nothing else'. Every story, every poem, every piece of literary writing carries a message, even if the writer doesn't know it's there. All works of literature are moral systems: they all, without exception and however slight, deal in the stuff of life and the nature of being.

Brough Girling, one of our most vocal publicists and promoters of children's books, has taken the appeal to 'fun and nothing else' a step further. He tells us that children's books are toys and should be sold as such. Just as I have trouble identifying what can be fun and nothing else in a book, so I have trouble with the concept of a book as a toy – which I take to mean, as Collins English Dictionary puts it, 'an object designed to be played with and which is a non-functioning replica of something else, especially a miniature one'. If that is what a toy is, then a book is something different. It is an object designed to contain meaning-communicating marks arranged in an authorised order as a means of enabling the reading of written language. We may find it fun to read a book, but it is not there for 'fun and nothing else', nor is it a replica of something else. There is a good deal of play involved in reading, but books are not intended as playthings in the usually accepted sense of that word, that is, as objects you invest with imaginary functions, as, for instance, turning sitting-room chairs into a spaceship that you imagine transporting you to another planet till teatime.

I'm making heavy weather of this point because it seems to me that we are doing books and children as readers a disservice just now in our anxiety to sell more books and promote reading by trying to transfer onto books the easy popularity of a different kind of object: toys as pastime entertainment. The danger is that it doesn't actually work. Books don't provide the kind of fun that toys do, and to suggest to children that they do will lead to disappointment because it raises the wrong expectations. Just as bad, it encourages a tendency to select as most worthy of attention – for publishers' promotions, reviewing, television exposure, and so on – those books which most nearly are like toys, which, where books are concerned, inevitably means the banal, the gimmicky, and the most toylike (think of the vogue for pop-ups a few years ago, and the increasing production of books that are only an adjunct of their more toyish stuff: games, videos, and what are called, always at the implied expense of books, 'activity' packages, as if reading were not itself an activity).

Children's books as toys for fun are tangled with another misunderstanding about books: that they are part of the entertainment industry, like TV and cinema and pop music, where success is judged by size of audience. In book publishing, this is expressed in the quantity of sales and the accountancy notion of the best-seller list. During the last few years, the decision-making power in many publishing houses has moved out of the hands of editors and into the hands of the sales department. Now books are referred to as units, they are often remaindered within months of publication if they don't quickly reach profitable sales figures, and the maintenance of a backlist is secondary to the volume of unit sales.

Let's unpick the confusions that have led to this destructive state of affairs. First, books do not belong to the entertainment industry. Some books, it is true, are intended as pastime amusements, but not the majority. Most books are intended to store and communicate information – everything from a child's first dictionary to the records of legal case histories, from school text books to Mandlebrot's *The Fractual Geometry of Nature.* It may be fun to read them if we are interested in their subject matter, but to provide 'fun and nothing else' could hardly be described as their purpose. And the observable fact is that when the vast majority of people want to be, as we say, simply entertained, they actually look to other forms of amusement than books, nowadays usually TV or a video. (Why? Because, by comparison, reading is always hard work.)

Second, there is the confusion about books as units of commerce, the success of which is determined by volume of sales. By this standard, Enid Blyton, Roald Dahl, Barbara Cartland and Jeffrey Archer are judged more successful than Jan Mark, Alan Garner, Brigid Brophy and William Trevor. But this is a misjudgement about what books are for. When we use the word 'book', we can think of it in two ways: as a singular work (for example, the novel we call *The Owl Service*) or as an object reproduced many many times (that is, the thousands of copies in various formats since 1967: hardback, cheap paperback, large-print, Braille, and school editions, other-language translations, and so on, all called *The Owl Service*). To judge success by large quantity sales is to confuse the book's easy reproducibility for its main purpose and to encourage the belief that those that sell a great many copies are better than those that sell only a few.

But of course, mass production is not the main purpose of a book.

Rather, a book is intended as a means of printing messages in a stable and unchangeable physical form – that is, to preserve an authorised communication – and to present the text in an object that can be conveniently read, and that can be easily transported across long distances and across time. The audience for a book is one. But so perfect is the design for its purpose, that the singular book can be easily reproduced as many times as necessary. Whether or not vast numbers of people want to own copies has nothing to do with the book's reason for being, but only to do with the desire of some people to make money. For them, it doesn't actually matter whether they are selling books or sweets or second-hand cars. As Alan Sugar, founder of the Amstrad (computer) Corporation, so famously put it in one of the pithiest statements of 1980s postmodern amorality, 'If there was a market in mass-produced portable nuclear weapons then we'd market them'.

Of course, there are others who claim they want to sell large numbers of books because they are interested in people, especially children, being readers, and I don't doubt their honesty. But we will succeed in that aim only if we concentrate on what makes books different from other saleable objects and do not talk them up as being something they aren't. Far from being toys made for nothing but fun, the success of which can be judged by sales, books make available a vast variety – hundreds of thousands – of individual, singular texts, each of which supplies a particular need (dictionaries, reference books, text-books) or offers a particular companionship (poetry, stories, novels, biography, essays) to a particular reader at a particular time.

This means that knowing how to select the ones we want is part of what it is to be a reader. And because there are so many to select from, this in turn means that those who help us are potently important to our well-being. Where children are concerned, therefore, the adults who are charged with the greater part of the responsibility of enabling children to become readers need to be clear about what they are doing and why. The responsible enablers are teachers and librarians. They can't afford to be confused or ignorant. Every child has only one chance: one chance to be three or four, or nine, or ten, or fourteen or fifteen. If enabling adults get it wrong, a school leaver can't say, 'You didn't do too well at helping me. Why don't I go back to being three and start again, and you can have another try.' Of course there are all sorts of impediments that get in the way over which teachers and librarians have no control. And I've written a good deal about the best that teachers can do. I won't repeat it here. But I do want to make a point about how we enable the enablers.

Children's and youth's librarians first. Their great asset has traditionally been a detailed knowledge of the books and their skill at working informally with children and parents. You'll recall that in *Young Fluent Readers* (1976), her seminal study of children who came to school already able to read, Margaret M. Clark wrote that the place of the children's librarian in the reading lives of those children and their families could not be overestimated. Since she wrote those words in the early 1970s, a change has been enforced that puts at risk the skills that made children's librarians so valuable. It is the change from training specialist children's librarians to training all librarians as generalists, with, at best, a short optional course for anyone who is interested in work with young readers. What being a generalist means is that you are mainly a systems processor rather than someone with an intimate knowledge of books.

Whatever the reasons for that change, one result is certain. In Britain now, young librarians leave their training institutions with little if any knowledge or understanding of the history of literature for the young, with an inadequate knowledge of even the contemporary books, and with no preparation in dealing with children or how to mediate books to them. They have to learn on the job. Learning on the job means learning at children's expense. A child who needs help needs it now. She or he can't wait while you mug up what you should know.

It is time to campaign for specialist training again.

For teachers things are a little better than they were. There is a much more widespread recognition now than there was in the early 1970s that teachers need courses in literature for children during their preservice training. From doing nothing at all, as was the case in my days as a student in the 1950s, many institutions, perhaps most, now try to do something – not enough, of course, and things have got harder since the British government began its demoralising attacks on the teaching profession and gave legal and economic force to its retrograde policies. We're all having to work desperately hard just to hold on to the achievements of the last forty years. The experience of my own part in those achievements is this: at the heart of all improvements in a teacher's skill as an enabler of young readers is knowledge of the books.

Let me give you an example. Recently I was looking round the bookshop in one of our major teacher-training institutions. There was a modest range of books for children on sale. Standing in front of a shelf of poetry books were a couple of young women who were discussing whether a picture book they were examining would be suitable for their purpose. I asked them what they wanted. They said they needed good strong verses that five- and six-year-olds would like. It turned out that they were just finishing their college course, would be taking up their first jobs in September, and meanwhile were going to help out in an infant school. As we talked, it became clear that they had been persuaded of the importance of reading aloud, had been taught the place of poetry in children's lives, had been given some preparation in classroom management, and had learned something of the growth and development of children in the early years of schooling. They'd been into the school where they were to help out, had talked to the teacher, and had sorted out together what it was they wanted to do. Now they needed the primary tools: they needed the books. They'd never heard of the Raymond Briggs *Mother Goose Treasury* (1969), or *The Puffin Book of Verse* (1966), or Jill Bennett's *Roger Was a Razor Fish* (1980), three old standards that would have got them going. Neither did they know of any aids like – dare I say it – the Thimble Press Signal Bookguide, *Poetry Books for Children*, which would have given them plenty of help. They had no reference points that would help them make a selection from the small stock in the bookshop. What they had not been given was knowledge of the books. Without that, they were stuck.

Since 1982, I've been a visiting lecturer at Westminster College, a preservice institution in Oxford. One of the things we've been trying to do is to discover the optimum number of books that a primary school teacher needs to know if he or she is to function satisfactorily from day one of the first job. It looks as if the answer hovers around the five hundred mark. And it also looks as if it takes most students two to three years to make that basic library their own if they are to do so by reading it with pleasure and with time to absorb it and think about it, while at the same time thinking about, and trying out in supervised practice, how best to put their knowledge to work in enabling children to become literary readers.

I don't claim that the Westminster courses are all they should be, and I might add that they did not come about by imposition from above but because of pressure from students. We began by offering an optional short course. Students who didn't take it began to demand it for themselves; many who had taken it demanded more. This happened for a number of reasons: because they enjoyed it, of course, but more important, because they found what they learned was immediately useful in their work with children, and because the professional advantage that those who had taken the course had over those who hadn't was evident.

I had guessed this would be so before we began; it was part of my own experience. One reason I hadn't guessed, however, was, to me at any rate, as valuable as any of the others. It was the effect on the students as readers for themselves. Time and again, when they were assessing the course at the end, students would report what had happened to them in phrases such as these: 'Through reading children's books, I've rediscovered myself as a reader,' 'For the first time since I was in primary school I've been reading again with pleasure just for myself,' 'Because of the children's books I've read now as an adult (well, nearly an adult), I find they have changed the way I read adult books like the Victorian novels I have to study for the rest of my courses, and it is a change for the better,' and 'I've realised that children's books are not just for children; they are for me, too.'

When children watch a film or the television or go to the theatre, they are engaged in a view of life interpreted by people who come between the writer and the audience. They see what they see at the pace the performers want to give it. They are not usually meant or allowed to stop and go back, or interrupt, or skip a part, or take a break when they feel like it. They are shown the world; they don't make their own version of it. And what they are engaged in is a visual representation of life.

When children read a book, they have in their own hands a vision composed (in English) of twenty-six abstract signs ordered into horizontal lines, where they are grouped and spaced and separated by other kinds of abstract marks that indicate how to orchestrate the pages in the theatre of their own heads, where they interpret the vision for themselves, taking it at the pace they want to, and flicking back and forth and skipping and stopping and starting when they feel like it. It is theirs in a way nothing else can be. No one comes between the mind that composed the vision and their own. It is communicated by abstract signs that the reader turns into a reality of his or her own. 'When we read a story,' Berger says, 'we inhabit it. The covers of a book are like a roof and four walls. What is to happen next is possible because the story's voice makes everything its own.'

Literature is about written language; that's what makes it different from everything else. And written language in book form is about sustained, passionate contemplation. As we read, we feel strongly and are affected by the vision that we inhabit and that inhabits us. Yet, mysteriously, at the same time, we can also stand back and consider what it is that is happening to us. We take part in the event – indeed, we *are* the event: it can take place nowhere else but in us – but we are outside it as well, looking on.

'My language is the sum total of myself,' Charles S. Peirce wrote.

'[People] become what they contemplate,' Austen Warren says.

Literature is made of authorised language meant for reader-controlled contemplation. That is the essence of the thing, the difference of literature from all else.

From *Children's Literature in Education* No. 88, 1993

Bibliography

Appleyard, J.A. *Becoming a Reader; the Experience of Fiction from Childhood to Adulthood.* Cambridge: Cambridge University Press, 1990

Auden, W.H. *Forewords and Afterwords.* New York: Random House, 1943

Auden, W.H. *A Choice of de la Mare's Verse.* London: Faber and Faber, 1963

Auden, W.H. *The Place of Value in a World of Facts.* Nobel Symposium 14 Stockholm: Almqvist and Wiksell, 1970

Bazalgette, Cary. 'All in fun: Su Pollard on Disneytime' in *Television Mythologies,* Len Masterman (ed.), pp. 29–33. London: Comedia, 1985

Bennett, Jill. *Roger was a Razor Fish.* London: Bodley Head, 1980

Berger, John. *Keeping a Rendezvous.* London: Granta Books, 1992

Bettelheim, Bruno. *The Uses of Enchantment: The Meaning and Importance of Fairy Tales.* London: Thames & Hudson, 1976

Blake, William. *Songs of Innocence.* 1789

Blake, William. *Songs of Experience.* 1794

Briggs, Raymond. *Mother Goose Treasury.* London: Hamish Hamilton, 1966

Briggs, Raymond. *The Snowman.* London: Hamish Hamilton, 1978

Britton, James. *Language and Learning: the importance of speech in children's development,* 2nd edn. London: Penguin, 1992

Broster, D.K. *The Flight of the Heron* (1925). London: Heinemann, 1952

Broster, D.K. *The Gleam in the North* (1927). London: Heinemann, 1952

Bruner, Jerome. *Actual Minds, Possible Worlds.* Cambridge, Mass.: Harvard University Press, 1986

Bulletin of the Center for Children's Books. Review of *Dangerous Spaces.* 1991, *44*(8), pp. 222–3

Burningham, John. *Mr Gumpy's Outing.* London: Cape, 1970

Calder, Jenni. *Stevenson, R.L.: A Life Study.* London: Hamilton, 1980; New York: Oxford University Press, 1980

Calvino, Italo. *If on a Winter's Night a Traveller.* London: Martin, Secker & Warburg, 1981

Calvino, Italo. *Six Memos for the Next Millennium.* London: Cape, 1992

Cass, Joan E. *Literature and the Young Child.* London: Longman, 1967

Chambers, Aidan. *Dance on My Grave.* London: Bodley Head, 1982

Chambers, Aidan. *The Toll Bridge.* London: Bodley Head, 1992

Chesterton, G.K. 'The Ethics of Elfland' (1908) in *G.K. Chesterton: A Selection from his Non-Fictional Prose* (ed. W.H. Auden). London: Faber and Faber, 1970

Chinery, Michael. *Spiders*. Gloucester: Whittet Books, 1993
Clark, Margaret M. *Young Fluent Readers*. London: Heinemann Educational Books, 1976
Comenius, Joannes Amos. Facsimile of the London edition 1672. *Orbis Sensualium Pictus*. Sydney: Sydney University Press, 1967
Cooper, Ilene. Review of *Dangerous Spaces* in *Booklist*. May 15, 1991, p. 1799
Daly, Lloyd W. (ed. and tr.). *Aesop Without Morals*. New York, 1961
Dann, Colin. *The Animals of Farthing Wood Omnibus*. London: Hutchinson, 1994
Davis, Lennard J. *Resisting Novels*. New York and London: Methuen, 1987
De la Mare, Walter. *Miss Jemima*. Oxford: Blackwell, 1925; New York: Artists and Writers Guild, 1935
Dégh, Linda. 'Grimms' *Household Tales*, and its place in the household: the social relevance of a controversial classic' in *Western Folklore* 1979, *38*(2), pp. 83–103
Duvall, Shelley (Producer), Curtis, Mark, and Ash, Rod (Writers). *The Three Little Pigs* (videotape). Hollywood: Platypus Productions, 1983
Duvall, Shelley (Producer), and Fiskin, Jeffrey (Writer). *The Sleeping Beauty* (videotape). Hollywood: Platypus Productions, 1983
Duvall, Shelley (Producer), and Jones, R.C. (Writer). *Snow White and the Seven Dwarfs* (videotape). Hollywood: Platypus Productions, 1983
Earnshaw, Brian. *Dragonfall Five and the Mastermind*. London: Methuen, 1975
Earnshaw, Brian. *Dragonfall Five and the Space Cowboys*. London: Methuen
Eliot, Charles, W. (Ed.). *Folklore and Fable*. New York, 1909
Eliot, T.S. *East Coker*. London: Faber and Faber, 1940
Favat, F. Andre. *Child and Tale: The Origins of Interest*. Illinois: National Council of Teachers of English, 1977
Fisher, Margery. *Matters of Fact: aspects of non-fiction for children*. Leicester: Brockhampton Press, 1972
Fisher, Margery. 'Life Course or Screaming Farce?' in *Children's Literature in Education*, Vol. 22, Autumn 1976
Forster, E.M. *Aspects of the Novel* (1927). London: Arnold, 1974; New York: Harcourt, 1974
Fox, Carol. *At the Very Edge of the Forest: the Influence of Literature on Storytelling by Children*. London: Cassell, 1993
French, Vivian and Voake, Charlotte. *Caterpillar, Caterpillar*. London: Walker Books, 1993
Fry, Donald. *Children Talk About Books: Seeing Themselves as Readers*. Milton Keynes: Open University Press, 1985
George, Jean Craighead. *Julie of the Wolves*. New York: Harper & Row, 1972

Gilbert, Henry. *Robin Hood and His Merry Men.* London: T.C. & E.C. Jack, 1912
Goble, Paul. *The Friendly Wolf.* New York: Bradbury Press, 1974
Graham, Eleanor (ed.). *The Puffin Book of Verse.* London: Penguin Books, 1969
Grahame, Kenneth. 'The Reluctant Dragon' in *Dream Days.* London: Lane, 1898
Graves, Robert. *I Claudius.* London: Methuen, 1934
Grimm, Jakob and Wilhelm. (trans. Randall Jarrell, 1973). 'The Golden Bird' in *The Juniper Tree and Other Tales from Grimm.* New York: Farrar, Strauss & Giroux
Handford, S.A. (trans.) *Fables of Aesop.* Baltimore: Penguin, 1954
Hansard, Peter and Casey, Patricia. *My Cat Jack.* London: Walker Books, 1994
Hardy, Barbara. *Novel: A forum on fiction.* Brown University, Fall 1968
Hatt, Frank. *The Reading Process: A Framework for Analysis and Description.* London: Clive Bingley, 1976
Hazard, Paul. (trans. Marguerite Mitchell) *Books, Children and Men.* Boston: The Horn Book, 1944
Hennessy, James Pope. *Robert Louis Stevenson.* London: Cape, 1974
Hindley, Judy and Chamberlain, Margaret. *A Piece of String is a Wonderful Thing.* London: Walker Books, 1993
Hindley, Judy and Chamberlain, Margaret. *The Wheeling and Whirling Around Book.* London: Walker Books, 1994
Hogarth, Peter and Clery, Val. *Dragons.* New York: Penguin, 1979
Hollindale, Peter. 'Spaces of the secret mind' in *The Times Educational Supplement,* 14 June 1991, p. 26
Hopkins, G.M. 'The Candle Indoors', *Poems of Gerard Manley Hopkins,* 2nd edn. Oxford: Oxford University Press, 1944
Horkenheimer, Max and Adorno, Theodor W. *Dialectic of Enlightenment,* (trans. John Cumming) New York: Herder & Herder, 1972; London: Allen Lane, 1973
Hughes, Ted. *The Iron Man.* London: Faber & Faber, 1968
Hughes, Ted. 'Myth in Education' in *Children's Literature in Education,* Vol. 1, No. 1, March 1970, pp. 55–70
Hull, Robert. 'Some Fictions of Non-fiction' in *Books for Keeps.* No. 60. January 1990, pp. 16–19
Jackson, Rosemary. *Fantasy: The Literature of Subversion.* New York and London: Methuen, 1981
Jacobs, Joseph. 'The Well of the World's End' in *English Fairy Tales.* London: David Nutt, 1890
Jung, Carl G. 'The phenomenology of the spirit in fairy tales' in *The*

Archetypes and the Collective Unconscious, 9, Part 1, pp. 207–254. New York: Pantheon, 1959

Just, Marcel Adam, and Carpenter, Patricia A. 'A theory of reading: From eye fixations to comprehension' in *Theoretical Models and Processes of Reading* (3rd. edn.), Harry Singer and Robert B. Ruddel, eds., pp. 174–208. Newark: International Reading Association, 1985

Kerins, Anthony. *Lost.* London: Puffin Books, 1991

Kipling, Rudyard. *The Jungle Book.* London: Macmillan, 1894; New York: Century, 1894

Kipling, Rudyard. *The Second Jungle Book.* London: Macmillan, 1895; New York: Century, 1895

Kipling, Rudyard. *Kim.* New York: Doubleday, 1901; London: Macmillan, 1901

Kipling, Rudyard. *Just So Stories for Little Children.* London: Macmillan, 1902; New York: Doubleday, 1902

Kipling, Rudyard. *Puck of Pook's Hill.* London: Macmillan, 1906; New York: Doubleday, 1906

Kipling, Rudyard. *Rewards and Fairies.* London: Macmillan, 1910; New York: Doubleday, 1910

Kohlberg, Lawrence. 'Stages of moral development as a basis for moral education' in *Moral Education*, C.M. Beck, ed., Toronto: University of Toronto, 1971

Kohlberg, Lawrence. 'Moral stages and moralisation: The cognitive developmental approach' in *Moral Development and Behaviour*, T. Likona, ed. London: Holt, Rinehart and Winston, 1976

Lambert, David. *The Ultimate Dinosaur Book.* London: Dorling Kindersley, 1993

Laski, Audrey. Review of *Dangerous Spaces* in *The School Librarian*, 1991, 39(3), 115

Le Guin, Ursula. 'Some Thoughts on Narrative' in *Dancing at the Edge of the World.* London: Paladin, 1992

Lewis, C.S. *Of Other Worlds: Essays and Stories.* New York: Harcourt, Brace and World, 1966

Lewis, David. 'Looking for Julius: two Children and a Picture Book' in Kimberley, K., Meek, M. and Miller, J. *New Reading: Contributions to an Understanding of Literacy.* London: A. & C. Black, 1992

Lukens, Rebecca J. *A Critical Handbook of Children's Literature.* Glenview, Illinois: Scott, Foresman, 1976

Mackey, Margaret. 'The New Basics: learning to Read in a Multi-media World' in *English in Education.* Vol. 28, No. 1, 1994, pp. 9–19

Mahy, Margaret. *The Haunting.* London: J.M. Dent, 1982

Mahy, Margaret. *The Changeover: A Supernatural Romance.* London: J.M. Dent, 1984
Mahy, Margaret. *The Tricksters.* London: J.M. Dent, 1986
Mahy, Margaret. *The Great White Man-Eating Shark: A Cautionary Tale.* Jonathan Allen, Illus. New York: Dial Books, 1992; London: Puffin Books, 1989
Mahy, Margaret. *Dangerous Spaces.* New York: Viking Penguin, 1991
Mallett, Margaret. *Making Facts Matter: Reading Non-Fiction 5–11.* London: Paul Chapman Publishing, 1992
McGann, Jerome J. *The Textual Condition.* Newark: Princeton Paperbacks, 1993
Medway, Peter. *From Information to Understanding: What children do with new ideas.* Schools Council and Institute of Education Joint Project. London Institute of Education, 1973
Meek, Margaret. *How Texts Teach What Readers Learn.* Stroud: The Thimble Press, 1988
Mitchison, Naomi. *The Conquered.* London: Cape, 1923
Mitchison, Naomi. *Cloud Cuckoo Land.* London: Cape, 1925
Mitchison, Naomi. *The Corn King and the Spring Queen.* London: Cape, 1931
Mowat, Farley. *Never Cry Wolf.* Toronto: McClelland & Stewart, 1963
Munsch, Robert. *The Paper Bag Princess.* Toronto: Annick, 1980
Nash, Ogden. *The Tale of Custard the Dragon and the Wicked Knight.* Boston: Little, Brown, 1961
Neate, Bobbie. *Finding Out about Finding Out: a practical guide to children's information books.* London: Hodder and Stoughton, 1992
Nesbit, Edith. *A Book of Dragons.* London and New York: Harper, 1900
Opie, Iona and Peter. *The Oxford Nursery Rhyme Book.* Oxford: Clarendon Press, 1967
Pappas, Christine C. 'Ontogenesis of the register of written language. Young children's use of the story and information book genres.' Paper given at NCTE Annual Convention, Baltimore, 1989
Peppard, Murray B. *Paths Through the Forest.* New York, 1971
Perry, Ben Edwin (trans.). *Babrius and Phaedrus.* Cambridge: Harvard University Press. 1965, p. xxxv
Piaget, Jean. 'The Mental Development of the Child'. *Six Psychological Studies* (trans. Anita Tenzer). New York: Vintage, 1967
Piaget, Jean. *The Moral Judgment of the Child.* London: Routledge, 1932
Plowden Report. *Children and their Primary Schools.* Central Advisory Committee for Education (England). H.M.S.O., 1967
Propp, Vladimir. *Morphology of the Folktale,* 2nd edn. Austin: University of Texas Press, 1968

Rose, Jacqueline. *The Case of Peter Pan.* London: Macmillan, 1984
Rosen, Philip. 'Adorno and film music: Theoretical notes on composing for the films' in *Yale French Studies*, 1980, *60*, 157–182
Rosenblatt, Louise. *The Reader, the Text, the Poem: The Transactional Theory of the Literary Work.* Carbondale, Il: Southern Illinois University Press, 1978
Ross, Tony. *Jack the Giantkiller.* London: Puffin Books, 1983
Scannell, Vernon. *New and Collected Poems 1950–1980.* Robson Books, 1980
Searle, John R. *Speech Acts.* Cambridge: Cambridge University Press, 1969
Sendak, Maurice. *Where the Wild Things Are.* London: Bodley Head, 1967
Sendak, Maurice. *Dear Mili.* London: Viking Kestrel, 1988
Snowman, The (film). Dianne Jackson, dir. Snowman Enterprises for Channel 4, 1982
Spark, Muriel. *The Prime of Miss Jean Brodie.* London: Macmillan, 1961; New York: Dell, 1964
Stevenson, Robert Louis. *Catriona* (1893). Edinburgh: Chambers, 1980; New York: Arrow, 1979
Stevenson, Robert Louis. *Kidnapped* (1886). Edinburgh: Chambers, 1980; New York: Signet Classics, 1981
Stevenson, Robert Louis. *Virginibus Puerisque* (1881)
Stone, Kay. '*Marchen* to fairy tales: An unmagical transformation' in *Western Folklore* 1981, 40(3), 232–244
Story, Rita. *Goldilocks and the Three Bears.* Amelia Rosario, illus. Beverley Hills: Mad Hatter Books, 1990; London: Puffin Books, 1991
Story of the Three Little Pigs, The. Burbank CA: Walt Disney Educational Media Company, 1978
Todorov, Tzvetan. *The Fantastic.* (trans. Richard Howard) Ithaca, NY: Cornell University Press, 1975
Tolkien, J.R.R. 'On Fairy Stories' in *Tree and Leaf.* London: Unwin, 1964
Trease, Geoffrey. *Trumpets in the West.* Oxford: Blackwell, 1953
Trease, Geoffrey. *Mist over Athelney.* London: Macmillan, 1958
Trease, Geoffrey. *The Crown of Violet.* London: Macmillan, 1959
Trease, Geoffrey. *Thunder of Valmy.* London: Macmillan, 1960
Trousdale, Ann M. 'The right story: A child's responses to fairy tales adapted for television by Faerie Tale Theatre'. Unpublished manuscript, 1986
Trousdale, Ann M. The telling of the tale: Children's responses to fairy tales presented orally and through the media of film. Doctoral dissertation, The University of Georgia, 1987
Trousdale, Ann M. 'Let the children tell us: The meanings of fairy tales for children' in *The New Advocate* 1989, 2(1) 37–48

Wallace, Karen and Bostock, Mike. *Think of an Eel.* London: Walker Books, 1993

Wallace, Karen and Manning, Mick. *Think of a Beaver.* London: Walker Books, 1993

White, Haydon. 'The Value of Narrativity in the Representation of Reality' in *On Narrative . . .*, ed. W.J.T. Mitchell. Chicago: University of Chicago Press, 1981

Whitehead, A.N. *Adventures of Ideas.* Cambridge: Cambridge University Press, 1933

Whitehead, Frank *et al. Children and Their Books.* London: Macmillan Educational, 1977

Wild, Margaret. *Let the Celebration Begin!* Julie Vivas, illus. New York: Orchard Books, 1991; London: Bodley Head, 1991

Wilder, Laura Ingalls. *Little House in the Big Woods.* New York: Harper, 1932

Yolen, Jane. 'The fault of the nightingale: Effects of fairy tales on children' in *California Media and Library Educators Association Journal* 1977, 8–12

Zipes, Jack. *Fairy Tales and the Art of Subversion.* New York: Wildman Press, 1983; London: Heinemann, 1983

INDEX